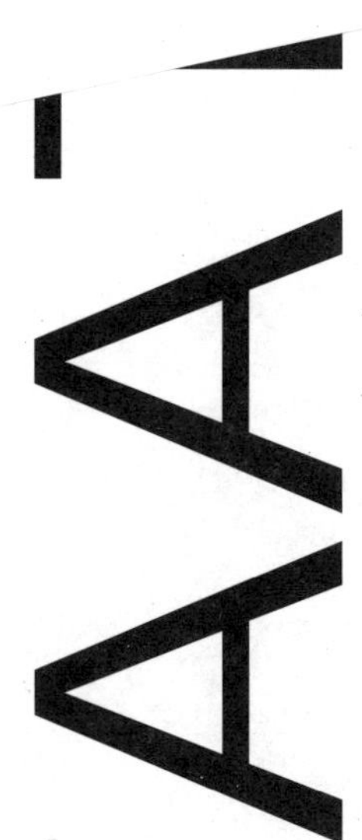

Technician Unit 18

Preparing Business Taxation Computations
Finance Acts 2005

For exams in June 2006
and December 2006

Combined Text and Kit

In this September 2005 edition

- Combined Text and Revision Kit written in a clear straightforward way
- Numerous new examples and activities
- Activities checklist to tie in each activity to specific knowledge and understanding, performance criteria and/or range statement
- June 2004 and December 2004 papers included as practice exams
- Thorough reliable updating of material to for the 2005 Finance Acts

FOR EXAM BASED ASSESSMENTS IN JUNE 2006 AND DECEMBER 2006 UNDER THE FINANCE ACTS 2005 TAX LEGISLATION

First edition August 2003
Third edition September 2005

ISBN 07517 2361 4 (previous ISBN 07517 1722 3)

British Library Cataloguing-in-Publication Data
A catalogue record for this book
is available from the British Library

Published by

BPP Professional Education
Aldine House, Aldine Place
London W12 8AW

www.bpp.com

Printed in Great Britain by
Page Bros. (Norwich) Ltd

We are grateful to the Lead Body for Accounting for permission to reproduce extracts from the Standards of Competence for Accounting, and to the AAT for permission to reproduce extracts from the mapping and Guidance Notes.

Contents

Introduction

How to use this Combined Text and Kit – Technician qualification structure – Unit 18 Standards of competence – Exam based assessment technique – Assessment strategy – Tax rates and allowances

Introduction

How to use this Combined Text and Kit

Aims of this Combined Text and Kit

To provide the knowledge and practice to help you succeed in the assessment for Technician Unit 18 *Preparing Business Tax Computations.*

To pass the assessment you need a thorough understanding of all areas covered by the standards of competence.

To tie in with the other components of the BPP Effective Study Package to ensure you have the best possible chance of success.

Combined Text and Kit

Parts A to E cover all you need to know for the exam based assessment for Unit 18 *Preparing Business Tax Computations.* Numerous activities throughout the text help you practise what you have just learnt.

When you have understood and practised the material in Parts A to E and reviewed the answers to activities in Part F, you will have the knowledge and experience to tackle Parts G to H of this combined Text and Kit for Unit 18 *Preparing Business Tax Computations.* These parts aim to get you through the exam by providing you with plenty of activities to practise and also some full exam based assessments.

Passcards

These short memorable notes are focused on key topics for Unit 18, designed to remind you of what the Combined Text and Kit has taught you.

Recommended approach to this Combined Text and Kit

(a) To achieve competence in Unit 18 (and all the other units) you need to be able to do **everything** specified by the standards. Study Parts A to E carefully and do not skip any of it.

(b) Learning is an **active** process. Do **all** the activities as you work through Parts A to E so you can be sure you really understand what you have read.

(c) Before you work through Parts G to H of this Combined Text and Kit, check that you still remember the material using the following revision plan for each of the chapters in Parts A to E.

  (i) Read and learn the **key learning points**, which are a summary of the chapter. This includes key terms and shows the sort of things likely to come up in the exam. Are there any gaps in your knowledge? If so, study the section again.

  (ii) Do the **quick quiz** again. If you know what you're doing, it shouldn't take long.

(d) Once you have completed your quick revision plan for each chapter, you are ready to tackle Parts G and H of this Combined Text and Kit.

  (i) Try the **Practice Activities**. These are short activities, linked to the Standards of Competences, to reinforce your learning and consolidate the practice that you have had doing the activities in parts A to E of this Combined Text and Kit.

  (ii) **Attempt the Exam Based Assessments**. These will help you develop techniques in approaching the assessments and allocating time correctly. For guidance on this, please see Exam Based Assessment Technique on page (xvi)

(e) Go through the **Passcards** as often as you can in the weeks leading up to your assessment.

This approach is only a suggestion. You or your college may well adapt it to suit your needs.

Remember this is a **practical** course.

(a) Try to relate the material to your experience in the workplace or any other work experience you may have had.

(b) Try to make as many links as you can to your study of the other Units at Technician level.

(c) Keep this text, (hopefully) you will find it invaluable in your everyday work too!

Lecturers' Resource Pack Activities

Part H of this Combined Text and Kit includes a number of chapter-linked activities without answers. We have also included one exam based assessment without answers. The answers for this section are in the BPP Lecturers' Resource Pack for this Unit.

Revenue forms

In your Examination you may have to either complete or take information from Revenue forms. The examiner has stated that in Unit 18 you may have to complete

(i) The self employment pages that accompany the income tax return form and/or

(ii) The CT600 short return

Please note that at the time this Text was printed 2005/06 versions of the self employment pages were not available. We have therefore updated the 2004/05 versions of the form and amended them where necessary to fit in with Finance Acts 2005 tax legislation. This necessarily involves us in making 'guesses' about how the 2005/06 forms will change. Although, it is unlikely that the 2005/06 versions of the forms will differ significantly from what we have included here, it is important that you contact the Revenue for updated copies before you take your examination.

If you have Internet access you should be able to find the 2005/06 forms on the Revenue's website (www.hmrc.gov.UK).

Technician qualification structure

The competence-based Education and Training Scheme of the Association of Accounting Technicians is based on an analysis of the work of accounting staff in a wide range of industries and types of organisation. The Standards of Competence for Accounting which students are expected to meet are based on this analysis.

The AAT issued new standards of competence in 2002, which took effect from 1 July 2003. This Combined Text and Kit reflects the **new standards.**

The Standards identify the key purpose of the accounting occupation, which is to operate, maintain and improve systems to record, plan, monitor and report on the financial activities of an organisation, and a number of key roles of the occupation. Each key role is subdivided into units of competence, which are further divided into elements of competences. By successfully completing assessments in specified units of competence, students can gain qualifications at NVQ/SVQ levels 2, 3 and 4, which correspond to the AAT Foundation, Intermediate and Technician stages of competence respectively.

Whether you are competent in a Unit is demonstrated by means of:

- *Either* an Exam Based Assessment (set and marked by AAT assessors)
- *Or* a Skills Based Assessment (where competence is judged by an Approved Assessment Centre to whom responsibility for this is devolved)

Below we set out the overall structure of the Technician (NVQ/SVQ Level 4) stage. In the next section there is more detail about the Exam Based Assessment for Unit 18.

NVQ/SVQ Level 4

Group 1 Core Units – All units are mandatory.

Unit 8 Contributing to the Management of Performance and the Enhancement of Value	Element 8.1 Collect, analyse and disseminate information about costs
	Element 8.2 Make recommendations and make recommendations to enhance value
Unit 9 Contributing to the Planning and Control of Resources	Element 9.1 Prepare forecasts of income and expenditure
	Element 9.2 Produce draft budget proposals
	Element 9.3 Monitor the performance of responsibility centres against budgets
Unit 10 Managing Systems and People in the Accounting Environment	Element 10.1 Manage people within the accounting environment
	Element 10.2 Identify opportunities for improving the effectiveness of an accounting system
Unit 22 Contribute to the Maintenance of a Healthy, Safe and Productive Working Environment	Element 22.1 Contribute to the maintenance of a healthy, safe and productive working environment
	Element 22.2 Monitor and maintain an effective and efficient working environment

NVQ/SVQ Level 4, continued

Group 2 Optional Units – Choose **one** of the following **four** units.

Unit 11 Drafting Financial Statements (Accounting Practice, Industry and Commerce)	Element 11.1 Draft limited company financial statements
	Element 11.2 Interpret limited company financial statements
Unit 12 Drafting Financial Statements (Central Government)	Element 12.1 Draft Central Government financial statements
	Element 12.2 Interpret Central Government financial statements
Unit 13 Drafting Financial Statements (Local Government)	Element 13.1 Draft Local Authority financial statements
	Element 13.2 Interpret Local Authority financial statements
Unit 14 Drafting Financial Statements (National Health Service)	Element 14.1 Draft NHS accounting statements and returns
	Element 14.2 Interpret NHS accounting statements and returns

NVQ/SVQ Level 4, continued

Group 3 Optional Units – Choose **two** of the following **four** units.

Unit 15 Operating a Cash Management and Credit Control System	Element 15.1	Monitor and control cash receipts and payments
	Element 15.2	Manage cash balances
	Element 15.3	Grant credit
	Element 15.4	Monitor and control the collection of debts
Unit 17 Implementing Audit Procedures	Element 17.1	Contribute to the planning of an audit assignment
	Element 17.2	Contribute to the conduct of an audit assignment
	Element 17.3	Prepare related draft reports
Unit 18 Preparing Business Taxation Computations	Element 18.1	Prepare capital allowances computations
	Element 18.2	Compute assessable business income
	Element 18.3	Prepare capital gains computations
	Element 18.4	Prepare Corporation Tax computations
Unit 19 Preparing Personal Taxation Computations	Element 19.1	Calculate income from employment
	Element 19.2	Calculate property and investment income
	Element 19.3	Prepare Income Tax computations
	Element 19.4	Prepare Capital Gains Tax computations

Unit 18 Standards of competence

The structure of the Standards for Unit 18

The Unit commences with a statement of the **knowledge and understanding** which underpin competence in the Unit's elements.

The Unit of Competence is then divided into **elements of competence** describing activities which the individual should be able to perform.

Each element includes:

(a) A set of **performance criteria.** This defines what constitutes competent performance.

(b) A **range statement.** This defines the situations, contexts, methods etc in which competence should be displayed.

The elements of competence for Unit 18: *Preparing Business Taxation Computations* are set out below. Knowledge and understanding required for the Unit as a whole are listed first, followed by the performance criteria and range statements for each element.

Unit 18: Preparing Business Taxation Computations

What is the Unit about?

This unit is about preparing tax computations for businesses and completing the relevant tax returns. There are four elements.

The first element requires you to prepare capital allowances computations, including adjustments for private use by the owners of a business.

In the second element you must prepare assessable business income computations for partnerships and self-employed individuals. This includes identifying the National Insurance Contributions payable.

The third element is concerned with preparing capital gains computations for companies and unincorporated businesses.

The final element requires you to prepare Corporation Tax computations for UK resident companies.

Throughout the unit you must show that you take account of current tax law and Revenue practice and make submissions within statutory timescales. You also need to show that you consult with the Revenue in an open and constructive manner, give timely and constructive advice to business clients and maintain client confidentiality.

Knowledge and understanding

To perform this unit effectively you will need to know and understand:

The business environment

1 The duties and responsibilities of the tax practitioner (Elements 18.1, 18.2, 18.3 & 18.4)

2 The issues of taxation liability (Elements 18.1, 18.2, 18.3 & 18.4)

3 Relevant legislation and guidance from the Revenue (Elements 18.1, 18.2, 18.3 & 18.4)

Taxation principles and theory

4 Basic law and practice relating to all issues covered in the range and referred to in the performance criteria (Elements 18.1, 18.2, 18.3 & 18.4)

5 Availability and types of capital allowance:
- first year allowance
- writing down allowance
- balancing allowance and charge (relevant to industrial buildings and plant and machinery including computers, motor vehicles and short life assets) (Element 18.1)

6 Treatment of capital allowances for unincorporated businesses including private use adjustments (Element 18.1)

7 Adjustment of trading profits and losses for tax purposes (Element 18.2)

8 Regulations relating to disallowed expenditure such as business entertaining, bad debt write-offs and provisions, private expenditure and capital expenditure (Element 18.2)

9 Basis of assessment of unincorporated businesses (Element 18.2)

10 Basic allocation of income between partners (Element 18.3)

11 Identification of business assets disposed of including part disposals (Element 18.3)

12 Calculation of gains and losses on disposals of business assets including indexation allowance (Element 18.3)

13 Capital gains exemptions and reliefs on business assets including rollover relief and taper relief but excluding retirement relief (Element 18.3)

14 Rates of tax payable on gains on business assets disposed of by individuals (Element 18.3)

15 The computation of profit for Corporation Tax purposes including income, capital gains and charges (Element 18.4)

16 Calculation of Corporation Tax payable by starting, small, large and marginal companies including those with associated companies (Element 18.4)

17 Set-off of trading losses incurred by companies (Element 18.4)

18 Calculation of National Insurance Contributions payable by self-employed persons and employers of not contracted-out employees (Elements 18.2 & 18.4)

19 Self assessment including payment of tax and filing of returns for unincorporated businesses and companies (Elements 18.2 & 18.4)

The organisation

20 How the taxation liabilities of an organisation are affected by its legal structure and the nature of its business transactions (Elements 18.1, 18.2, 18.3 & 18.4)

21 The organisation's legal structure and its business transactions (Elements 18.1, 18.2, 18.3 & 18.4)

Element 18.1 Prepare capital allowances computations

Performance criteria

In order to perform this element successfully you need to:

A Classify expenditure on capital assets in accordance with the statutory distinction between capital and revenue expenditure

B Ensure that entries and calculations relating to the computation of capital allowances for a company are correct

C Make adjustments for private use by business owners

D Ensure that computations and submissions are made in accordance with current tax law and take account of current Revenue practice

E Consult with Revenue staff in an open and constructive manner

F Give timely and constructive advice to clients on the maintenance of accounts and the recording of information relevant to tax returns

G Maintain client confidentiality at all times

Range statement

Performance in this element relates to the following contexts:

- Self-employed individuals – Partnerships

Element 18.2 Compute assessable business income

Performance criteria

In order to perform this element successfully you need to:

A Adjust trading profits and losses for tax purposes

B Make adjustments for private use by business owners

C Divide profits and losses of partnerships amongst partners

D Apply the basis of assessment for unincorporated businesses in the opening and closing years

E Identify the due dates of payment of Income Tax by unincorporated businesses, including payments on account

F Identify the National Insurance Contributions payable by self-employed individuals

G Complete correctly the self-employed and partnership supplementary pages to the Tax Return for individuals, together with relevant claims and elections, and submit them within statutory time limits

H Consult with Revenue staff in an open and constructive manner

I Give timely and constructive advice to clients on the maintenance of accounts and the recording of information relevant to tax returns

J Maintain client confidentiality at all times

Range statement

Performance in this element relates to the following contexts:

- Sole traders – Partnerships

Element 18.3 Prepare capital gains computations

Performance criteria

In order to perform this element successfully you need to:

A Identify and value correctly any chargeable assets that have been disposed of

B Identify shares disposed of by companies

C Calculate chargeable gains and allowable losses

D Apply reliefs, deferrals and exemptions correctly

E Ensure that computations and submissions are made in accordance with current tax law and take account of current Revenue practice

F Consult with Revenue staff in an open and constructive manner

G Give timely and constructive advice to clients on the maintenance of accounts and the recording of information relevant to tax returns

H Maintain client confidentiality at all times

Range statement

Performance in this element relates to the following contexts:

- Chargeable assets that have been:

  Sold
  Gifted
  Lost
  Destroyed

- Reliefs:

  Rollover relief
  Relief for gifts

Element 18.4 Prepare Corporation Tax computations

Performance criteria

In order to perform this element successfully you need to:

A Enter adjusted trading profits and losses, capital allowances, investment income and capital gains in the Corporation Tax computation

B Set-off and deduct loss reliefs and charges correctly

C Calculate Corporation Tax due, taking account of marginal relief

D Identify and set-off Income Tax deductions and credits

E Identify the National Insurance Contributions payable by employers

F Identify the amount of Corporation Tax payable and the due dates of payment, including payments on account

G Complete Corporation Tax returns correctly and submit them, together with relevant claims and elections, within statutory time limits

H Consult with Revenue staff in an open and constructive manner

I Give timely and constructive advice to clients on the maintenance of accounts and the recording of information relevant to tax returns

J Maintain client confidentiality at all times

Range statement

Performance in this element relates to the following contexts:

- Loss reliefs relating to:

  Trade losses – Non-trade losses

Exam Based Assessment technique

Completing exam based assessments successfully at this level is half about having the knowledge, and half about doing yourself full justice on the day. You must have the right **technique**.

The day of the exam based assessment

1. Set at least one **alarm** (or get an alarm call) for a morning exam.
2. Have **something to eat** but beware of eating too much; you may feel sleepy if your system is digesting a large meal.
3. Allow plenty of **time to get to where you are sitting the exam**; have your route worked out in advance and listen to news bulletins to check for potential travel problems.
4. **Don't forget** pens, pencils, rulers, erasers.
5. Put **new batteries** into your calculator and take a spare set (or a spare calculator).
6. **Avoid discussion** about the exam with other candidates outside the venue.

Technique in the exam based assessment

1. **Read the instructions (the 'rubric') on the front of the exam carefully**

   Check that the format hasn't changed. It is surprising how often assessors' reports remark on the number of students who do not attempt all the tasks.

2. **Read the paper twice**

   Read through the paper twice – don't forget that you are given 15 minutes' reading time. Check carefully that you have got the right end of the stick before putting pen to paper. Use your 15 minutes' reading time wisely.

3. **Check the time allocation for each section of the exam**

   Suggested time allocations are given for each section of the exam. When the time for a section is up, you should go on to the next section.

4. **Read the task carefully and plan your answer**

   Read through the task again very carefully when you come to answer it. Plan your answer to ensure that you **keep to the point**. Two minutes of planning plus eight minutes of writing is virtually certain to produce a better answer than ten minutes of writing. Planning will also help you answer the exam question efficiently, for example by identifying workings that can be used for more than one task.

5. **Produce relevant answers**

   Particularly with written answers, make sure you **answer what has been set**, and not what you would have preferred to have been set. Do not, for example, answer a question on **why** something is done with an explanation of **how** it is done.

6. **Work your way steadily through the exam**

   Don't get bogged down in one task. If you are having problems with something, the chances are that everyone else is too.

7 **Produce an answer in the correct format**

The assessor will state **in the requirements** the format which should be used, for example in a report or memorandum.

8 **Do what the assessor wants**

You should ask yourself what the assessor is expecting in an answer; many tasks will demand a combination of technical knowledge and business commonsense. Be careful if you are required to give a decision or make a recommendation; you cannot just list the criteria you will use, but you will also have to say whether those criteria have been fulfilled.

9 **Lay out your numerical computations and use workings correctly**

Make sure the layout is in a style the assessor likes.

Show all your **workings** clearly and explain what they mean. Cross reference them to your answer. This will help the assessor to follow your method (this is of particular importance where there may be several possible answers).

10 **Present a tidy paper**

You are a professional, and it should show in the **presentation of your work**. You should make sure that you write legibly, label diagrams clearly and lay out your work neatly.

11 **Stay until the end of the exam**

Use any spare time **checking and rechecking** your script. Check that you have answered all the requirements of the task and that you have clearly labelled your work. Consider also whether your answer appears reasonable in the light of the information given in the question.

12 **Don't worry if you feel you have performed badly in the exam**

It is more than likely that the other candidates will have found the exam difficult too. As soon as you get up to leave the venue, **forget** that exam and think about the next – or, if it is the last one, celebrate!

13 **Don't discuss an exam with other candidates**

This is particularly the case if you **still have other exams to sit**. Even if you have finished, you should put it out of your mind until the day of the results. Forget about exams and relax!

Assessment strategy

This Unit is assessed by **exam based assessment** only.

Exam based assessment

An exam based assessment is a means of collecting evidence that you have the **essential knowledge and understanding** which underpins competence. It is also a means of collecting evidence across the **range of contexts** for the standards, and of your ability to **transfer skills**, knowledge and understanding to different situations. Thus, although exams contain practical tests linked to the performance criteria, they also focus on the underpinning knowledge and understanding. You should, in addition, expect each exam to contain tasks taken from across a broad range of the standards.

Format of exam

There will be a three hour exam in two sections.

Section 1: Element 18.2 (taxation of sole traders and partnerships)
Section 2: Element 18.4 (taxation of limited companies)

Elements 18.1 and 18.3 can appear in either section.

There will be an additional 15 minutes' reading time.

Further guidance

The Standard is divided into four elements. Element 18.1 is called Prepare capital allowances computations, Element 18.2 is called Compute assessable business income, Element 18.3 is called Prepare capital gains computations and Element 18.4 is called Prepare Corporation Tax computations.

Element 18.1 is not to be seen in isolation. It has an impact on both Element 18.2 and 18.4. This is because both 18.2 and 18.4 require the calculation of **trading** profits or losses, and capital allowances need to be deducted as an allowable expense.

Specific areas that need to be covered are:

1. Awareness of the kind of expenditure on which capital allowances will be available: What is plant and machinery? What is an industrial building? When is expenditure for capital purposes and when is it for revenue purposes?

2. The ability to calculate capital allowances on: Plant and machinery. This includes special rules on: Motor vehicles; Short life assets; Computers; First year allowances; Private use assets (unincorporated businesses only); Industrial buildings allowance (this only includes buildings that have continuously been used for industrial purposes).

These calculations need to be made for both unincorporated and incorporated businesses. The rules governing opening, continuing and ceasing organisations need to be considered.

Writing down allowances, balancing allowances and balancing charges are required.

Students must consider the rationale behind these calculations, so that they can provide a written explanation of the calculations, for instance, when dealing with client queries.

The purpose of **Element 18.2** is to demonstrate the ability to calculate **trading** profits or losses.

Firstly, students should be able to determine whether trading is taking place, for instance, through the use of the badges of trade.

In calculating the adjusted trading profit or loss of the business, a sound knowledge is required of how to adjust the accounting profit or loss. Only a few of the adjustments required are specifically mentioned in the Knowledge and Understanding. This list should be viewed as being indicative, rather than exhaustive. Part of these adjustments is the ability to correctly identify, and adjust for, private usage of expenditure as shown in the accounting profit and loss account.

If the trade is being carried on by a partnership, students need to be able to determine how profits are to be split between the partners according to the rules laid down by the Revenue. This includes changes in the profit-sharing agreement or a change in the composition of the partnership, such as when a partner joins or leaves the business.

For both a sole trader and a partnership, a sound knowledge is required of the rules for opening, continuing and closing years of trade. This includes overlap profits. However, the rules for the change of accounting date are excluded. Such calculations will be expected in round tax months, not in days.

Once determined, students need to demonstrate understanding of the use of the profit or loss in the inclusion of the income tax return. The dates for submission of the return and payment of income tax must be considered, together with the implications of making a late filing of the return. However, the completion of the actual income tax return and completion of the income tax computation is assessable under Unit 19.

If the trading profits figure results in a loss, students must have knowledge of the ways in which such a loss can be relieved. S.385, S.380, S.381 and S. 388 ICTA 1988 should all be covered, but detailed and complex loss relief provisions will not be assessed. Excluded from this are losses for partnerships.

For National Insurance Contributions, knowledge of both Class 2 and Class 4 is required.

Element 18.3 deals with the calculation of capital gains for businesses only. This includes chargeable disposals by individuals and companies of business assets, and of the business itself. Disposal of private assets held by individuals is assessable under Unit 19. Taper relief is therefore included where an individual disposes of a business asset, but the treatment of capital gains for a partnership is excluded.

Capital gains computations may include:

Shares and securities, including rights issues and bonus issues, FA 1985 pool and matching rules
Chattels
Part disposal of assets
Improvement expenditure
Indexation allowance
Tapering relief as appropriate to individuals

A capital gain computation will not be required on any assets acquired before 31 March 1982.

In addition, students should have an understanding of business reliefs, including rollover relief and relief for gifts. Students should be able to demonstrate knowledge about the conditions for such reliefs and be able to complete basic calculations. Complex calculations will not be required, for example assets with non-business use or depreciating assets. Calculations on partial reinvestment or gift relief will be straight forward. The capital tax implications for leases are also excluded.

Under **Element 18.4**, the student must be able to compute the trading profit (called Schedule D Case I profits) or loss of a company using the same rules for capital allowances and adjustment of profit as detailed in Elements 18.1 and 18.2 respectively. A capital gains computation from Element 18.3 may also be included in a full Corporation Tax computation. For periods of accounts, students should be able to understand how those shorter or longer than twelve months affect the CT computation.

If the company has made a loss, knowledge is expected of how to deal with that loss under S.393 (1) and S393A (1) ICTA 1988. This includes computational aspects of loss relief, together with the ability to provide clients with advice on the best option to take for the most tax effective way of handling the loss, albeit in a simple way. The impact of charges on loss relief is restricted to non-trade charges only, given the change in classification of patent royalties from 1 April 2002. Students should be able to deal with company losses other than Schedule D Case I, such as capital losses and Schedule A (property income).

When determining the amount of Corporation Tax payable, the following knowledge is required: the impact of the starting rate, the use of upper and lower limits for small company rate purposes, the use of the marginal relief calculation, together with the impact of associated companies on the limits for the marginal relief, the deduction of income tax and the calculation of Mainstream Corporation Tax payable.

The FA 2004 introduced new rules for non company distributions. This is assessable, but only the basic rules.

Students should also be able to state the due date of payment and be able to explain the self-assessment rules. Translation of these figures to the short version of Form CT600 may also be required.

For National Insurance Contributions, students should be able to compute the NIC payable by companies for their employees who are not contracted out. This includes an understanding of the definition of earnings, on which the NIC will be based.

Excluded topics from this element are: close companies and close investment holding companies, investment companies, groups and consortium structures, group capital gains tax, overseas aspects, including double tax relief, calculation of property income rental income (assessable under Unit 19).

Typical tasks in the first section

- Trading profits computation, leading to either a profit or a loss. This could be for either a sole trader or a partnership
- Set-off of income tax losses for individuals
- Capital allowances computation for industrial buildings and/or plant and machinery
- Capital gains computation for business asset disposals for an individual
- National Insurance Contributions for the self-employed
- Opening and closing rules for unincorporated businesses, including overlap profits
- Completion of the supplementary pages to the Tax Return for individuals

Typical tasks in the second section

- Schedule D Case I computation, leading to either a profit or a loss
- Set-off of Schedule D Case I losses, restricted to a scenario involving four years
- Capital allowances computation for industrial buildings and/or plant and machinery
- Capital gains computation for limited companies
- Calculation of the Corporation Tax payable, including small company marginal relief, MCT and the dates of payment
- National Insurance Contributions for the employees of companies
- Completion of the Corporation Tax returns

It is not anticipated that students will be required to compute certain topics more than once during the examination. For instance, capital allowances for industrial buildings and plant and machinery will only be assessed once in either Section 1 or Section 2. The same principle applies for capital gains, although it may be appropriate to assess the disposal of a business in Section 1 and the disposal of shares in Section 2.

Tax rates and allowances

A Income tax

1 Rates

	2005/06		2004/05	
	£	%	£	%
Starting rate	1 – 2,090	10	1 – 2,020	10
Basic rate	2,091 – 32,400	22	2,021 – 31,400	22
Higher rate	32,401 and above	40	31,401 and above	40

Savings (excl. Dividend) income is taxed at 20% if it falls in the basic rate band. Dividend income in both the starting rate and the basic rate bands is taxed at 10%. Dividend income within the higher rate band is taxed at 32.5%.

2 Allowances

	2005/06	2004/05
	£	£
Personal allowance	4,895	4,745

3 Capital allowances

	%
Plant and machinery	
Writing down allowance	25
First year allowance (acquisitions after 2.7.98)	40
First year allowances for small enterprises (1.4.04 – 31.3.05 or 6.4.04 – 5.4.05)	50
First year allowance (information and communication technology equipment – period 1.4.00 – 31.3.04, energy/water saving equipment)	100
Industrial buildings allowance	
Writing down allowance:	4

B Corporation tax

1 Rates

Financial year	*Full rate*	*Small companies rate*	*Starting rate*	*Starting rate marginal relief fraction*	*Lower limit for starting rate*	*Upper limit for starting rate*	*Small companies' rate marginal relief*	*Lower limit for SCR*	*Upper Limit for SCR*
	%	%			£	£		£	£
2002	30	19	0	19/400	10,000	50,000	11/400	300,000	1,500,000
2003	30	19	0	19/400	10,000	50,000	11/400	300,000	1,500,000
2004	30	19	0	19/400	10,000	50,000	11/400	300,000	1,500,000
2005	30	19	0	19/400	10,000	50,000	11/400	300,000	1,500,000

2 Marginal relief

$(M - P) \times I/P \times$ Marginal relief fraction

C Capital gains tax

1 Annual exemption (individuals)

	£
2004/05	8,200
2005/06	8,500

2 Taper relief

Number of complete years after 5.4.98 for which asset held	*Business assets % of gain chargeable*
0	100
1	50
2	25
3	25
4	25
5	25
6	25
7	25

D National insurance (not contracted out rates) 2005/06

Class 1 contributions

Employer

Earnings threshold	£4,895 (£94 pw)
Employer contributions	12.8% on earnings above earnings threshold

Class 1A contributions

Rate 12.8%

Class 2 contributions

Rate	£2.10 pw
Small earnings exception	£4,345 pa

Class 4 contributions

Main rate between LEL and UEL	8%
Additional rate above UEL	1%
Lower earnings limit	£4,895
Upper earnings limit	£32,760

P A R T A

Business taxation

chapter 1

Introduction to business taxation

Contents

Performance criteria

This is an introductory chapter and there are no specific performance criteria applicable to it.

Range statement

This chapter is an introductory chapter dealing with knowledge that is core to all four elements in Unit 18.

Knowledge and understanding

2 The issues of taxation liability (Elements 18.1, 18.2, 18.3, 18.4)

3 Relevant legislation and guidance from the Revenue (Elements 18.1, 18.2, 18.3, 18.4)

4 Basic law and practice (Elements 18.1, 18.2, 18.3, 18.4)

1 Business taxes

A business may be carried on by:

(i) a **sole trader** (ie a self employed individual), or
(ii) a **partnership** (ie a group of self employed individuals), or
(iii) a **limited company**

Sole traders and partnerships are unincorporated businesses. This means that there is no legal separation between the individual(s) carrying on the business and the business itself. As a result **the individual(s) concerned must pay income tax on any income arising from the business and capital gains tax on any gains arising on the disposal of business assets.** You will study income tax and capital gains tax in the first part of this text.

Companies are incorporated businesses. This means that they are taxed as separate legal entities independently of their owners. **Companies must pay corporation tax on their total profits**. Total profits include income arising from all sources and gains arising on the disposal of any assets. You will study corporation tax in the second part of this text.

As a general rule, income is a receipt that is expected to recur (such as business profits), whereas a gain is a one off profit on the disposal of a capital asset (eg the profit on the sale of a factory used in the business).

2 Relevant legislation and guidance from the Revenue

The main tax law is incorporated into the following Acts of Parliament.

(i) The Income and Corporation Taxes Act 1988
(ii) The Taxation of Chargeable Gains Act 1992
(iii) The Income Tax (Trading and Other Income) Act 2005

These Acts are amended by the Annual Finance Acts which incorporate proposals set out each year in the Chancellor's Budget Speech. **This text includes the provisions of the Finance Act 2005 and the Finance (No 2) Act 2005. The Finance Acts 2005 will be examined in June 2006 and December 2006.**

The above statute is interpreted and amplified by **case law**. The Revenue also issue:

(a) **statements of practice**, setting out how they intend to apply the law

(b) **extra–statutory concessions**, setting out circumstances in which they will not apply the strict letter of the law

(c) a wide range of **explanatory leaflets**

(d) **business economic notes**. These are notes on particular types of business, which are used as background information by the Revenue and are also published

(e) the **Tax Bulletin**. This is a newsletter giving the Revenue's view on specific points. It is published every two months

(f) the **Internal Guidance**, a series of manuals used by Revenue staff

However, none of these Revenue publications has the force of law.

A great deal of information and the Revenue publications can now be found on the Revenue's Internet site (www.hmrc.gov.uk).

3 Sources of income

We saw above that individuals must pay income tax on their income whilst companies must pay corporation tax on income.

There are different rules for calculating the taxable income, depending on the source of income. Historically the rules divide income into different schedules, and some schedules were further divided into cases. This terminology has been abolished for income tax, but it is still used for corporation tax.

The categories of income that you may need to be aware of at Unit 18 are as follows:

- Taxable trading profits, including profits from professions and vocations (Schedule D Case I income for companies)
- Property income, such as rents etc from land and buildings in the UK (Schedule A income for companies)
- Interest, such as from banks and buildings societies, and other savings income (Schedule D Case III for companies)
- Other incomes, not being in one of the above categories (Schedule D Case VI for companies)

4 The aggregation of income

Although the examination for Unit 18 is concerned with business taxation, you may need to know broadly how to compute an individual's income tax liability in order to give advice on, for example, utilising business losses. The remainder of this chapter, therefore, gives brief details of this computation. If you study Unit 19 *Preparing Personal Tax Computations* you will deal with the personal tax computations in more detail.

4.1 Statutory total income

An individual's income from all sources is brought together in a personal tax computation. We split income into non-savings income, savings (excl. dividend) income and dividend income. This means that when preparing an income tax computation you need three columns headed as follows:

Non-savings income	Savings (excluding dividend) income	Dividend income
£	£	£

The total of an individual's income from all sources is known as **statutory total income.**

Interest and dividends are **'savings income'** All other income is non-savings income.

4.2 Personal allowance

All persons are entitled to the personal allowance of £4,895.

The personal allowance is deducted from **statutory total income** to give **taxable income**. It comes off non-savings income first, then savings (excl. dividend) income and then dividend income.

4.3 Layout of personal tax computation

Here is a complete proforma computation of taxable income. We include it here as you might find it useful to refer back to later.

	Non-savings	*Savings (excluding dividend) income*	*Dividend*	*Total*
	£	£	£	£
Business profits	X			
Less losses set against business profits	(X)			
	X			
Other non-savings	X			
Interest		X		
Dividends			X	
	X	X	X	
Less losses set against general income	(X)	(X)	(X)	
STI	X	X	X	X
Less personal allowance	(X)	(X)	(X)	
Taxable income	X	X	X	X

The following is an example of how a personal tax computation should be laid out. We will look at the computation of business income in more detail later in this text.

Example

RICHARD: INCOME TAX COMPUTATION 2005/06

	Non-savings income	*Savings (excl dividend) income*	*Dividend income*	*Total*
	£	£	£	£
Business profits	38,000			
Building society interest		1,320		
UK dividends			1,000	
Statutory total income (STI)	38,000	1,320	1,000	40,320
Less: personal allowance	(4,895)			
Taxable income	33,105	1,320	1,000	35,425

Now follow the above layout to try the next activity for yourself.

Activity 1.1

An individual has the following income in 2005/06.

	£
Business profits	16,000
Building society interest	6,000
Dividends	8,750

His personal allowance is £4,895. What is his total taxable income?

5 Calculation of income tax liability

5.1 Income tax bands

The first step in calculating the income tax liability is to divide the total **taxable income** into three bands:

(i) the first £2,090 of income; this is called income in the **starting rate band**
(ii) the next £30,310 of income; this is income in the **basic rate band**
(iii) the remaining income over the **higher rate threshold** of £32,400

The rate of tax applied to the income in each band depends on whether the income is non-savings income, savings (excluding dividend) income or dividend income.

There is only one set of income tax bands used for all three types of income. These bands **must be allocated to income in the following order:**

(i) **non-savings income**
(ii) **savings** (excluding dividend) **income**
(iii) **dividend income**

Example

Zoë has total taxable income of £33,000. Of this £19,000 is non-savings income, £12,000 is interest and £2,000 is dividend income.

The first £2,090 of non-savings income is in the starting rate band. The remaining £16,910 of non-savings income is in the basic rate band. This leaves £13,400 (£30,310 – £16,910) of the basic rate band.

The next £12,000 of the basic rate band is used by interest income, leaving £1,400 (£13,400 - £12,000) of the basic rate band to be used by dividend income.

The remaining dividend income £600 (£2,000 – £1,400) is income above the higher rate threshold.

5.2 Tax rate

Non-savings income in the starting rate band is taxed at 10%. Next any non-savings income in the basic rate band is taxed at 22%, and finally non-savings income above the higher rate threshold is taxed at 40%.

Savings (excl dividend) income is dealt with after non-savings income. If any of the starting or basic rate bands remain **after taxing non-savings income** they can be used here. Savings (excl dividend) income is taxed at 10% in the starting rate band. If savings (excl dividend) income falls within the basic rate band it is taxed at 20% (not 22%). Once income is above the higher rate threshold, it is taxed at 40%.

Lastly, tax dividend income. If dividend income falls within the starting or basic rate bands, it is taxed at 10% (never 20% or 22%). If, however, the dividend income exceeds the basic rate threshold of £31,400, it is taxed at 32.5%

Example

Continuing Zoë's income tax computation above, the tax liability is:

	£
Income tax	
Non savings income	
£2,090 × 10%	209
£16,910 × 22%	3,720
£19,000	
Savings (excl. dividend) income	
£12,000 × 20%	2,400
Dividend income	
£1,400 × 10%	140
£600 × 32.5%	195
2,000	
Tax liabilities	6,664

Activity 1.2

An individual has total taxable income of £50,000 for 2005/06. All of his income is non-savings income. What is the total income tax liability?

6 Examples of personal tax computations

Now let us work through some complete computations of an individual's income tax liability.

(a) Kathe has business profits of £10,000 and dividends of £5,000.

	Non-savings	*Dividends*	*Total*
	£	£	£
Business profits	10,000		
Dividends		5,000	
STI	10,000	5,000	15,000
Less personal allowance	(4,895)		
Taxable income	5,105	5,000	10,105

	£
Income tax	
Non savings income	
£2,090 × 10%	209
£3,015 × 22%	663
Dividend income	
£5,000 × 10%	500
Tax liability	1,372

The dividend income falls within the **basic rate band** so it is taxed at 10% (*not* 22%).

(b) Jules has business profits of £48,000, dividends of £7,500 and building society interest of £3,750.

	Non-savings	*Savings (excl dividend)*	*Dividends*	*Total*
	£	£	£	£
Business profits	48,000			
Dividends			7,500	
Building society interest		3,750		
STI	48,000	3,750	7,500	59,250
Less personal allowance	(4,895)			
Taxable income	43,105	3,750	7,500	54,355

	£
Income tax	
Non savings income	
£2,090 × 10%	209
£30,310 × 22%	6,668
£10,705 × 40%	4,282
	11,159
Savings (excl. dividend) income	
£3,750 × 40%	1,500
Dividend income	
£7,500 × 32.5%	2,438
	15,097

Savings (excl. dividend) income and dividend income fall above the basic rate threshold so they are taxed at 40% and 32.5% respectively.

Key learning points

- ☑ Businesses may be operated by a **sole trader**, **partnerships** or **companies**.
- ☑ Individuals trading as sole traders or in partnerships suffer **income tax** and **capital gains tax**.
- ☑ Companies suffer **corporation tax**.
- ☑ All of an individual's sources of income are **aggregated** in a **personal tax computation** to arrive at **statutory total income.**
- ☑ Income is divided into **non-savings** income, **savings (excluding dividend)** income and **dividend** income.
- ☑ The **personal allowance** is deducted from Statutory Total Income.
- ☑ The rate of income tax charged depends on which income tax band the income falls into. There is one set of **income tax bands** which applies to all the income.
- ☑ The **non-savings income is taxed first**, then the **savings (excluding dividends) income** and **finally dividend income**.

Quick quiz

1 What are the main UK taxes suffered by businesses?

2 At what rates is income tax charged on non-savings income?

3 Why do you need to know the source of income?

Answers to quick quiz

1 Income tax and capital gains tax by individuals, corporation tax by companies.

2 10%, 22% and 40%

3 Different tax rules apply to the computation of income depending on its source, and different income tax rates apply to different types of income.

Activity checklist

This checklist shows which knowledge and understanding point is covered by each activity in this chapter. Tick off each activity as you complete it.

Activity

1.1	☐	This activity deals with Knowledge and Understanding point 2: the issues of tax liability.
1.2	☐	This activity deals with Knowledge and Understanding point 2: the issues of tax liability.

chapter 2

Computing trading income

Contents

Performance criteria

18.1 A Classify expenditure on capital assets in accordance with the statutory distinction between capital and revenue expenditure

18.2 A Adjust trading profits and losses for tax purposes

18.2 B Make adjustments for private use by business owners

Range statement

18.2 Clients: sole traders, partnerships

Knowledge and understanding

4 Basic Law and Practice (Elements 18.1, 18.2, 18.3, 18.4)

7 Adjustment of trading profits and losses for tax purposes (Element 18.2)

8 Regulations relating to disallowed expenditure such as business entertaining, bad debt write-offs and provisions, private expenditure and capital expenditure (Element 18.2)

1 The badges of trade

1.1 Nature of 'trade'

A trade is defined in the legislation only in an unhelpful manner as including every trade, manufacture, adventure or concern in the nature of a trade. It has therefore been left to the courts to provide guidance. This guidance is often summarised in a collection of principles known as the **'badges of trade'**. These are set out below.

If a person carries on a trade he will have **trading income which is subject to tax**. The question of whether or not a trade is being carried on is therefore an important one.

1.2 Traditional badges of trade

1.2.1 The subject matter

Whether a person is trading or not may sometimes be decided by examining the subject matter of the transaction. Some assets are commonly held as investments for their intrinsic value: an individual buying some shares or a painting may do so in order to enjoy the income from the shares or to enjoy the work of art. Any subsequent disposal, even at a profit, may produce a gain of a capital nature rather than a trading profit. But **where the subject matter of a transaction is such as would not be held as an investment** (for example 34,000,000 yards of aircraft linen (*Martin v Lowry 1927*) or 1,000,000 rolls of toilet paper (*Rutledge v CIR 1929*)), **it is to be presumed that any profit on resale is a trading profit.**

1.2.2 The frequency of transactions

Transactions which may be treated in isolation as being of a capital nature will be interpreted as trading transactions where their **frequency indicates the carrying on of a trade**. It was decided that whereas normally the purchase of a mill-owning company and the subsequent stripping of its assets might be a capital transaction, where the taxpayer was embarking on the same exercise for the fourth time he must be carrying on a trade (*Pickford v Quirke 1927*).

1.2.3 The length of ownership

It may be decided that a trade is being carried on where items purchased are sold soon afterwards.

1.2.4 Supplementary work and marketing

When work is done to make an asset more marketable, or steps are taken to find purchasers, the courts will be more ready to ascribe a trading motive. When a group of accountants bought, blended and recasked a quantity of brandy they were held to be taxable on a trading profit when the brandy was later sold (*Cape Brandy Syndicate v CIR 1921*).

1.2.5 A profit motive

The absence of a profit motive will not necessarily preclude an income tax assessment on trading income, but its presence is a strong indication that a person is trading. The purchase and resale of £20,000 worth of silver bullion by the comedian Norman Wisdom, as a hedge against devaluation, was held to be a trading transaction (*Wisdom v Chamberlain 1969*).

1.2.6 The way in which the asset sold was acquired

If goods are acquired deliberately, trading may be indicated. If goods are acquired unintentionally, for example by gift or inheritance, their later sale is unlikely to constitute trading.

1.3 The taxpayer's intentions

Where a transaction clearly amounts to trading on objective criteria, **the taxpayer's intentions are irrelevant**. If, however, a transaction has (objectively) a dual purpose, the taxpayer's intentions may be taken into account. An example of a transaction with a dual purpose is the acquisition of a site partly as premises from which to conduct another trade, and partly with a view to the possible development and resale of the site.

This intentions test is not one of the traditional badges of trade, but it may be just as important.

Activity 2.1

Gareth inherited some land. He then bought some adjoining land, drained the combined plot, applied for planning permission and sold the combined plot at a profit. Which badges of trade would indicate that he was trading?

1.4 Alternative charges to income tax

If income is received by an individual and on applying the badges of trade the Revenue do not conclude that the income is 'trading income' then they can potentially treat it as other income or a capital gain.

2 The adjustment of profits

The net profit before taxation shown in a businesses accounts provides a starting point in computing the taxable trading profit. However, many adjustments may be required to the accounts profit to find the actual taxable trading profit.

Note that professions and vocations are taxed in exactly the same way as trades.

There are four main reasons why adjustments may be needed to the accounts profit.

2.1 Expenditure deducted in arriving at the accounts profit is not deductible in computing taxable trading profits

Expenditure on entertaining clients, for example, cannot be deducted from income in arriving at taxable trading profits. If that expenditure has been deducted in arriving at the accounts profit, the expenditure must be **'added back'** to the accounts profit to find taxable trading profits.

Expenditure which cannot be deducted in arriving at taxable trading profits is known as **'disallowable'** or **'non-deductible'** expenditure. We look at various types of non-deductible expenditure below.

2.2 Income included in accounts profit is not taxable as trading income

Some income included within the accounts profit may not be taxable as trading income. For example, rental income is taxed under separate rules as property income, not trading income. If such income is included in as the accounts profit it must be deducted from the accounts profit to arrive at the taxable trading profits.

There are three types of receipts which may be found in the accounting profits but which must be excluded from the computation of taxable trading profits. These are:

(a) **capital receipts**
(b) **income taxed in another way**
(c) **income specifically exempt from tax**

Note that compensation received in one lump sum for the loss of income is likely to be treated as income.

2.3 Items specifically deductible from taxable trading profits is not deducted in arriving at the accounts profit

Capital allowances (see later in this text) are an example of a deduction allowed by statute in arriving at taxable trading profits that will not have been not deducted in arriving at account profits. Therefore an adjustment to accounts profit is needed to arrive at taxable trading profits.

2.4 Items taxable as trading income is not included in the accounts

The usual example is when a proprietor takes goods for his own use. In such circumstances the normal selling price of the goods is added to the accounting profit. In other words, the proprietor is treated for tax purposes as having made a sale to himself. This rule does not apply to supplies of services, which are treated as sold for the amount (if any) actually paid (but the cost of services to the trader or his household is not deductible).

2.5 Illustrative adjustment

Here is an illustrative adjustment.

	£	£
Net profit per accounts		140,000
Add: expenditure charged in the accounts which is not deductible from taxable trading profits	50,000	
income taxable as trading income which has not been included in the accounts	30,000	
		80,000
		220,000
Less: profits included in the accounts but which are not trading income	40,000	
expenditure which is deductible from taxable trading profits but has not been charged in the accounts	20,000	
		(60,000)
Profit adjusted for tax purposes		160,000

You may refer to **deductible and non-deductible** expenditure as **allowable and disallowable** expenditure respectively. The two sets of terms are interchangeable.

Individuals and companies are taxed on taxable trading profits income. However, the computation of taxable trading profits for companies differs slightly to the computation for individuals. We mention this at relevant points in this chapter. Companies are dealt with in more detail later in this text.

3 Deductible and non-deductible expenditure

3.1 Payments contrary to public policy and illegal payments

Fines and penalties are not deductible. However, the Revenue usually allow employees' parking fines incurred in parking their employer's cars while on their employer's business. Fines relating to proprietors, however, are never allowed. (Similarly, a company would not be able to deduct fines relating to directors – companies are covered later in this text.)

A payment is (by statute) not deductible if making it constitutes an offence by the payer. This covers protection money paid to terrorists, and also bribes. Statute law also prevents any deduction for payments made in response to blackmail or extortion.

3.2 Capital expenditure

Income tax is a tax solely on income and so capital expenditure is not deductible. The most contentious items of expenditure will often be repairs (revenue expenditure) **and improvements** (capital expenditure).

- The cost of restoration of an asset by, for instance, replacing a subsidiary part of the asset will be treated as revenue expenditure. It was held that expenditure on a new factory chimney replacement was allowable since the chimney was a subsidiary part of the factory (*Samuel Jones & Co (Devondale) Ltd v CIR 1951.* However, in another case a football club demolished a spectators' stand and replaced it with a modern equivalent. This was held not to be repair, since repair is the restoration by renewal or replacement of subsidiary parts of a larger entity, and the stand formed a distinct and *separate* part of the club (*Brown v Burnley Football and Athletic Co Ltd 1980*

- The cost of initial repairs to improve an asset recently acquired to make it fit to earn profits is disallowable capital expenditure. In *Law Shipping Co Ltd v CIR 1923* the taxpayer failed to obtain relief for expenditure on making a newly bought ship seaworthy prior to using it.
- The cost of initial repairs to remedy normal wear and tear of recently acquired assets will be treated as allowable. *Odeon Associated Theatres Ltd v Jones 1971* can be contrasted with the *Law Shipping* judgement. Odeon were allowed to charge expenditure incurred on improving the state of recently acquired cinemas.

Two exceptions to the 'capital' rule are worth noting.

(a) The costs of **registering patents and trade marks** are deductible.

(b) **Incidental costs of obtaining loan finance**, or of attempting to obtain or redeeming it, are deductible other than a discount on issue or a premium on redemption (which are really alternatives to paying interest). This deduction for incidental costs does not apply to companies because they get a deduction for the costs of borrowing in a different way. We will look at companies later in this text.

Activity 2.2

Sue bought a new tractor for use in her farming business on 1 July 2005. Sue began to use the tractor in her business immediately. Six months later she spent £600 on buying new tyres for the tractor. Explain to Sue how the expenditure on the tyres will be treated in the tax computation giving reasons for the treatment.

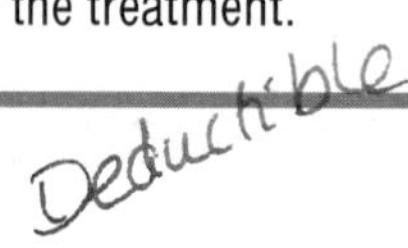

3.3 Depreciation

Depreciation or amortisation may be charged in the accounts on fixed and current assets. Depreciation **is not deductible** in the computation of taxable trading profits and therefore **must be added back** to the accounts profit. Instead capital allowances (see the next chapter) may be given on the assets involved.

3.4 Appropriations

Salary or interest on capital paid to a sole trader or partner, are not deductible.

3.5 Private payments

The private proportion of payments for motoring expenses, rent, heat and light and telephone expenses of a proprietor is not deductible. Where the payments are to or on behalf of employees, the full amounts are deductible but the employees are taxed on the benefits.

Activity 2.3

Sana runs her business from home. Sana has deducted all of her heating and lighting bills of £800 in computing her accounts profit. 30% of the heating and lighting bills relate to be business. What amounts must be added back in computing taxable trading profits?

£560

3.6 Provisions

General provisions are not deductible. A specific provision against a particular trade debt is deductible if it is a reasonable estimate of the likely loss.

3.7 Patent and copyright royalties

Royalties (also known as charges on income) are dealt with in the personal tax computation, so they cannot also be deducted in computing trading profits. Any charges deducted in the accounts must be added back in computing taxable trading profits. You do not need to worry about the deduction of charges in the personal tax computations in this Unit. You will study this if you take Unit 19.

3.8 Entertaining and gifts

Entertaining for and gifts to employees are normally deductible although where gifts are made, or the entertainment is excessive, a charge to tax may arise on the employee under the benefits legislation.

Gifts to customers not costing more than £50 per donee per year are allowed if they carry a conspicuous advertisement for the business and are not food, drink, tobacco or vouchers exchangeable for goods.

Gifts to charities may also be allowed although many will fall foul of the 'wholly and exclusively' rule below.

There is a scheme for giving known as the 'gift aid' scheme. If a gift aid declaration is made in respect of a gift, income tax relief will be given under the gift aid scheme, **not as a deduction from taxable trading profits**. You will learn how this relief is given for gift aid donations if you study Unit 19. You do not need to study it at Unit 18. However, you may need to add the gift aid donations back to accounts profit in computing taxable trading profits.

All other expenditure on entertaining and gifts is non-deductible.

Activity 2.4

The entertainment account of Green and Co showed:

	£
Staff tennis outing for 30 employees	1,800
2,000 tee shirts with firm's logo given to race runners	4,500
Advertising and sponsorship of an athletic event	2,000
Entertaining customers	7,300
Staff Christmas party (30 employees)	2,400

What amount must be added back in arriving at taxable trading profits?

3.9 Expenditure not wholly and exclusively for the purposes of the trade

Expenditure is not deductible if it is not for the purposes of the trade (the remoteness test), or if it reflects more than one purpose (the duality test). If an exact apportionment is possible (as with motor expenses) relief is given on the business element.

The remoteness test is illustrated by the following cases.

- *Strong & Co of Romsey Ltd v Woodifield 1906*

  A customer injured by a falling chimney when sleeping in an inn owned by a brewery claimed compensation from the company. The compensation was not deductible: 'the loss sustained by the appellant was not really incidental to their trade as innkeepers and fell upon them in their character not of innkeepers but of householders'.

- *Bamford v ATA Advertising Ltd 1972*

  A director misappropriated £15,000. The loss was not allowable: 'the loss is not, as in the case of a dishonest shop assistant, an incident of the company's trading activities. It arises altogether outside such activities'.

- Expenditure which is wholly and exclusively to benefit the trades of several companies (for example in a group) but is not wholly and exclusively to benefit the trade of one specific company is not deductible *(Vodafone Cellular Ltd and others v Shaw 1995)*.

- *McKnight (HMIT) v Sheppard (1999)* concerned expenses incurred by a stockbroker in defending allegations of infringements of Stock Exchange regulations. It was found that the expenditure was incurred to prevent the destruction of the taxpayer's business and that as the expenditure was incurred for business purposes it was deductible. It was also found that although the expenditure had the effect of preserving the taxpayer's reputation, that was not its purpose, so there was no duality of purpose.

The **duality test** is illustrated by the following cases.

- *Caillebotte v Quinn 1975*

  A self-employed carpenter spent an average of 40p per day when obliged to buy lunch away from home but just 10p when he lunched at home. He claimed the excess 30p. It was decided that the payment had a dual purpose and was not deductible: 'a Schedule D taxpayer must eat to live not eat to work'.

- *Mallalieu v Drummond 1983*

  Expenditure by a lady barrister on black clothing to be worn in court (and on its cleaning and repair) was not deductible. The expenditure was for the dual purpose of enabling the barrister to be warmly and properly clad as well as meeting her professional requirements.

- *McLaren v Mumford 1996*

  A publican, traded from a public house which had residential accommodation above it. He was obliged to live at the public house but he also had another house which he visited regularly. It was held that the private element of the expenditure incurred at the public house on electricity, rent, gas, etc was not incurred for the purpose of earning profits, but for serving the non-business purpose of satisfying the publican's ordinary human needs. The expenditure, therefore had a dual purpose and was disallowed.

However, the cost of overnight accommodation when on a business trip may be deductible and reasonable expenditure on an evening meal and breakfast in conjunction with such accommodation is then also deductible.

3.10 Subscriptions and donations

There is a general 'wholly and exclusively' rule which determines the deductibility of expenses. Subscriptions and donations are not deductible unless the expenditure is for the benefit of the trade. The following are the main types of subscriptions and donations you may meet and their correct treatments.

(a) Trade subscriptions (such as to a professional or trade association) are generally deductible.

(b) Charitable donations are deductible only if they are small and to local charities. Tax relief may be available for donations under the gift aid scheme (see above). However, gift aid donations are not a deductible trading expense.

(c) Political subscriptions and donations are generally not deductible. However, if it can be shown that political expenditure is incurred for the survival of the trade then it may be deducted. This follows a case in which it was held that expenditure incurred in resisting nationalisation was allowable on the grounds that it affected the survival of the business (*Morgan v Tate and Lyle Ltd 1954)*

3.11 Legal and professional charges

Legal and professional charges relating to capital or non-trading items are not deductible. These include charges incurred in acquiring new capital assets or legal rights, issuing shares, drawing up partnership agreements and litigating disputes over the terms of a partnership agreement.

Charges incurred are deductible when they relate directly to trading. Deductible items include:

- legal and professional charges incurred defending the taxpayer's title to fixed assets
- charges connected with an action for breach of contract
- expenses of the **renewal** (not the original grant) of a lease for less than 50 years;
- charges for trade debt collection
- normal charges for preparing accounts and assisting with the self assessment of tax liabilities

Accountancy expenses arising out of an enquiry into the accounts information in a particular year's return are not allowed where the enquiry reveals discrepancies and additional liabilities for the year of enquiry, or any earlier year, which arise as a result of negligent or fraudulent conduct. Where, however, the enquiry results in no addition to profits, or an adjustment to the profits for the year of enquiry only and that assessment does not arise as a result of negligent or fraudulent conduct, the additional accountancy expenses are allowable.

Accountancy expenses relating to specialist consultancy work are not deductible.

Activity 2.5

A manufacturing business spends the following amounts on legal and professional services.

		£
Debt collection:	trade debts	500
	loan to former employee (covered in Section 3.12)	230
Defending action for faulty goods		1,900
Preparing accounts		450
Specialist tax consultancy		700
		3,780

How much must be added back in computing the taxable profits?

Activity 2.6

A sole trader incurred legal fees during his twelve month accounting period ended 31 December 2005 on the following:

	£
Directors' service contracts	12,000
On a loan to be used to acquire a new factory	9,000
Defending an action for faulty workmanship	6,000
Bringing a tax appeal to the High Court	16,000
Obtaining planning permission to extend a factory	8,000

In arriving at the taxable trading profits, the amount added back will be:

A £25,000
B £31,000
C £33,000
D £39,000

3.12 Bad and doubtful debts

Only bad debts incurred in the course of a business are deductible for taxation purposes.

Loans to employees written off are not deductible unless the business is that of making loans, or it can be shown that the writing-off of the loan was an emolument laid out for the benefit of the trade.

General doubtful debt provisions are not deductible, but specific provisions and write-offs against individual debts are deductible. The only adjustment needed to the accounts profit is to add back an increase (or deduct a decrease) in the general provision.

Activity 2.7

The bad and doubtful debts account of a sole trader was as follows:

	£		£
Debts written off		Balances brought forward	
Trade	9,300	General provision	15,300
Loan to customer	1,400	Specific provision	7,800
Balances carried forward		Bad debts recovered (previously allowed)	5,400
General provision	12,200	Profit and loss account	1,600
Specific provision	7,200		
	30,100		30,100

What adjustment must be made to the accounts profit for tax purposes?

3.13 Interest

Interest paid by an individual on borrowings for trade purposes is deductible as a trading expense on an accruals basis, so no adjustment to the accounts figure is needed.

Individuals cannot deduct interest on overdue tax. Therefore you must add back any interest on overdue tax which has been charged in the accounts.

Companies have different rules for the cost of borrowing. We will look at these later in this text.

3.14 Miscellaneous deductions

Here is a list of various other items that you may meet.

Item	Treatment	Comment
Costs of seconding employees to charities or educational establishments	Allow	
Expenditure incurred in the seven years prior to the commencement of a trade	Allow	Provided expenditure is of a type that would have been allowed had the trade started. Treat as an expense on the first day of trading
Educational courses for staff	Allow	
Educational courses for proprietor	Allow	If to update existing knowledge or skills, not if to acquire new knowledge or skills
Removal expenses (to new business premises)	Allow	Only if not an expansionary move
Travelling expenses to the trader's place of business	Disallow	*Ricketts v Colquhoun 1925*: unless an itinerant trader (*Horton v Young 1971*)
Redundancy payments	Allow	On the earlier of the day of payment and the last day of trading. If the trade does not end, they can be deducted as soon as they are provided for, so long as the redundancy was decided on within the period of account, the provision is accurately calculated and the payments are made within nine months of the end of the period of account If the trade ceases, the limit on allowability is 3 × the statutory amount (in addition to the statutory amount)
Compensation for loss of office and ex gratia payments	Allow	If for benefit of trade.
Contributions to any of: local enterprise agencies; training and enterprise councils; local enterprise companies; business link organisations	Allow	
Pension contributions (to schemes for employees and company directors)	Allow	If paid, not if only provided for; special contributions may be spread over the year of payment and future years
Premiums for insurance: against an employee's death or illness to cover locum costs or fixed overheads whilst the policyholder is ill	Allow	Receipts are taxable
Payments to employees for restrictive undertakings	Allow	Taxable on employee
Damages paid	Allow	If not too remote from trade: *Strong and Co v Woodifield 1906*
Improving an individual's personal security	Allow	Trader must be an individual or a partnership (not a company). Provision of a car, ship or dwelling is excluded

In the exam you could be given a copy of a business's profit and loss account and asked to calculate 'taxable trading profits'. You will have to look at every expense charged in the accounts to decide if it is (or isn't) a 'tax deductible expense'. To help you to achieve this you must become familiar with the many expenses you are likely to see and the correct tax treatment. Look at the above paragraphs again noting what expenses are (and are not) allowable for tax purposes.

Activity 2.8

Here is the profit and loss account of S Pring, a trader.

	£	£
Gross operating profit		30,000
Rental income received		860
		30,860
Wages and salaries	7,000	
Rent and rates	2,000	
Depreciation	1,500	
Specific bad debts written off	150	
Provision against a fall in the price of raw materials	5,000	
Entertainment expenses	750	
Patent royalties	1,200	
Bank interest	300	
Legal expenses on acquisition of new factory	250	
		(18,150)
Net profit		12,710

(a) Salaries include £500 paid to Mrs Pring who works full time in the business. X

(b) No staff were entertained.

(c) The provision of £5,000 is a general provision charged because of an anticipated trade recession.

Compute the taxable trading profit.

Sch D I

Net Profit per A/cs		12,710
Add disallowed Exp		
Depreciation	1500	
General Provision	5000	
Entertainment	750	
Patent Royalty	1200	
Legal (new factory capital)	250	
		8700
		21,410
~~Add~~ less Allowable Income under DI		(860)
Adjusted trading Profit		20550

4 End of chapter activity

Activity 2.9

The profit and loss account of Mr Brillo for the year ended 31 December 2005 shows the following.

		£		£
Staff wages		2,416	Gross profit from trading account	10,326
Wife's wages		624	Profit on sale of plant	240
Rent		630	Profit on sale of investment	1,032
Light and heat		171	Bank interest received	54
Motor car expenses		336		
Telephone		79		
Postage, stationery and wrapping		80		
Repairs and renewals		476		
Bad debts written off		100		
Miscellaneous expenses		346		
Advertising		24		
Loan interest		130		
Depreciation: plant	480			
motor car	120	600		
Net profit		5,640		
		11,652		11,652

Notes

(a) One third of the expenditure on rent, light and heat relates to living accommodation at the business premises.

(b) One seventh of the motor expenses relate to private motoring.

(c) Repairs and renewals comprise the following.

	£
Painting shop internally	155
Plant repairs	220
Building extension to stockroom	101
	476

(d) BAD DEBTS ACCOUNT

2005		£	*2005*		£
31 Dec	Bad debts written off	102	1 Jan	Balances b/f	
	Balances c/f			General	200
	General	400		Specific	360
	Specific	398			560
			31 Dec	Bad debt recovered	240
				Profit & loss account	100
		900			900

(e) Miscellaneous expenses comprise the following.

	£
Donations to the Spastics Society	10
Subscription to the Chamber of Commerce	8
Entertaining customers	90
Christmas gifts to customers:	
bottles of gin costing £8.75 each, one per customer with 'Mr Brillo' labels	70
Payments to employees in lieu of notice	50
Legal expenses re debt collecting	15
Sundries: all allowable	103
	346

(f) The profit on the sale of an investment relates to the sale of a holding of ordinary shares in a company quoted on the Stock Exchange. The capital gain on these shares was £7,690.

(g) Mrs Brillo assists full time in the business.

(h) Gross profit is 15% of selling price and Brillo estimates that he has withdrawn goods costing £340 for his own use. No entry has been made in the accounts in respect of this.

(i) The staff wages include £260 paid to Brillo.

Task

Compute Mr Brillo's tax adjusted trading profit for the year ended 31 December 2005. Explain your reasons for treating any items as disallowable/not taxable.

5640

Plus

Key learning points

☑ The **badges of trade** can be used to decide whether or not a trade exists.

☑ If there is a trade, the **accounts profits need to be adjusted** in order to **calculate taxable trading profits.**

Add back any of the following expenditure which has been charged in the accounts:

☑ **Entertaining** of anyone other than staff

☑ **Depreciation**

☑ An **increase in general bad debt provision**

☑ **Fines and penalties**

☑ Legal and professional charges relating to **capital items**

☑ **Wages or salary paid to a proprietor**

The following expenditure is allowable:

☑ **Gifts costing not more than £50 per donee per year providing they carry a conspicuous advertisement for the business and are not food, drink, tobacco or vouchers exchangeable for goods**

☑ **Staff entertaining**

☑ **Specific bad debts**

Income not taxable as trading income but included in the accounts profit must be deducted eg.

☑ **Rental income** – taxable as property income

☑ **Capital profits** – may be subject to capital gains tax

Deduct items specifically deductible from taxable trading profits which have not been deducted in the accounts, eg

☑ **Capital allowances**

Quick quiz

1 List the six traditional badges of trade.

2 Victor has a trading profit of £220,000 after charging entertainment expenses of £3,200, (including £1,000 for a staff dance), legal fees of £4,500 (of which £800 related to the purchase of a property) and depreciation of £32,000.

Victor's taxable trading profits are:

A £252,000
B £252,800
C £255,000
D £268,800

3 Mr Jones provides an analysis of his business legal expenses as follows:

	£
Successful tax appeal to commissioners	1,600
New employment contract for manager	700
Renewal of 18 year lease	950
Interest paid on a loan to buy a factory for use in the trade	850
Fine for breach of Factories Act	200

The amount to be added back in arriving at his taxable profits is:

A £Nil
B £200
C £1,600
D £1,800

4 Jane, a sole trader, took goods for her own use in the year to 31 March 2006.

	£
Cost of goods taken	100
Market value of goods taken	120
Amount paid by Jane for the goods	85

What amount for tax purposes should be added back to the accounting profit?

5 Which of the following cannot be deducted in computing taxable trading profits for a sole trader?

A Pre-trading expenditure incurred in the seven years prior to the commencement of trade
B Staff entertaining
C Specific bad debts
D Legal fees incurred in relation to the purchase of property

6 The following legal costs were incurred by Jamie during the year ended 31 March 2006:

	£
Re: Employment contracts	1,000
Re: Abortive work on prospective property purchase	2,000
Re: Debt collection	750
	3,750

What amount is an allowable from taxable trading profits?

Answers to quick quiz

1. Subject matter
   Frequency of transactions
   Length of ownership
   Supplementary work and marketing
   Profit motive
   Way the goods were acquired

2. C

		£
Trading profit		220,000
Add:	Entertaining	2,200
	Legal fees	800
Depreciation		32,000
Taxable trading profits		255,000

3. D

	£
Appeal	1,600
Fine	200
	1,800

The legal fees incurred in renewing a short lease are specifically allowable.

4. When a sole trader takes goods for their own use we must ensure that the normal profit is recorded.

   Therefore £120 – £85 = £35

5. D Legal fees incurred in relation to the purchase of a property are a capital item. The other expenses are deductible in computing taxable trading profits.

6. The correct answer is £1,750.

   £1,750 (£1,000 + £750)

   Explanation: Property purchase is capital in nature, therefore disallowed.

Activity checklist

This checklist shows which performance criteria or knowledge and understanding point is covered by each activity in this chapter. Tick off each activity as you complete it.

Activity		
2.1	☐	This activity deals with Knowledge and Understanding point 4: basic law and practice.
2.2	☐	This activity deals with Performance Criteria 18.1.A: classify expenditure on capital assets in accordance with the statutory distinction between capital and revenue expenditure.
2.3	☐	This activity deals with Performance Criteria 18.2.B: make adjustments for private use by business owners.
2.4	☐	This activity deals with Performance Criteria 18.2.A: adjust trading profits and losses for tax purposes.
2.5	☐	This activity deals with Performance Criteria 18.2.A: adjust trading profits and losses for tax purposes.
2.6	☐	This activity deals with Performance Criteria 18.2.A: adjust trading profits and losses for tax purposes.
2.7	☐	This activity deals with Performance Criteria 18.2.A: adjust trading profits and losses for tax purposes.
2.8	☐	This activity deals with Performance Criteria 18.2.A: adjust trading profits and losses for tax purposes.
2.9	☐	This activity deals with Performance Criteria 18.1.A: classify expenditure on capital assets in accordance with the distinction between capital and revenue expenditure, 18.2.A and 18.2.B: adjust trading profits and losses for tax purposes: make adjustments for private use by business owners.

chapter 3

Capital allowances

Contents

Performance criteria

18.1 A Classify expenditure on capital assets in accordance with the statutory distinction between capital and revenue expenditure

18.1 B Ensure that entries and calculations relating to the computation of capital allowances for a company are correct

18.1 C Make adjustments for private use by business owners

Range statement

18.1 Business owners: self-employed individuals, partnerships

Knowledge and understanding

5 Availability and types of capital allowances:
- first year allowances
- writing down allowances
- balancing allowance and charge (relevant to industrial buildings and plant and machinery including computers, motor vehicles and short life assets) (Element 18.1)

6 Treatment of capital allowances for unincorporated businesses including private use adjustments (Element 18.1)

1 Capital allowances in general

Capital expenditure is not in itself an allowable deduction in computing taxable trading profits, but it *may* attract capital allowances. Capital allowances are treated as a trading expense and are deducted in arriving at taxable trading profits. Balancing charges, effectively negative allowances, are added in arriving at those profits.

Capital expenditure on plant and machinery qualifies for capital allowances. Expenditure on industrial buildings may also qualify for allowances.

Both unincorporated businesses (sole traders and partnerships) and companies are entitled to capital allowances. For completeness, in this chapter we will look at the rules for companies alongside those for unincorporated businesses. We will look at companies in more detail later in this text.

For unincorporated businesses, capital allowances are calculated for periods of account. These are simply the periods for which the trader chooses to make up accounts.

For companies, capital allowances are calculated for accounting periods. (See later in this text.)

For capital allowances purposes, expenditure is generally deemed to be incurred when the obligation to pay becomes unconditional. This will often be the date of a contract, but if for example payment is due a month after delivery of a machine, it would be the date of delivery. However, amounts due more than four months after the obligation becomes unconditional are deemed to be incurred when they fall due.

2 The definition of plant

2.1 Introduction

There are two sources of the rules on what qualifies as plant and is therefore eligible for capital allowances. (Machinery is also eligible, but the word 'machinery' may be taken to have its everyday meaning.) **Statute** lists items which do not qualify, but it does not give a comprehensive list of other items which do qualify. There are several **cases** in which certain items have been accepted as plant. A few items such as thermal insulation and computer software are specifically defined as plant by statute.

2.2 The statutory exclusions

2.2.1 Buildings

Expenditure on a building and on any asset which is incorporated in a building or is of a kind normally incorporated into buildings does not qualify as expenditure on plant unless the asset falls within the list of exceptions given below. Even if an asset falls within that list, it does not follow that it is plant although it usually will be.

The following assets may **be plant**.

- Any machinery not within any other item in this list.
- Electrical, cold water, gas and sewerage systems:
  - (i) Provided mainly to meet the particular requirements of the trade, or
  - (ii) Provided mainly to serve particular machinery or plant used for the purposes of the trade.

- Space or water heating systems and powered systems of ventilation.
- Manufacturing and display equipment.
- Cookers, washing machines, refrigeration or cooling equipment, sanitary ware and furniture and furnishings.
- Lifts etc.
- Sound insulation provided mainly to meet the particular requirements of the trade.
- Computer, telecommunication and surveillance systems.
- Sprinkler equipment, fire alarm and burglar alarm systems.
- Strong rooms in bank or building society premises; safes.
- Partition walls, where movable and intended to be moved.
- Decorative assets provided for the enjoyment of the public in the hotel, restaurant or similar trades; advertising hoardings.
- Glasshouses which have, as an integral part of their structure, devices which control the plant growing environment automatically.
- Swimming pools (including diving boards, slides).
- Caravans provided mainly for holiday lettings
- Movable buildings intended to be moved in the course of the trade

Activity 3.1

One side wall of a building consists of a single sheet of wood, 2cm thick, and advertisements are displayed on the outside. Could this wall qualify as plant?

No, as part of Building.

2.2.2 Structures

Expenditure on structures and on works involving the alteration of land **does not normally qualify as expenditure on plant.**

A 'structure' is a fixed structure of any kind, other than a building.

2.2.3 Land

Land does not qualify as plant and machinery. However, expenditure on altering land for the purpose only of installing machinery or plant may qualify.

2.3 Case law

The original case law **definition of plant** (applied in this case to a horse) **is 'whatever apparatus is used by a businessman for carrying on his business: not his stock in trade which he buys or makes for sale; but all goods and chattels, fixed or movable, live or dead, which he keeps for permanent employment in the business'** (*Yarmouth v France 1887*).

Subsequent cases have refined the original definition and have largely been concerned with the **distinction between plant actively used in the business (qualifying) and the setting in which the business is carried on (non-qualifying). This is the 'functional' test**. Some of the decisions have now been enacted as part of statute law, but they are still relevant as examples of the principles involved.

The whole cost of excavating and installing a swimming pool was allowed to the owners of a caravan park: the pool performed **the function** of giving 'buoyancy and enjoyment' to the persons using the pool (now covered by statute) (*Cooke v Beach Station Caravans Ltd 1974*).

A barrister succeeded in his claim for his law library: 'Plant includes a man's tools of his trade. It extends to what he uses day by day in the course of his profession. It is not confined to physical things like the dentist's chair or the architect's table' (*Munby v Furlong 1977*).

Office partitioning was allowed. Because it was movable it was not regarded as part of the setting in which the business was carried on (now covered by statute) (*Jarrold v John Good and Sons Ltd 1963*).

A ship used as a floating restaurant was regarded as a 'structure in which the business was carried on rather than apparatus employed ... '. No capital allowances could be obtained (*Benson v Yard Arm Club 1978*). The same decision was made in relation to a football club's spectator stand. The stand performed no function in the actual carrying out of the club's trade (*Brown v Burnley Football and Athletic Club 1980*).

At a motorway service station, false ceilings contained conduits, ducts and lighting apparatus. **They did not qualify because they did not perform a function in the business. They were merely part of the setting in which the business was conducted** (*Hampton v Fortes Autogrill Ltd 1979*).

Light fittings, decor and murals can be plant. A company carried on business as hoteliers and operators of licensed premises. The function of the items was the creation of an atmosphere conducive to the comfort and well being of its customers (decorative assets used in hotels etc, now covered by statute) (*CIR v Scottish and Newcastle Breweries Ltd 1982*).

On the other hand, it has been held that when an attractive floor is provided in a restaurant, the fact that the floor performs the function of making the restaurant attractive to customers is not enough to make it plant. It functions as premises, and the cost therefore does not qualify for capital allowances (*Wmpey International Ltd v Warland 1988*).

General lighting in a department store is not plant, as it is merely setting. Special display lighting, however, can be plant (*Cole Brothers Ltd v Phillips 1982*).

Free-standing decorative screens installed in the windows of a branch of a building society qualified as plant. Their function was not to act a part of the setting in which the society's business was carried on; it was to attract local custom, and accordingly the screens formed part of the apparatus with which the society carried on its business (*Leeds Permanent Building Society v Proctor 1982*).

2.4 Expenditure deemed to be on plant and machinery

Plant and machinery capital allowances are also available on:

- Expenditure incurred by a trader in complying with fire regulations for a building which he occupies
- Expenditure by a trader on thermal insulation of an industrial building
- Expenditure by a trader in meeting statutory safety requirements for sports ground
- Expenditure (by an individual or a partnership, not by a company) on *security assets* provided to meet a special threat to an individual's security that arises wholly or mainly due to the particular trade concerned. Cars, ships, aircraft and dwellings are specifically excluded from the definition of a security asset

On disposal, the sale proceeds for the above are deemed to be zero, so no balancing charge (see below) can arise.

2.5 Computer software

Capital expenditure on computer software qualifies as expenditure on **plant and machinery**.

However, if software is expected to have a useful economic life of less than two years, its cost may be treated as revenue expenditure.

Activity 3.2

Would lights in a factory qualify as plant if they were:

(a) normal background illumination? No - normal Environment

(b) powerful spotlights to assist workers engaged in delicate work? Yes - specific function

3 Allowances on plant and machinery

3.1 Pooling expenditure

Most expenditure on plant and machinery is put into a pool of expenditure on which capital allowances may be claimed. An addition increases the pool whilst a disposal decreases it. The pool is known as the 'general pool'.

Exceptionally the following items are not pooled.

(i) cars costing more than £12,000

(ii) assets with private use by the proprietor

(iii) short life assets where an election has been made.

Each of these items is dealt with in further detail below.

3.2 Writing down allowances

3.2.1 Introduction

A writing down allowance (WDA) is given on pooled expenditure **at the rate of 25% a year** (on a reducing balance basis). The WDA is calculated on the written down value (WDV) of pooled plant, after adding the current period's additions and taking out the current period's disposals.

Example

Elizabeth has a balance of unrelieved expenditure on her general pool of plant and machinery of £16,000 on 1.4.05. In the year to 31 March 2006 she disposed of an asset for £4,000.

Calculate the capital allowances available for the year.

	£
WDV b/f	16,000
Less: disposal proceeds	(4,000)
	12,000
WDA @ 25%	(3,000)
WDV c/f	9,000

3.2.2 Disposals

When plant is sold, proceeds are taken out of the pool. Provided that the trade is still being carried on, the pool balance remaining is written down in the future by WDAs, even if there are no assets left (see below).

Activity 3.3

Jameel has a balance of £20,000 brought forward on 1 April 2005 on his general pool of plant and machinery. In the year to 31 March 2006 he disposed of an asset for £12,000.

Calculate the capital allowances for the year.

The most common disposal value at which assets are entered in a capital allowances computation is the sale proceeds. However, there is an overriding rule that the capital allowances **disposal value cannot exceed the original purchase price of the asset.**

Activity 3.4

At the start of its accounting period from 1 January to 31 December 2005, a company had a balance on its plant pool of £123,000. Plant which had cost £27,000 was sold for £32,000 on 1 August 2005. What were the capital allowances for this accounting period?

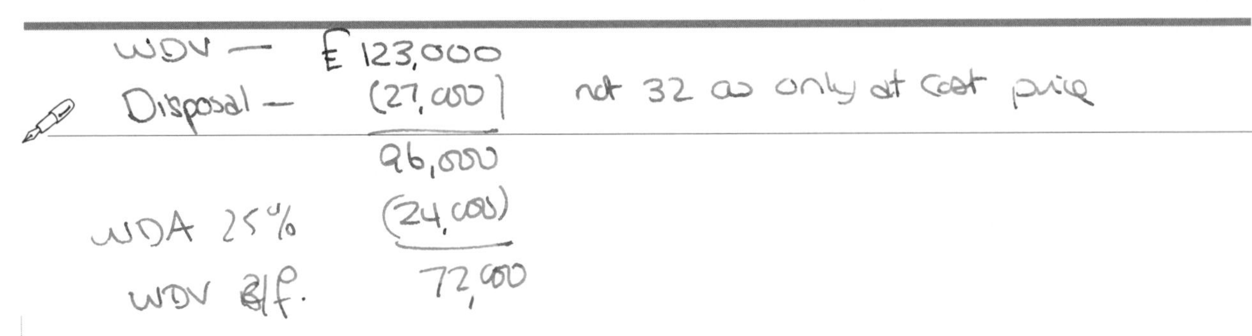

3.2.3 Pro-rating allowances in short or long periods

WDAs are 25% × months/12:

(a) For unincorporated businesses where the period of account is longer or shorter than 12 months

(b) For companies where the accounting period is shorter than 12 months (a company's accounting period for tax purposes is never longer than 12 months): Remember that we will be studying companies in detail later in this text.

Activity 3.5

Nialah had a tax written down value brought forward on her general pool of plant and machinery on 1 July 2005 of £60,000.

Nialah prepared accounts for the six months to 31 December 2005. Compute Nialah's capital allowances for this period, assuming there were no disposals or additions in the period.

Expenditure on plant and machinery by a person about to begin a trade is treated as incurred on the first day of trading. Assets previously owned by a trader and then brought into the trade (at the start of trading or later) are treated as bought for their market values at the times when they are brought in.

Allowances are claimed in the tax return.

Note that from a tax planning point of view any business can claim less than the full allowances. **Adjusting capital allowances may be advantageous, if, for example, a trader wants to avoid making such a large loss claim as to lose the benefit of the personal allowance (see later in this text).** Higher capital allowances will then be available in later years because the WDV carried forward will be higher.

3.3 First year allowances

3.3.1 Spending by small and medium sized enterprises

Expenditure incurred on plant and machinery on or after 2 July 1998 **by medium sized enterprises, in general, qualifies for a first year allowance** (FYA) of 40%.

Expenditure incurred on plant and machinery by **small** enterprises on or after 2 July 1998 also qualifies for a 40% FYA. However, the rate of FYA for small enterprises was increased to 50% for a one year period. The one year period commences on 1 April 2004 for companies and on 6 April 2004 for unincorporated businesses.

In your examination you will be told if a business is a small or medium sized enterprise.

3.3.2 Calculation of FYAs

First year allowances are given in the place of writing down allowances. For subsequent years a WDA is given on the balance of expenditure at the normal rate. You should therefore have a separate column for FYA but transfer the balance of the expenditure to the general pool at the end of the first period.

Example

ABC and Co, a small enterprise for capital allowance purposes, had a balance on its general pool of plant and machinery of £18,000 on 1 April 2005. In June 2005 it bought new plant for £8,000.

Calculate the total capital allowances claimable for the year to 31 March 2006.

Solution

	FYA @ 40%	*General pool*	*Allowances*
	£	£	£
WDV b/f		18,000	
WDA @ 25%		(4,500)	4,500
		13,500	
Additions			
Qualifying for FYA	8,000		
FYA @ 40%	(3,200)		3,200
		4,800	7,700
WDV c/f		18,300	

As ABC and Co is a small enterprise, FYA are available at 40%.

3.3.3 Short and long periods

FYAs are given for incurring expenditure. It is irrelevant whether the basis period of expenditure is twelve months or not. **FYAs are not scaled up or down by reference to the length of the period.**

Example

Sonny, a sole trader, had a balance of £16,000 on his general pool of plant and machinery brought forward at 1 April 2005. He bought new plant for £6,000 on 1 June 2005.

Sonny's business qualifies as a small enterprise for capital allowance purposes.

Sonny prepared accounts for the three months to 30 June 2005. What capital allowances are available for this three month period?

Solution

	FYA	*General pool*	*Allowance*
	£	£	£
WDV b/f		16,000	
WDA @ 25% × $^3/_{12}$		(1,000)	1,000
		15,000	
Addition	6,000		
FYA @ 40%	(2,400)		
		3,600	2,400
WDV c/f		18,600	3,400

Writing down allowances are pro rated in a short period but first year allowances are not.

Activity 3.6

The tax written down value brought forward on GWC's general pool of plant and machinery on 1 July 2005 was £48,000. The only addition in the six month period to 31 December 2005 was printing press costing £20,000.

GWC is a medium sized enterprise for capital allowance purposes.

What are the maximum capital allowances GWC will be entitled to claim in the six month period to 31 December 2005?

3.3.4 100% FYAs

Expenditure by **small enterprises on information and communication technology equipment in the four year period from 1 April 2000 to 31 March 2004 qualifies for a 100% FYA.**

In addition, 100% FYAs are given to all businesses:

(a) on certain energy saving plant, such as boilers
(b) on cars with CO_2 emissions not exceeding 120 g/km
(c) on certain water efficient plant

In your examination you will be told when 100% FYAs are available.

Activity 3.7

Walton started a trade on 1 March 2002 and prepared his first accounts to 31 July 2003. Thereafter accounts were prepared to 31 July annually. Plant was bought as follows.

Date	*Cost*
	£
1.3.02 (Grinding machine)	13,000
1.6.02 (Grinding machine)	9,603
1.6.04 (Drilling machine)	6,000
31.12.04 (Low emission car)	10,000

On 1 May 2004, the grinding machine which cost £9,603 is sold for £4,000.

Walton's business is a small enterprise for FYA purposes. Both of the grinding machines qualified for a 40% FYA and the drilling machine for a 50% FYA. The low emission car qualified for 100% FYA.

Show the capital allowances arising in the first three periods of account.

3.4 Balancing charges and allowances

Balancing charges occur when the disposal value deducted exceeds the balance remaining in the pool. The charge equals the excess and is effectively a negative capital allowance, increasing profits. Most commonly this happens when the trade ceases and the remaining assets are sold. It may also occur, however, whilst the trade is still in progress.

Balancing allowances on the capital allowance pools of expenditure arise only when the trade ceases. The balancing allowance is equal to the remaining unrelieved expenditure after deducting the disposal value of all the assets. Balancing allowances also arise on items which are not pooled (see below) whenever those items are disposed of.

3.5 The cessation of a trade

When a business ceases to trade no FYAs or WDAs are given in the final period of account (unincorporated businesses) or accounting period (companies - see later in this text). Each asset is deemed to be disposed of on the date the trade ceased (usually at the then market value). Additions in the relevant period are brought in and then the disposal proceeds (limited to cost) are deducted from the balance of qualifying expenditure. If the proceeds exceed the balance then a balancing charge arises. If the balance of qualifying expenditure exceeds the proceeds then a balancing allowance is given.

4 Assets which are not pooled

Certain assets are not pooled

A separate record of allowances and WDV must be kept for each asset which is not pooled and when it is sold a balancing allowance or charge emerges.

4.1 Cars

Motor cars costing more than £12,000 are not pooled. The maximum WDA is £3,000 a year. The limit is £3,000 × months/12:

(a) For short or long periods of account of unincorporated businesses
(b) For short accounting periods of companies

FYAs are not available on cars (except for certain low emission or electric cars – see above).

Activity 3.8

A company started to trade on 1 July 2002, making up accounts to 31 December 2002 and each 31 December thereafter. On 1 August 2002 it bought a car for £15,500. The car was sold in July 2005 for £4,000. What are the capital allowances?

4.2 Private use assets

An asset (for example, a car) which is used partly for private purposes by a sole trader or a partner is not pooled)(See below). **Make all calculations on the full cost but claim only the business use proportion of the allowances**. An asset with some private use by an employee (not a proprietor), however, suffers no such restriction. The employee may be taxed on a benefit so the business gets capital allowances on the full cost of the asset. The private use of an asset never restricts the capital allowances due to a company. (Companies are covered later in this text.)

Example

On 1 August 2003 Sana, a sole trader who prepares accounts for 30 September each year, bought a car for £16,000. She used it 30% for private purposes and 70% for business purposes. Show the capital allowances available in the three periods to 30 September 2005.

	Private use asset	*Allowances*
	£	£
Year ended 30.9.03		
Addition	16,000	
WDA @ 25% (max £3,000)	(3,000) × 70%	2,100
TWDV C/F	13,000	
Year ended 30.9.04		
WDA @ 25% (max (£3,000)	(3,000) × 70%	2,100
TWDV C/F	10,000	
Year ended 30.9.05		
WDA @ 25% (max (£3,000)	(2,500) × 70%	1,750
TWDV C/F	7,500	

Note that full allowances are deducted in the private use asset column but that the allowances (in the allowances column) that can be deducted in computing taxable trading profits are restricted to the business proportion of the allowances.

4.3 Short-life assets

A trader can elect that specific items of plant be kept separately from the general pool. The election is irrevocable. For an unincorporated business, the time limit for electing is the 31 January which is 22 months after the end of the tax year in which the period of account of the expenditure ends. (For a company, it is two years after the end of the accounting period of the expenditure.) **Any asset subject to this election is known as a 'short-life asset'**, and the election is known as a **'de-pooling election'**.

Provided that the asset is disposed of within four years of the end of the period of account or accounting period in which it was bought, it is a **short life asset** and a balancing charge or allowance is made on its disposal.

If the asset is not disposed of in the correct time period, its tax written down value is added to the general pool at the end of that time.

Activity 3.9

Caithin bought an asset on 1 May 2001 for £12,000 and elected for de-pooling. His accounting year end is 30 April. Calculate the capital allowances due if:

(a) The asset is scrapped for £300 in August 2005.
(b) The asset is scrapped for £200 in August 2006.

Short-life asset treatment cannot be claimed for:

- Motor cars
- Plant used partly for non-trade purposes
- Plant brought into use for the trade following non-business use

5 Hire purchase and leasing

5.1 Assets on hire purchase

Any asset (including a car) bought on hire purchase (HP) is treated as if purchased outright for the cash price. Therefore:

(a) The buyer normally obtains **capital allowances on the cash price** when the agreement begins.
(b) He may write off the **finance charge as a trade expense** over the term of the HP contract.

5.2 Leased assets

Under a lease, the lessee merely hires the asset over a period. The hire charge can normally be deducted in computing taxable trading profits.

An expensive car (one costing over £12,000) will attract WDAs limited to £3,000 a year if bought. If it is leased instead, the maximum allowable deduction from trading profits for lease rentals is

$$\frac{£12,000 + P}{2P} \times R$$

where P = the purchase price (if bought outright)
R = the annual rental

5.3 Example: leased cars

A car is used by a business under a lease. The purchase price would have been £20,000. The annual rental is £5,000. The rental allowed for tax purposes is

$$\frac{£12,000 + £20,000}{2 \times £20,000} \times £5,000 = £4,000$$

Since £5,000 is deducted in the profit and loss account, £5,000 - £4,000 = £1,000 is added back in computing taxable profits.

6 Industrial buildings – types

6.1 Introduction

A special type of capital allowance (an **industrial buildings allowance** or IBA) is available in respect of **expenditure on industrial buildings**.

The allowance is available to traders as a deduction from taxable trading profits.

6.2 Definition of industrial buildings

Industrial buildings include:

(a) All factories and ancillary premises used in:

  (i) A manufacturing business
  (ii) A trade in which goods and materials are subject to any process
  (iii) A trade in which goods or raw materials are stored

(b) Staff welfare buildings (such as workplace nurseries and canteens, but not directors' restaurants) where the trade is qualifying

(c) Sports pavilions used by any trade

Dwelling houses, retail shops, showrooms and offices are not industrial buildings.

Warehouses used for storage often cause problems in practice. A warehouse used for storage which is merely a transitory and necessary incident of the conduct of the business is not an industrial building. Storage is only a qualifying purpose if it is an end in itself.

Any building is an industrial building if it is constructed for the welfare of employees of a trader whose trade is a qualifying one (that is, the premises in which the trade is carried on are industrial buildings).

Sports pavilions provided for the welfare of employees qualify as industrial buildings. In this case, it does not matter whether the taxpayer is carrying on a trade in a qualifying building or not. Thus a retailer's sports pavilion would qualify for IBAs.

Drawing offices which serve an industrial building are regarded as industrial buildings themselves (*CIR v Lambhill Ironworks Ltd 1950*).

Activity 3.10

A retailer buys a shop, a staff canteen, a staff sports pavilion and a warehouse. Will any of them qualify as industrial buildings?

6.3 Eligible expenditure

IBAs are computed on the amount of eligible expenditure incurred on qualifying buildings. The eligible expenditure is:

- The original cost of a building if built by the trader, or
- The purchase price if the building was acquired from a person trading as a builder.

If the building was acquired other than from a person trading as a builder, the eligible expenditure is the lower of the purchase price and the original cost incurred by the person incurring the construction expenditure.

Where part of a building qualifies as an industrial building and part does not, the whole cost qualifies for IBAs, provided that the cost of the non-qualifying part is not more than 25% of the total expenditure. If the non-qualifying part of the building does cost more than 25% of the total, its cost must be excluded from the IBA computation.

The cost of land is disallowed but expenditure incurred in preparing land for building does qualify.

Activity 3.11

Sue purchased an industrial building for £2,500,000. This cost was made up of:

	£
Factory	2,100,000
Land	400,000
	2,500,000

The costs attributable to showrooms and offices within the factory were £400,000 and £200,000 respectively.

What is the expenditure qualifying for industrial buildings allowances?

Professional fees, for example architects' fees, incurred in connection with the construction of an industrial building qualify. The cost of repairs to industrial buildings also qualifies, provided that the expenditure is not deductible as a trading expense.

7 Allowances on industrial buildings

7.1 Writing down allowances

A writing down allowance (WDA) is given for a period provided that the industrial building was in use as such on the last day of the period concerned.

If the building was not in use as an industrial building at the end of the relevant period it may have been:

- **Unused** for any purpose, or
- Used for a non-industrial purpose.

The distinction is important in ascertaining whether WDAs are due to the taxpayer. **If any disuse is temporary and previously the building had been in industrial use, WDAs may be claimed in exactly the same way as if the building were in industrial use.** The legislation does not define 'temporary' but in practice, any subsequent qualifying use of the building will usually enable the period of disuse to be regarded as temporary.

Non-industrial use has different consequences, but you will not be expected to deal with these in your examination.

The WDA is 4% of the eligible expenditure incurred by the taxpayer.

The allowance is calculated on a straight line basis (in contrast to WDAs on plant and machinery which are calculated on the reducing balance), starting when the building is brought into use.

The WDA is 4% × months/12 if the period concerned is not 12 months long.

Buildings always have a **separate computation for each building**. They are never pooled.

Activity 3.12

Fraser Ltd acquired a factory for £600,000 and started to use it for industrial purposes on 1 July 2005. What industrial buildings allowances are available to Fraser Ltd in its nine month accounting period to 30 September 2005?

7.2 Balancing adjustments on sale

7.2.1 The tax life

The 'tax life' of an industrial building is 25 years (hence the 4% straight line WDA) after it is first used. Balancing adjustments apply *only* if a building is sold within its tax life of 25 years.

7.2.2 Sales of industrial buildings

The seller's calculation is quite straightforward. It takes the following form;

	£
Cost	X
Less allowances previously given	(X)
Residue before sale	X
Less proceeds (limited to cost)	(X)
Balancing (charge)/allowance	(X)

The buyer obtains annual straight line WDAs for the remainder of the building's tax life (25 years). This life is calculated to the nearest month. The allowances are granted on the residue after sale which is computed thus;

	£
Residue before sale	X
Plus balancing charge or less balancing allowance	X
Residue after sale	X

This means that **the second owner will write off the lower of his cost or the original cost.**

Activity 3.13

Frankie, who prepares accounts to 31 December, bought an industrial building for £100,000 (excluding land) on 1 October 2001. He brought it into use as a factory immediately. On 1 September 2005 he sells it for £120,000 to Holly, whose accounting date is 30 September and who brought the building into industrial use immediately. Show the IBAs available to Frankie and to Holly.

The Revenue allow IBAs equal to the fall in value of a building over the trader's use of that building. As a general rule if an industrial building is sold for more than its original cost a balancing charge equal to the allowances given to date will arise. This is because there was no fall in value so no allowances are actually due.

If it is sold for less than original cost we could calculate the fall in value of the building and that would equal the allowances available for this building. If we compare this to the allowances already given, the difference would be the balancing adjustment due on the sale.

In the above question if Frankie sold the building Holly for £90,000:

	£
Fall in value (£100,000 – £90,000) = allowances due	10,000
Less: allowances already given to Frankie	16,000
Balancing adjustment = Balancing charge	6,000

Over the use of the building by Frankie £16,000 of IBAs were claimed. On the sale of the building the fall in value is calculated as £10,000. Thus Frankie should only have received £10,000 of allowances not £16,000. So £6,000 is paid back as a balancing charge.

8 End of chapter activities

Now attempt the two activities below. The first is concerned with capital allowances on plant and machinery whilst the second is concerned with industrial buildings allowances.

Activity 3.14

Vivace makes up his accounts to 31 December each year.

After claiming allowances based on the period ended 31 December 2002, the balance of his general pool stood at £8,000.

During the years ended 31 December 2003, 2004 and 2005 Vivace recorded the following capital transactions.

14	September 2003	He sold machinery which originally cost £1,800 for £700.
16	September 2003	He bought a new car for a salesman for £4,000. The employee uses it privately for 25% of all its mileage.
1	December 2003	He bought secondhand machinery for £7,693.
21	March 2004	He sold plant which cost £2,000 in 2000 for £2,500.
22	March 2004	He sold the salesman's car for £3,200.
5	July 2004	He bought a Mercedes car for his own use costing £22,000. Vivace uses the car 60% for business purposes.
4	February 2005	He bought a new machine on hire purchase. A deposit of £1,800 was paid immediately. Four further instalments of £1,000 are payable annually in future years. The cash price would have been £4,000.
5	February 2005	He bought a car for the accountant for £3,000. There is no private use.
15	June 2005	He replaced his car. The Mercedes was sold for £4,000; a Volvo was bought for £18,000. 60% business use continued.
30	June 2005	Plant and equipment which originally cost £10,000 was sold for £2,602.
30	June 2005	He bought plant for £3,000.

Set out Vivace's capital allowance computations for the periods of account ended 31 December 2003, 2004 and 2005, assuming that maximum claims are made. Assume Vivace's business qualifies as a small enterprise for capital allowances purposes where appropriate. For one year from 6.4.04 small enterprises are entitled to a 50 % FYA. Before 6.4.04 and after 5.4.05 they are entitled to a FYA of 40%.

no first year Allowance on car

Activity 3.15

Cuckold Ltd makes up accounts to 31 March each year. It is considering the purchase of an additional, secondhand factory on 1 April 2006. It has decided to spend £150,000 and the following details refer to four possible factories which could each be acquired for that sum. All are equally suitable for Cuckold Ltd's purposes and all have been used for qualifying industrial purposes throughout their lives.

	Original cost to first owner	*Date of first use*
	£	
(i)	100,000	31 March 1982
(ii)	80,000	31 March 1981
(iii)	160,000	31 March 2004
(iv)	120,000	31 March 1998

Advise Cuckold Ltd of the amount of industrial buildings allowances which would be available as a result of purchasing each of the above factories, indicating the periods for which the allowances would be available. Which building would you advise it to purchase?

Key learning points

- ☑ Statutory rules generally exclude specified items from treatment as plant, rather than include them as plant.
- ☑ There is substantial case law dealing with the **function/setting** distinction.
- ☑ The main point about capital allowances is to **get the layout right**. Then the figures should drop into place.
- ☑ Most expenditure on plant and machinery qualifies for a **25% writing down allowance (WDA) on the reducing balance** every 12 months.
- ☑ First year allowances (FYAs) may be available on certain expenditure.
- ☑ **FYAs are never reduced or increased for short or long periods of account.**
- ☑ **Private use assets** by sole traders and partners have **restricted capital allowances.**
- ☑ Short life asset elections can bring forward the allowances due on an asset.
- ☑ Allowances for industrial buildings (IBAs) equal the fall in value of the building whilst in industrial use.
- ☑ **IBAs are 4% a year on straight line basis.**
- ☑ The **tax life of an industrial building is 25 years**, after that there are no allowances available.
- ☑ **IBAs are only available if a building is in industrial use at the end of an accounting period.**

Quick quiz

1 The tax written down value brought forward on Mr Green's general pool of plant and machinery on 1 July 2005 was £24,000. The only addition in the six month period of account to 31 December 2005 was of a printing press costing £20,000. Mr Green's business is a small enterprise for capital allowance purposes.

What are the maximum capital allowances that Mr Green will be entitled to claim in the period to 31 December 2005?

A £16,000
B £13,000
C £7,000
D £11,000

2 JD Ltd prepares accounts for the year to 31 March 2006. During the year the company made the following purchases of capital assets:

1.7.05	Car for managing director (50% private use)	£18,000
1.10.05	New computer	£5,000

The balance on JD Ltd's general pool for capital allowance purposes on 1 April 2005 was £10,000. There were no other balances brought forward. JD Ltd qualifies as a small enterprise for capital allowance purposes.

What are the maximum capital allowances that JD Ltd can claim for the year?

A £6,000
B £7,500
C £10,500
D £8,000

3 When may balancing allowances arise?

4 An asset must be disposed of within .... years of the end of the period of account or accounting period to be treated as a short life asset. Fill in the blank.

5 Mr Newell bought a factory on 1 June 2005 for £500,000. The purchase price comprised:

	£
Land	100,000
Drawing office	20,000
General offices	85,000
Factory	295,000
	500,000

On what amount may IBAs be claimed?

A £295,000
B £315,000
C £400,000
D £500,000

6 Louise bought a secondhand factory on 1 July 2005 for £200,000. The factory which had always been used for industrial purposes, originally cost £140,000 on 1 July 2000.

What IBAs will be available to Louise in her year ended 31 December 2005?

Answers to quick quiz

1 D

	£	£	£
WDV b/f		24,000	
WDA @ 25% × $^6/_{12}$		(3,000)	3,000
		21,000	
Addition	20,000		
FYA @ 40%	(8,000)		8,000
		12,000	
		33,000	11,000

WDA is pro-rated in a short period of account but the FYA is not.

2 B

	£	Pool £	Car £	£
TWDV b/f		10,000		
WDA @ 25%		(2,500)		2,500
		7,500		
Car addition			18,000	
WDA – restricted			(3,000)	3,000
Computer	5,000			
FYA @ 40%	(2,000)	3,000		2,000
		10,500	15,000	7,500

The private use of an asset has no impact on the capital allowances available to a *company*.

3 Balancing allowances may arise in respect of pooled expenditure only when the trade ceases. They may arise on non-pooled items whenever they are disposed of.

4 An asset must be disposed of within **four** years of the end of the period of account or accounting period to be treated as a short life asset.

5 C IBAs are never allowed on the cost of land.

IBAs are available on drawing offices.

IBAs are available on the general offices as they constitute less than 25% of the qualifying expenditure: 25% × £400,000 = £100,000.

6 IBAs are available on lower of:

- original cost (£140,000)
- purchase price (£200,000)

Over the remaining tax life: $\frac{140{,}000}{20}$ = £7,000 pa

IBAs of £7,000 will be available to Louise.

Activity checklist

This checklist shows which performance criteria or knowledge and understanding point is covered by each activity in this chapter. Tick off each activity as you complete it.

Activity		
3.1	☐	This activity deals with Performance Criteria 18.1.A: classify expenditure on capital assets in accordance with the distinction between capital and revenue expenditure.
3.2	☐	This activity deals with Performance Criteria 18.1.A: classify expenditure on capital assets in accordance with the distinction between capital and revenue expenditure.
3.3	☐	This activity deals with Knowledge and Understanding point 5: availability and types of capital allowances
3.4	☐	This activity deals with Knowledge and Understanding point 5: availability and types of capital allowances
3.5	☐	This activity deals with Knowledge and Understanding point 5: availability and types of capital allowances
3.6	☐	This activity deals with Knowledge and Understanding point 5: availability and types of capital allowances
3.7	☐	This activity deals with Knowledge and Understanding point 5: availability and types of capital allowances
3.8	☐	This activity deals with Knowledge and Understanding point 5: availability and types of capital allowances.
3.9	☐	This activity deals with Knowledge and Understanding point 5: availability and types of capital allowances
3.10	☐	This activity deals with Knowledge and Understanding point 5: availability and types of capital allowances
3.11	☐	This activity deals with Knowledge and Understanding point 5: availability and types of capital allowances
3.12	☐	This activity deals with Knowledge and Understanding point 5: availability and types of capital allowances
3.13	☐	This activity deals with Knowledge and Understanding point 5: availability and types of capital allowances
3.14	☐	This activity deals with Performance Criteria 18.1.C: make adjustments for private use by business owners and Knowledge and Understanding point 6: treatment of capital allowances for unincorporated businesses
3.15	☐	This activity deals with Performance Criteria 18.1.B: ensure that entries and calculations relating to the computation on capital allowance for a company are correct.

chapter 4

Basis of assessment for unincorporated businesses

Contents

Performance criteria

18.2 D Apply the basis of assessment for unincorporated businesses in opening and closing years

Range statement

18.2 Clients, sole traders, partnerships

Knowledge and understanding

9 Basis of assessment for unincorporated businesses (Element 18.2)

1 Basis periods: continuing businesses

1.1 Introduction

Individuals must pay tax for tax years. The **tax year**, or **fiscal year**, or **year of assessment** runs from 6 April to 5 April. For example, 2005/06 runs from 6 April 2005 to 5 April 2006.

A tax year runs from 6 April to 5 April, but most businesses do not have periods of account ending on 5 April. **Thus there must be a link between a period of account of a business and a tax year.** The procedure is to **find a period to act as the basis period for a tax year. The profits for a basis period are taxed in the corresponding tax year**. The **basis period** is normally the **period ending in the tax year**. This is known as the **current year basis of assessment.**

Example

Ayesha, a sole trader, prepares accounts to 31 December each year.

Ayesha's basis period for **2005/06** is the year ended 31 December 2005 as this is her period of account ending in 2005/06. Ayesha will be taxed on the profits of the year to 31 December 2005 in 2005/06.

Activity 4.1

Jameel, a grocer, prepares accounts to 30 June each year. What is Jameel's basis period for 2005/06?

2 Basis periods: opening and closing years

We will now look at the basis period rules that apply in the opening and closing years of a business when there is no change of accounting date. Special rules are needed when a trader changes his accounting date but you will not be examined on these in Unit 18 so they are not considered here.

2.1 The first tax year

The first tax year is the year during which the trade commences. For example, if a trade commences on 1 June 2005 the first tax year is 2005/06.

The **basis period for the first tax year runs from the date the trade starts to the next 5 April** (or to the date of cessation if the trade does not last until the end of the tax year).

For example, if a trade starts on 1 December 2005 the first tax year will be 2005/06 and the basis period for 2005/06 will be 1 December 2005 to 5 April 2006.

2.2 The second tax year

- **If the accounting date falling in the second tax year is at least 12 months after the start of trading, the basis period is the 12 months to that accounting date.**

Example

Vivien, a hairdresser, commenced business on 1 September 2004. She prepares her first accounts for the sixteen months to 31 December 2005.

Vivien's basis periods for her first two tax years are:

Year	*Basis period*	
2004/05	1.9.04 – 5.4.05	(commencement to following 5 April)
2005/06	Year to 31.12.05	(12 months ended in second tax year)

- **If the accounting date falling in the second tax year is less than 12 months after the start of trading, the basis period is the first 12 months of trading.**

Example

Niahlah commences business on 1 September 2004 and prepares accounts to 30 June 2005 and annually thereafter.

Niahlah's basis periods for the first two tax years of her business are:

Year	*Basis period*	
2004/05	1.9.04 – 5.4.05	(commencement to next 5 April)
2005/06	Year to 31.8.05	(first 12 months)

- **If there is no accounting date falling in the second tax year**, because the first period of account is a very long one which does not end until a date in the third tax year, **the basis period for the second tax year is the year itself (from 6 April to 5 April).**

Example

Azrina commences business on 1 December 2004 and prepares accounts for the 18 months to 31 May 2006.

Azrina's basis periods for her first two years of trading are:

Year	*Basis period*
2004/05	1.12.04 – 5.4.05
2005/06	6.4.2005 – 5.4.2006

The following flowchart may help you determine the basis period for the second tax year.

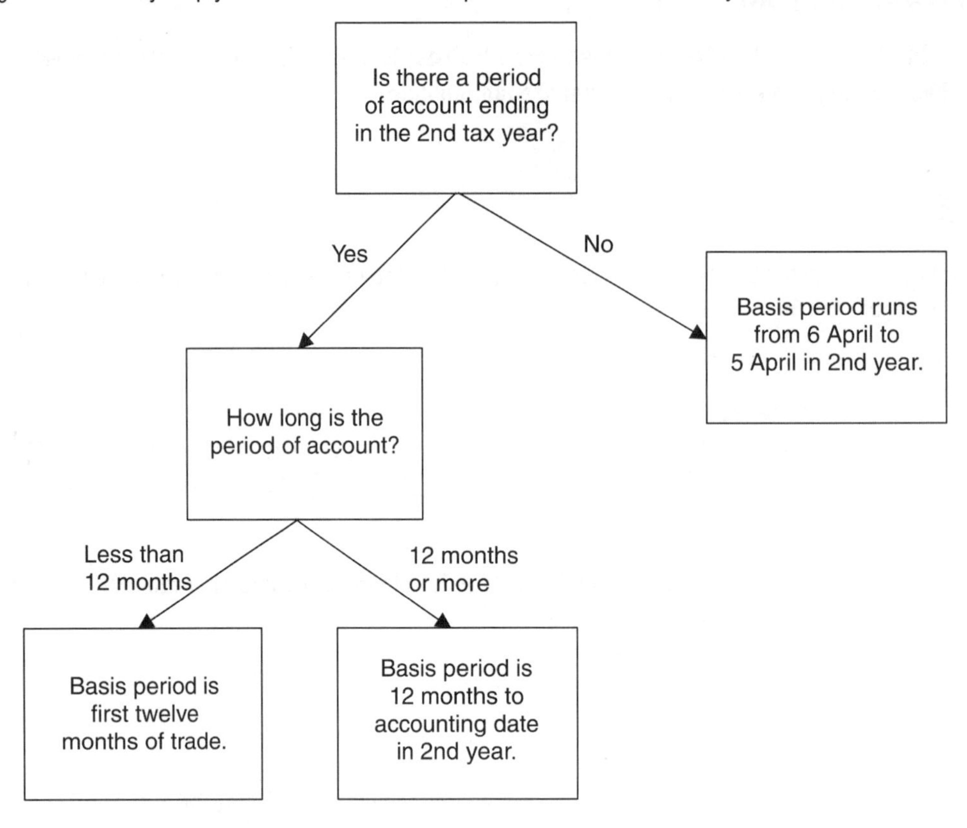

2.3 The third tax year

If there is an accounting date falling in the second tax year, the basis period for the third tax year is the period of account ending in the third tax year.

If there is no accounting date falling in the second tax year, the basis period for the third tax year is the 12 months down to the accounting date falling in the third tax year.

2.4 Later tax years

For later tax years, except the year in which the trade ceases, **the basis period is the period of account ending in the tax year**. As described above, this is known as the **current year basis of assessment**.

2.5 Apportioning profits to tax years

If you need to time apportion the profits of a period of account into a basis period for tax purposes, you should time apportion the profits on a monthly basis.

Activity 4.2

Mavis started in business as a newsagent on 1 July 2005. She made up accounts to 30 June and had the following results.

y/e 30.6.06	£10,000
y/e 30.6.07	£15,000
y/e 30.6.08	£18,000

Show the taxable profits for the year 2005/06 to 2008/09.

2.6 The final year

If a trade starts and ceases in the same tax year, the basis period for that year is the whole lifespan of the trade.

If the final year is the second year, the basis period runs from 6 April at the start of the second year to the date of cessation. This rule overrides the rules that normally apply for the second year.

If the final year is the third year or a later year, **the basis period runs from the end of the basis period for the previous year to the date of cessation**. This rule overrides the rules that normally apply in the third and later years.

Activity 4.3

Maud was in business as a dressmaker for many years. The business had the following results to closure on 31.12.06:

y/e 30.9.04	£10,000
y/e 30.9.05	£7,000
y/e 30.9.06	£6,000
p/e 31.12.06	£2,000

Show the taxable profits for the years 2004/05 to 2006/07 inclusive before considering any overlap relief (see below).

3 Overlap profits

Profits which have been taxed more than once are called **overlap profits**.

When a business starts, some profits may be taxed twice because the basis period for the second year includes some or all of the period of trading in the first year or because the basis period for the third year overlaps with that for the second year.

Example

Thelma starts to trade on 1 March 2004. Her first accounts, covering the 16 months to 30 June 2005, show a profit of £36,000. The taxable profits for the first three tax years and the overlap profits are as follows.

Year	Basis period	Working	*Taxable profits* £
2003/04	1.3.04 – 5.4.04	£36,000 × 1/16	2,250
2004/05	6.4.04 – 5.4.05	£36,000 × 12/16	27,000
2005/06	1.7.04 – 30.6.05	£36,000 × 12/16	27,000

The overlap profits are the profits from 1 July 2004 to 5 April 2005: £36,000 × 9/16 = £20,250. These profits are taxed in both 2004/05 and 2005/06.

When the trade ceases overlap profits are deducted from the final year's taxable profits. Any deduction of overlap profits may create or increase a loss. The usual loss reliefs (covered later in this text) are then available.

Example

Jenny trades from 1 July 2000 to 31 December 2005, with the following results.

Period	*Profit* £
1.7.00 – 31.8.01	7,000
1.9.01 – 31.8.02	12,000
1.9.02 – 31.8.03	15,000
1.9.03 – 31.8.04	21,000
1.9.04 – 31.8.05	18,000
1.9.05 – 31.12.05	5,600
Actual profits	78,600

The profits to be taxed in each tax year from 2000/01 to 2005/06, and the total of these taxable profits are calculated as follows.

Year	*Basis period*	*Working*	*Taxable profit* £
2000/01	1.7.00 – 5.4.01	£7,000 × 9/14	4,500
2001/02	1.9.00 – 31.8.01	£7,000 × 12/14	6,000
2002/03	1.9.01 – 31.8.02		12,000
2003/04	1.9.02 – 31.8.03		15,000
2004/05	1.9.03 – 31.8.04		21,000
2005/06	1.9.04 – 31.12.05	£(18,000 + 5,600 – 3,500)	20,100
			78,600

The overlap profits are those in the period 1 September 2000 to 5 April 2001, a period of seven months. They are £7,000 × 7/14 = £3,500. Overlap profits are deducted from the final year's taxable profit when the business ceases. Over the life of the business, the total taxable profits equal the total actual profits.

Activity 4.4

Peter trades from 1 September 2000 to 30 June 2005, with the following results.

Period	Profit £
1.9.00 – 30.4.01	8,000
1.5.01 – 30.4.02	15,000
1.5.02 – 30.4.03	9,000
1.5.03 – 30.4.04	10,500
1.5.04 – 30.4.05	16,000
1.5.05 – 30.6.05	950
	59,450

Show the profits to be taxed in each year from 2000/01 to 2005/06, the total of these taxable profits and the overlap profits.

4 Revenue forms

A self employed taxpayer must submit 'self employment pages' with his annual tax return. A copy of the supplementary pages to the income tax return that have to be completed by self employed taxpayers are included in Activity 45 later in this text. In Unit 18 you will be expected to be aware of how business income is entered in these supplementary pages. Have a look at these pages now. You can practise filling them in when you come to activity 45 and certain practice exams later in this text. Please see page (vii) for a note regarding these pages.

5 End of chapter activity

Activity 4.5

Debbie started trading as a freelance author on 1 May 2003. She prepared accounts to 31 December each year and made the following taxable trading profits:

	£
Period to 31 December 2003	24,000
Year to 31 December 2004	40,000
Year to 31 December 2005	60,000

Tasks

(a) Calculate Debbie's taxable trading profits for 2003/04, 2004/05, and 2005/06.

(b) Calculate the overlap profits that arose for Debbie in her opening years of trading.

(c) Explain to Debbie what overlap profits are and how they might be relieved.

Key learning points

- ☑ **Basis periods** are used to link **periods of account** to **tax years**.
- ☑ For a continuing business, the **profits of a period of account ending in a tax year are taxed in that year**.
- ☑ In the **first tax year**, the **basis period is the date the business starts to the following 5 April**.
- ☑ If a **period of account of 12 months or more ends in the second tax year, the basis period for the second tax year is the 12 months to the end of that period of account.**
- ☑ If a **period of account of less than 12 months ends in the second tax year, the basis period for the second tax year is the first 12 months from the start of trading**.
- ☑ If **no period of account ends in the second year, the basis period for that year is 6 April to 5 April in the year.**
- ☑ In the **final year** of a business the **basis period runs from the end of the previous basis period to the date of cessation**.
- ☑ Certain profits may be **taxed twice** ('**overlap profits**').
- ☑ **Overlap profits** can be **relieved on cessation**.

Quick quiz

1 Steven starts in business on 1 December 2005. He makes up his first set of accounts to 30 November 2006 showing a profit of £15,000. What is his taxable profit for 2005/06?

2 What are Steven's taxable profits for 2006/07?

3 What are Steven's overlap profits?

4 Darren has been in business for many years preparing accounts to 30 June each year. He had overlap profits of £5,000 on the start of his business. His results to the cessation of his business were:

y/e 30.6.05	£10,000
3 months to 30.9.05	£1,500

What are Darren's taxable profits for the final tax year of trading?

Answers to quick quiz

1 Basis period 1.12.05 – 5.4.06 = 4 months

(First year: date of commencement to following 5 April)

Taxable profit 2005/06 is 4/12 x £15,000 = £5,000

2 Taxable profit 2006/07 will be the whole of the y/e 30.11.06 i.e. £15,000

3 The profits between 1.12.05 – 5.4.06 will be taxed twice

Overlap profits are therefore 4/12 x £15,000 = £5,000

4 Basis period for 2005/06 is 1.7.04 – 30.9.05

Taxable profits are £(10,000 + 1,500 – 5,000) = £6,500

Overlap profits are relieved on cessation

Activity checklist

This checklist shows which performance criteria or knowledge and understanding point is covered by each activity in this chapter. Tick off each activity as you complete it.

Activity		
4.1	☐	This activity deals with Knowledge and Understanding point 9: Basis of assessment for unincorporated businesses.
4.2	☐	This activity deals with Performance Criteria 18.2.D: apply the basis of assessment for unincorporated businesses in the opening and closing years.
4.3	☐	This activity deals with Performance Criteria 18.2.D: apply the basis of assessment for unincorporated businesses in the opening and closing years.
4.4	☐	This activity deals with Performance Criteria 18.2.D: apply the basis of assessment for unincorporated businesses in the opening and closing years.
4.5	☐	This activity deals with Performance Criteria 18.2.D: apply the basis of assessment for unincorporated businesses in the opening and closing years.

chapter 5

Trading losses

Contents

Performance criteria

18.2 A Adjust trading profits and losses for tax purposes

Range statement

18.2 Clients: sole traders

Knowledge and understanding

2 Issues of tax liability
7 Adjustment of trading profits and losses for tax purposes (Element 18.2)
9 Basis of assessment for unincorporated businesses

1 Losses

This chapter considers how losses are calculated and how a loss-suffering taxpayer can use a trading loss to reduce his tax liability. Losses arising in professions and vocations are treated in exactly the same way.

The rules covered in this chapter apply only to individuals, trading alone or in partnership. Loss reliefs for companies are completely different and are covered later in this text.

Losses of one spouse cannot be relieved against income of the other spouse.

When computing tax adjusted trading profits, profits may turn out to be negative, that is a loss has been made in the basis period. **A loss is computed in exactly the same way as a profit**, making the same adjustments to the accounts profit or loss.

If there is a loss in a basis period, the taxable income for the tax year based on that basis period is nil.

2 Carry forward of trading losses: s 385 ICTA 1988

2.1 Introduction

A trading loss not relieved in any other way may be **carried forward to set against the first available profits of the same trade**. Losses may be carried forward for any number of years.

Example: carrying forward losses

B has the following results.

Year ending	£
31 December 2003	(6,000)
31 December 2004	5,000
31 December 2005	11,000

B's taxable trading profits, assuming that he claims loss relief only under s 385 are:

	2003/04		*2004/05*		*2005/06*
	£		£		£
Taxable trading profits	0		5,000		11,000
Less s 385 relief	(0)	(i)	(5,000)	(ii)	(1,000)
Profits	0		0		10,000

Loss memorandum		£
Trading loss, y/e 31.12.03		6,000
Less: claim in y/e 31.12.04	(i)	(5,000)
claim in y/e 31.12.05 (balance of loss)	(ii)	(1,000)
		0

3 Setting trading losses against total income: s 380 ICTA 1988

3.1 Introduction

Instead of carrying a loss forward against future trading income, it may be relieved against statutory total income of all types.

3.2 Relieving the loss

Relief under s 380 **is against the statutory total income of the tax year in which the loss arose. In addition or instead,** relief may be claimed **against statutory total income of the preceding year**.

Claim for a loss must be made by the 31 January which is 22 months after the end of the tax year of the loss: thus by 31 January 2008 for a loss in 2005/06.

The taxpayer cannot choose the amount of loss to relieve: thus the loss may have to be set against income, part of which would have been covered by the personal allowance. However, the taxpayer can choose whether to claim full relief in the current year and then relief in the preceding year for any remaining loss, or the other way round.

Set the loss against non-savings income then against savings (excluding dividend) income and finally against dividend income.

Relief is available by carry forward under s 385 for any loss not relieved under s 380.

Activity 5.1

In 2005/06 Nicola has a loss of £18,000. Her statutory total income in 2005/06 is non-savings investment income totalling £14,000, and her personal allowance for that year is £4,895. She has no other source of income for any year. If she obtains loss relief as soon as possible, what loss is carried forward under s 385 ICTA 1988?

Activity 5.2

Janet started to trade on 1 June 2005 and made a loss of £25,000 in her first period of account to 31 March 2006. Her other income is £18,000 rental income a year, and she wishes to claim loss relief for the year of loss and then for the preceding year. Show her taxable income for each year, and comment on the effectiveness of the loss relief.

3.3 Capital allowances

The trader may adjust the size of the total s 380 claim by not claiming all the capital allowances he is entitled to: a reduced claim will increase the balance carried forward to the next year's capital allowances computation.

3.4 Trading losses relieved against capital gains

Where relief is claimed against total income of a given year, the taxpayer may include **a further claim to set the loss against his chargeable gains for the year** less any allowable capital losses for the same year or for previous years. This amount of net gains is computed ignoring taper relief and the annual exempt amount. We will look at chargeable gains later in this text.

The trading loss is first set against total income of the year of the claim, and only any excess of loss is set against capital gains (see later in this text). The taxpayer cannot specify the amount to be set against capital gains, so the annual exempt amount may be wasted.

3.5 Restrictions on s 380 relief

Relief cannot be claimed under s 380 unless a business is conducted on a commercial basis with a view to the realisation of profits; this condition applies to all types of business.

3.6 The choice between loss reliefs

When a trader has a choice between loss reliefs, he should aim to obtain relief both quickly and at the highest possible tax rate.

Another consideration is that a trading loss cannot be set against the capital gains of a year unless relief is first claimed under s 380 against income of the same year. It may be worth making the claim against income and wasting the personal allowance in order to avoid a CGT liability.

Before recommending S 380 loss relief consider whether it will result in the waste of the personal allowance. Such waste is to be avoided if at all possible.

4 End of chapter activity

Activity 5.3

Shula has been trading for a number of years. Her taxable profits and losses have been as follows:

	£
Year ended 31 March 2005	8,000 profit
Year ended 31 March 2006	(10,000) loss
Year ended 31 March 2007 (projected)	9,000 profit

Shula's other income from rental properties is as follows:

	£
2004/05	NIL
2005/06	21,000

Task

Write a memorandum to your tax manager explaining the alternative methods by which Shula may obtain relief for the loss in the year to 31 March 2006. State the advantages/disadvantages of each method of obtaining relief.

Key learning points

☑ **Trading losses** may be **relieved in various ways.**

☑ A **trading loss not relieved in any other way** can be **carried forward** to set against the **first available profits** of the **same trade**.

☑ Losses can be set against **total income** in the **year the loss arises** or the **preceding year**.

Quick quiz

1 Trading losses can be carried forward and set off against .... Fill in the blank.

2 Keith makes a loss in his accounts made up for the year to 31 July 2005. In which years can he relieve the loss under s 380 ICTA 1988?

Answers to quick quiz

1 Trading losses can be carried forward and set off against **the first available profits of the same trade.**

2 The year of the loss (2005/06) and the preceding year (2004/05).

Activity checklist

This checklist shows which performance criteria, range statement or knowledge and understanding point is covered by each activity in this chapter. Tick off each activity as you complete it.

Activity

5.1	☐	This activity deals with Knowledge and Understanding point 2: issues of tax liability.
5.2	☐	This activity deals with Performance Criteria 18.2.A: adjust trading profits and losses for tax purposes. Knowledge and Understanding point 2: issues of tax liability.
5.3	☐	This activity deals with Knowledge and Understanding point 2: issues of tax liability.

chapter 6

Partnerships

Contents

Performance criteria

18.2 C Divide profits and losses of partnerships amongst partners

18.2 D Apply the basis of assessment for unincorporated businesses in opening and closing years

Range statement

18.2 Clients: partnerships

Knowledge and understanding

9 Basis of assessment for unincorporated businesses

10 Basic allocation of income between partners (Element 18.2)

1 Introduction

A partnership exists where two or more individuals (partners) carry on a trade together.

A partnership prepares business accounts in exactly the same way as a sole trader would. The business accounts show the profits for the partnership as a whole. The partners may agree to divide the profits of the partnership between themselves in any way they wish. We look further at how to divide the profits of a partnership between the partners below.

2 Computing taxable trading profits of partnerships

A partnership is treated like a sole trader for the purpose of computing its taxable trading profits. This means that you must take the net profits in the partnership's accounts and adjust them for tax purposes in exactly the same way as you would for a sole trader.

Any partners' salaries or interest on capital deducted in the accounts must be added back for tax purposes. These items are disallowable expenses because they are a form of drawings.

3 Dividing taxable trading profits between partners

Partners may divide partnership profits between themselves in any way they wish. The partnership agreement, therefore, determines how you should divide taxable trading profits between partners. **If the agreed profit sharing arrangements change during a period of account you should time apportion the profits to before and after the change and deal with each period separately**.

Example

Bernard and Clive are in partnership. Until 30 June 2005 profits are shared equally. From 1 July 2005 the partners agree that the profits should be shared 3:1. Taxable trading profits of the partnership for the year ended 31 December 2005 are £40,000.

Calculate Bernard and Clive's taxable trading profits for the year to 31 December 2005.

Solution

	Total	*Bernard*	*Clive*
1.1.05 – 30.6.05	£	£	£
6/12 × £40,000 = £20,000	20,000	10,000	10,000
1.7.05 – 31.12.05			
6/12 × £40,000 = £20,000	20,000	15,000	5,000
	40,000	25,000	15,000

Bernard's taxable trading profits for the year to 31 December 2005 are, therefore, £25,000 and Clive's taxable trading profits for the year to 31 December 2005 are £15,000.

Activity 6.1

Pratish and Jameel are in partnership. The taxable trading profits of the partnership for the year to 31 March 2006 are £100,000. Until 31 December 2005 the profits were shared 2:1. Thereafter they are shared 4:1. Calculate the taxable trading profits for each partner for the year to 31 March 2006.

3.1 Interest on capital and salaries

Sometimes a partnership agreement may provide for partners to be paid salaries and/or interest on the capital they have contributed to a partnership. As noted above, although these items may have been deducted in computing the accounts profits they must be added back for tax purposes as they are effectively drawings of the proprietors.

When allocating the taxable trading profits of the partnership between partners your first step should be to deal with any salaries or interest on capital. The balance of any taxable trading profit or loss should then be divided between the partners.

Example

Gunjeet and Elif are in partnership. Gunjit is paid a salary of £30,000 per annum and Elif is paid a salary of £16,000 per annum. The partnership agreement provides for any remaining profits or losses to be divided equally between the partners. The taxable trading profits for the partnership for the year ended 30 September 2005 were £60,000. Show how the profits are divided between the partners.

Solution

	Total	*Gunjit*	*Elif*
	£	£	£
Salary	46,000	30,000	16,000
Profit (£60,000 – £30,000 – £16,000)	14,000	7,000	7,000
	60,000	37,000	23,000

For the year ended 30 September 2005 Gunjit has taxable trading profits of £37,000 and Elif has taxable trading profits of £23,000.

Activity 6.2

Kumar and Bal are in partnership. The partnership agreement provides for salaries of £40,000 per annum to be paid to each of them. Thereafter profits are divided in the ratio 3:2. Taxable trading profits for the year to 30 June 2005 are £130,000. Show how these profits are divided between the partners.

Here is an example where the partners are paid interest on their capital.

Example

Doreen and Derek are in partnership. Doreen contributed capital of £100,000 to the partnership and Derek contributed capital of £60,000. The partnership agreement provides for the partners to be paid interest of 5% per annum on their capital. Thereafter partnership profits are divided in the ratio of 2:1. Taxable trading profits for the year ended 31 March 2006 were £140,000. Show how these profits are divided between the partners.

Solution

	Total	*Doreen*	*Derek*
	£	£	£
Interest on capital (5%)	8,000	5,000	3,000
Profits (£140,000 – 5,000 – 3,000)	132,000	88,000	44,000
Taxable trading profits	140,000	93,000	47,000

The profits remaining after allocating the interest on the capital are divided in the ratio 2:1.

Activity 6.3

Shuan and Matthew are in partnership. They contributed capital of £20,000 and £70,000 respectively to the partnership. The partnership agreement provides for interest on capital of 6% and salaries of £40,000 to be paid to each partner. Remaning profits are divided in the ratio 3:1. For the year to 31 December 2005 taxable trading profits were £180,000. Show how these profits are allocated between the partners.

If there is a change in the rate at which salaries or interest are paid part way through a period of account you should time apportion the profits before and after the change and deal with each period separately. Remember that the salaries and interest will need to be time apportioned too. You should make any time apportionments on a monthly basis.

Activity 6.4

Jameel and Shammima are in partnership. Until 30 June 2005 profits were shared equally after payment of salaries of £20,000 per annum to each partner. On 1 July 2005 Jameel's salary was increased to £50,000 per annum and Shammima's salary was increased to £30,000 per annum. Remaining profits continued to be shared equally. Taxable trading profits of the partnership for the year ended 31 December 2005 were £200,000. Show how this amount is divided between the partners.

4 The tax positions of individual partners

We have seen how to allocate taxable trading profits for a period of account between partners. Once you have done this you must decide which tax year the profits are taxed in.

A partner is taxed in the same way as a sole trader. This means taxable trading profits for the year ended 31.12.05 will usually form the basis year for 2005/06 and a partner will be taxed on his share of the profits arising in the year ended 31 December 2005 in 2005/06.

4.1 Changes in membership

When a trade continues but partners join or leave (including cases when a sole trader takes in partners or a partnership breaks up leaving only one partner as a sole trader), **the special rules for basis periods in opening and closing years do not apply to the people who were carrying on the trade both before and after the change. They carry on using the period of account ending in each tax year as the basis period for the tax year. The commencement rules only affect joiners, and the cessation rules only affect leavers.**

4.2 Assets owned individually

Where the partners own assets (such as their cars) individually, a capital allowances computation must be prepared for each partner in respect of the assets he owns (not forgetting any adjustment for private use). **The capital allowances must go into the partnership's tax computation.**

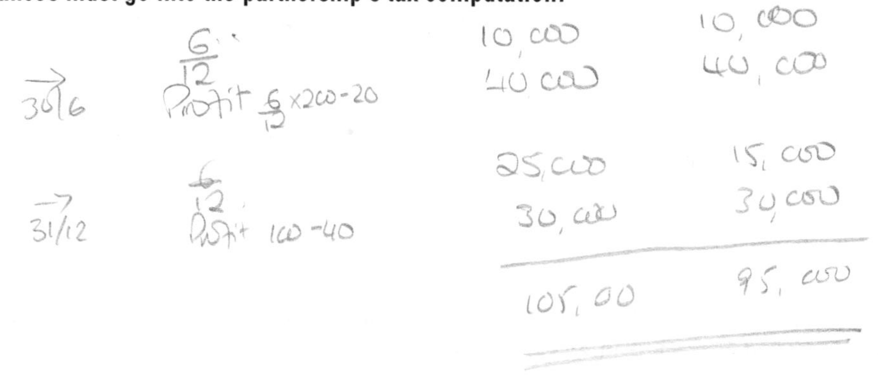

Example: a partnership

Alice and Bertrand start a partnership on 1 July 2002, making up accounts to 31 December each year. Profits are shared equally.

On 1 May 2004, Charles joins the partnership. Profits are shared in the ratio 2:2:1. On 1 November 2005, Charles leaves. The profits are then shared 3:2.

Profits and losses as adjusted for tax purposes are as follows.

Period	*Profit(loss)*
	£
1.7.02 – 31.12.02	22,000
1.1.03 – 31.12.03	51,000
1.1.04 – 31.12.04	39,000
1.1.05 – 31.12.05	15,000

Show the taxable trading profits for each partner for 2002/03 to 2005/06.

Solution

We must first share the profits and losses for the periods of account between the partners.

	Total	*Alice*	*Bertrand*	*Charles*
	£	£	£	£
1.7.02 – 31.12.02				
Profits 50:50				
Total (P/e 31.12.02)	22,000	11,000	11,000	
Year ended 31.12.03				
Profits 50:50				
Total	51,000	25,500	25,500	
Year ended 31.12.04				
January to April (4/12)				
Profits	13,000	6,500	6,500	
May to December (8/12)				
Profits	26,000	10,400	10,400	5,200
Total for y/e 31.12.04	39,000	16,900	16,900	5,200
Year ended 31.12.05				
January to October (10/12)				
Profits	12,500	5,000	5,000	2,500
November and December (2/12)				
Profits	2,500	1,500	1,000	
Total for y/e 31.12.05	15,000	6,500	6,000	2,500

The next stage is to work out the basis periods and hence the taxable profits for the partners. All of them are treated as making up accounts to 31 December, but Alice and Bertrand are treated as starting to trade on 1 July 2002, Charles as

trading only from 1 May 2004 to 31 October 2005. Applying the usual rules gives the following basis periods and taxable profits.

Alice

Year	*Basis period*	*Working*	*Taxable profits*
			£
2002/03	1.7.02 – 5.4.03	£11,000 + (£25,500 × 3/12)	17,375
2003/04	1.1.03 – 31.12.03		25,500
2004/05	1.1.04 – 31.12.04		16,900
2005/06	1.1.05 – 31.12.05		6,500

Alice will have overlap profits for the period 1 January to 5 April 2003 (£25,500 × 3/12 = £6,375) to deduct when she ceases to trade.

Bertrand

Year	*Basis period*	*Working*	*Taxable profits*
			£
2002/03	1.7.02 – 5.4.03	£11,000 + (£25,500 × 3/12)	17,375
2003/04	1.1.03 – 31.12.03		25,500
2004/05	1.1.04 – 31.12.04		16,900
2005/06	1.1.05 – 31.12.05		6,000

Bertrand's overlap profits are £25,500 × 3/12 = £6,375.

Charles

Year	*Basis period*	*Working*	*Taxable profits*
			£
2004/05	1.5.04 – 5.4.05	£5,200 + (£2,500 × 3/10)	5,950
2005/06	6.4.05 – 31.10.05	£2,500 × 7/10	1,750

Because Charles ceased to trade in his second tax year of trading, his basis period for the second year starts on 6 April and he has no overlap profits.

Activity 6.5

A partnership makes profits as follows.

Year ended 31 December	£
2004	34,200
2005	45,600

A partner joins on 1 September 2004, and is entitled to 20% of the profits. What are his taxable profits for 2004/05 and 2005/06?

Remember, partners are effectively taxed in the same way as sole traders with just one difference. Before you tax the partner you need to take each set of accounts (as adjusted for tax purposes) and divide the profit (or loss) between each partner.

Then carry on as normal for a sole trader – each partner is that sole trader in respect of his profits or losses for each accounting period.

5 End of chapter activity

Activity 6.6

Adam, Bert and Charlie started in partnership as secondhand car dealers on 6 April 2002, sharing profits in the ratio 2:2:1, after charging annual salaries of £1,500, £1,200 and £1,000 respectively.

On 5 July 2003 Adam retires and Bert and Charlie continue, taking the same salaries as before, but dividing the balance of the profits in the ratio 3:2.

The profits of the partnership as adjusted for tax purposes are as follows.

		Profits
		£
Year ending 31 March	2003	10,200
	2004	20,800
	2005	12,600
	2006	18,000

Task

Show the taxable trading profits for each partner for 2002/2003 to 2005/06 inclusive.

Key learning points

- ☑ **A partnership** is a **source of profits and losses** for **trades being carried on** by **individual partners**.
- ☑ The first step is to **divide the profit** (or loss) of each set of accounts **between the partners**.
- ☑ The second step is to **allocate the profit** for each partner for the accounting period to the **correct tax year**.
- ☑ **Commencement** and **cessation** rules apply to partners individually when they join or leave.

Quick quiz

1. Rod and Steve have been in partnership for many years. Profits are shared equally. For the year ended 31 December 2004, the partnership made a profit of £40,000 and for the year ended 31 December 2005 the profit was £50,000. Show the profit taxable on Rod and Steve for 2005/06.
2. How would your answer to question 1 be different if Rod took a salary of £10,000?
3. Ethel and Mildred have been in partnership for many years. On 1 December 2005, Maud joins the partnership and profits are shared 40:40:20. For the year to 30 November 2006, the partnership makes a profit of £60,000. Show the profits assessable on Maud in 2005/06 and 2006/07.

Answers to quick quiz

1. The profits of the year to 31 December 2005 are assessable in 2005/06 ie £25,000 each.
2.

	£
Profits y/e 31.12.05	50,000
Less: salary for Rod	(10,000)
Profits to allocate	40,000
Rod £(10,000 + 20,000)	30,000
Steve	20,000

3. y/e 30.11.06 20% of the profits are allocated to Maud ie £12,000

2005/06	
1.12.05 – 5.4.06	
4/12 x £12,000	£4,000
2006/07	
1.12.05 – 30.11.06	£12,000

Activity checklist

This checklist shows which performance criteria is covered by each activity in this chapter. Tick off each activity as you complete it.

Activity		
6.1	☐	This activity deals with Performance Criteria 18.2 C: divide profits and losses of partnerships amongst partners.
6.2	☐	This activity deals with Performance Criteria 18.2 C: divide profits and losses of partnerships amongst partners.
6.3	☐	This activity deals with Performance Criteria 18.2 C: divide profits and losses of partnerships amongst partners.
6.4	☐	This activity deals with Performance Criteria 18.2 C: divide profits and losses of partnerships amongst partners.
6.5	☐	This activity deals with Performance Criteria 18.2 C: divide profits and losses of partnerships amongst partners.
6.6	☐	This activity deals with Performance Criteria 18.2 C: divide profits and losses of partnerships amongst partners. Performance Criteria 18.2.D: apply the basis of assessment for unincorporated businesses in opening and closing years.

PART B

Chargeable gains

chapter 7

Chargeable gains: an outline

Contents

Performance criteria

18.3 A Identify and value correctly any chargeable assets that have been disposed of

18.3 D Apply reliefs, deferrals and exemptions correctly

Range statement

18.3 Chargeable assets that have been: sold, gifted, lost, destroyed

Knowledge and understanding

11 Identification of business assets disposed of including part disposals (Element 18.3)

13 Capital gains exemptions and reliefs on business assets including rollover relief and taper relief (Element 18.3)

14 Rates of tax payable on gains on business assets disposed of by individuals (Element 18.3)

1 The charge to tax

1.1 Individuals

An individual pays CGT on any taxable gains arising in the tax year. **Taxable gains are the net chargeable gains (gains minus losses) of the tax year reduced by unrelieved losses brought forward from previous years, a taper relief and the annual exemption.**

There is an annual exemption for each tax year. For 2005/06 it is £8,500. It is the last deduction to be made in the calculation of taxable gains.

1.2 Calculating CGT

Taxable gains are chargeable to capital gains tax as if the gains were an extra slice of savings (excl dividend) income for the year of assessment concerned. This means that CGT may be due at 10%, 20% or 40%.

The rate bands are used first to cover income and then gains.

Example

Sase had taxable income in 2005/06 of £22,400. She made taxable gains (ie gains after deduction of the annual exemption) in the year of £15,000.

Sase's taxable income uses all the starting rate band and £20,310 of the basic rate band. This means £10,000 of the basic rate band remains to be used by the taxable gains. The remaining gain is taxed at 40%.

Capital gains tax payable

	£
£10,000 × 20%	2,000
£5,000 × 40%	2,000
	4,000

Activity 7.1

In 2005/06, Carol, a single woman, has the following income and net chargeable gains. Find the CGT payable.

	£
Taxable trading profits	33,980
Net chargeable gains	18,400

*In 2005/2006 Carol is entitled to a personal allowance of £4,895 and a capital gains annual exemption of £8,500.

Net Gain = 18400 - 8500 = 9900

Trading Income 33980

(4895)

29085

2090 × 10% =

26995 × 22% =

32400 - 26995

3315 × 20% = 663

6585 × 40% = 2634

9900

3297

Activity 7.2

In 2005/06, Amy had taxable trading profits of £24,150 and gains (before the annual exemption) of £22,300. What is her CGT payable for 2005/06?

1.3 Companies

Companies are not liable to CGT as such but any net chargeable gains which arise in an accounting period, minus unrelieved losses brought forward from previous accounting periods, form part of their profits chargeable to corporation tax. Gains and losses are calculated, broadly, in the same way as for individuals (but see below).

The gains of companies are charged at normal corporation tax rates. **Companies do not get the annual exemption or taper relief** (see below). We have included this paragraph here for completeness: you will study the computation of corporation tax later in this text.

2 Chargeable persons, disposals and assets

2.1 Chargeable persons

The following are chargeable persons.

- Individuals
- Partnerships
- Companies

2.2 Chargeable disposals

The following are chargeable disposals.

- Sales of assets or parts of assets
- Gifts of assets or parts of assets
- Receipts of capital sums following the surrender of rights to assets
- The appropriation of assets as trading stock
- The loss or destruction of assets

A chargeable disposal occurs on the date of the contract (where there is one, whether written or oral), or the date of a conditional contract becoming unconditional.

Where a disposal involves an acquisition by someone else, the date of acquisition is the same as the date of disposal.

The following are exempt disposals.

- Transfers of assets on death (the heirs inherit assets as if they bought them at death for their then market values, but there is no capital gain or allowable loss on death)
- Transfers of assets as security for a loan or mortgage
- Gifts to charities and national heritage bodies

2.3 Chargeable assets

All forms of property, wherever in the world they are situated, are chargeable assets unless they are specifically designated as exempt.

The following are exempt assets (thus gains are not taxable and losses on their disposal are not in general allowable losses).

- Motor vehicles suitable for private use
- Works of art, scientific collections and so on given for national purposes
- Gilt-edged securities (when disposed of by individuals)
- Qualifying corporate bonds (QCBs) (when disposed of by individuals)
- Certain chattels
- Debts (except debts on a security)

Activity 7.3

In 1997, J Ltd bought a vintage motor car as an investment. Nobody in the company ever drove it. The car was sold in 2005, making a gain of £75,000. Is the gain chargeable?

3 Losses

3.1 Set-off of losses

Deduct allowable capital losses from chargeable gains in the tax year in which they arise. Any loss which cannot be set off is carried forward to set against future chargeable gains. Losses must be used as soon as possible (subject to the following paragraph). Losses may not normally be set against income.

Allowable losses brought forward are only set off to reduce current year chargeable gains less current year allowable losses to the annual exempt amount. No set-off is made if net chargeable gains for the current year do not exceed the annual exempt amount. (Companies do not have an annual exempt amount so no such restriction on the set off of losses applies to them.)

Example: the use of losses

(a) George has chargeable gains for 2005/06 of £10,000 and allowable losses of £6,000. As the losses are *current year losses* they must be fully relieved against the £10,000 of gains to produce net gains of £4,000, despite the fact that net gains are below the annual exemption.

(b) Bob has gains of £12,400 for 2005/06 and allowable losses brought forward of £6,000. Bob restricts his loss relief to £3,900 so as to leave net gains of £(12,400 – 3,900) = £8,500, which will be exactly covered by his annual exemption for 2005/06. The remaining £2,100 of losses will be carried forward to 2006/07.

(c) Tom has chargeable gains of £5,000 for 2005/06 and losses brought forward from 2004/05 of £4,000. He will leapfrog 2005/06 and carry forward all of his losses to 2006/07. His gains of £5,000 are covered by his annual exemption for 2005/06.

4 Taper relief

4.1 Taper relief for business assets

Taper relief may be available to reduce gains realised after 5 April 1998 by individuals. It is not available to reduce gains realised by companies.

Taper relief reduces the percentage of the gain chargeable according to how many complete years the asset had been held since acquisition, or 6 April 1998 if later. Taper relief is more generous for business assets than for non-business assets. In Unit 18 you will only be expected to compute gains on the disposal of business assets.

The percentages of gains which remain chargeable after taper relief are set out below.

Business assets *Number of complete years after 5.4.98* *for which asset held*	*% of gain chargeable*
0	100
1	50
2 or more	25

The above percentages will be given in the tax tables at the beginning of the examination.

Example: complete years held for taper relief

Peter buys a business asset on 1 January 2003 and sells it on 1 July 2005. For the purposes of the taper Peter is treated as if he had held the asset for two complete years after 5 April 1998.

This means that only 25% of the gain remains chargeable after taper relief.

4.2 Taper relief and losses

Taper relief is applied to net chargeable gains after the deduction of current year and brought forward losses. The annual exemption is then deducted from the tapered gains.

Example

Suppose in the above example, a gain of £50,000 was made on the asset sold and Peter had **losses** brought forward of £10,000.

The brought forward losses are set against the gain to give net chargeable gains before taper relief of 40,000.

Taper relief is then applied to give a gain after taper relief of 25% x £40,000 = £10,000.

Finally the annual exemption is deducted to give a taxable gain of £1,500 (£10,000 - £8,500)

Activity 7.4

William sold a business asset in December 2005 realising a chargeable gain of £40,600 before taper relief. He had purchased the asset in May 1997. In January 2006 William sold another business asset realising a loss of £1,300 but had made no other disposals in 2005/06. What are William's taxable gains (after the annual exemption) for 2005/06?

Losses are dealt with **before** taper relief. However losses brought forward are only deducted from net current gains to the extent that the gains exceed the CGT annual exemption.

Activity 7.5

Sally sold a business asset in July 2005 which she had purchased in January 2004. She realised a chargeable gain (before taper relief) of £17,800. She also sold a business asset in 2005/06 realising a capital loss of £6,000. She has a capital loss brought forward from 2004/05 of £10,000. What are Sally's taxable gains (after the annual exemption) for 2005/06?

4.3 The allocation of losses

Allocate losses to gains in the way that produces the lowest tax charge. Losses should therefore be deducted from the gains attracting the lowest rate of taper (ie where the highest percentage of the gain remains chargeable).

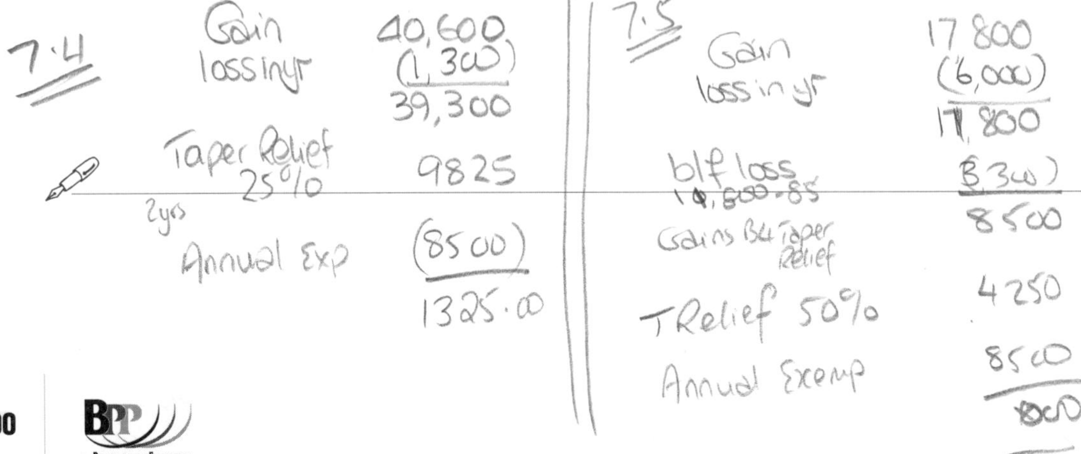

Example: allocation of losses to gains

Alan made the following capital losses and gains in 2005/06:

	£
Loss	10,000
Gains (before taper relief)	
Asset A (business asset)	50,000
Asset B (business asset)	18,000

Asset A was purchased in December 2003 and sold in January 2006. Taper relief reduces the gain to 25% of the original gain (2 years business asset). Asset B was purchased on 5 November 2004 and sold on 17 December 2005. Taper relief reduces the gain to 50% of the original gain (1 year business asset).

The best use of the loss is to offset it against the gain on asset B:

	£	£
Gain – Asset A	50,000	
Gain after taper relief (£50,000 × 25%)		12,500
Gain – Asset B	18,000	
Less loss	(10,000)	
	8,000	
Gain after taper relief (£8,000 × 50%)		4,000
Gains after taper relief		16,500
Less annual exemption		(8,500)
Taxable gains		8,000

4.4 Other points

There are certain special situations which will affect the operation of taper relief:

(a) where there has been a transfer of assets between spouses (or civil partners)(a no loss/no gain transfer; see below) the taper on a subsequent disposal will be based on the combined period of holding by the spouses (or civil partners).

(b) where gains have been relieved under a provision which reduces the cost of the asset in the hands of a new owner (such as gift relief, see later in this text) the taper will operate by reference to the holding period of the new owner.

4.5 Business assets

A business asset is:

(a) an asset **used for the purposes of a trade** carried on by an individual (either alone or in partnership) or by a qualifying company of that individual

(b) an asset **held for the purposes of any office or employment** held by that individual with a person carrying on a trade

(c) **shares in a qualifying company** held by an individual

A **qualifying company** is a trading company (or holding company of a trading group) where:

(a) the company is **not listed** on a recognised stock exchange nor is a 51% subsidiary of a listed company (companies listed on the Alternative Investment Market (AIM) are unlisted for this purpose)

(b) the shareholder is an **officer or employee** of the company (full-time or part-time), or of a company with a **relevant connection**

(c) the shareholder holds at least **5% of the voting rights** in the company

A company has a **relevant connection** with another company if:

(a) The companies are both members of a 51% group, or

(b) The companies are under common control and they carry on a complementary business which can reasonably be regarded as one composite undertaking, or

(c) One company (X Ltd) is a joint enterprise company in which 75% or more of the ordinary shares capital is held by five or fewer persons and the other company (Y Ltd) holds 10% or more of the ordinary share capital in X Ltd.

5 Married couples

5.1 Husband and wife

A husband and wife are taxed as two separate people. Each has an annual exemption, and losses of one spouse cannot be set against gains of the other.

Disposals between spouses who are living together give rise to no gain and no loss, whatever actual price (if any) **was charged by the person transferring the asset** to their spouse. A couple are treated as living together unless they are separated under a court order or separation deed, or are in fact separated in circumstances which make permanent separation likely.

The acquiring spouse normally takes over the taper relief position of the disposing spouse. This means the acquiring spouse is treated as acquiring the asset when the disposing spouse did.

Where an asset is jointly owned, the beneficial interests of the spouses will determine the treatment of any gain on disposal. If, for example, there is evidence that the wife's share in an asset was 60%, then 60% of any gain or loss on disposal would be attributed to her. If there is no evidence of the relative interests, the Revenue will normally accept that the asset is held in equal shares. Where a declaration of how income from the asset is to be shared for income tax purposes has been made, there is a presumption that the same shares will apply for CGT purposes.

If a spouse whose marginal tax rate is 40% wishes to dispose of an asset at a gain and the other spouse would only be taxed on the gain at a lower rate, the asset should first be transferred to the spouse with the lower tax rate. Similarly, assets or parts of assets should be transferred between spouses to use both CGT annual exemptions.

5.2 Civil partnerships

From 5 December 2005 same sex partnerships can be registered under the Civil Partnerships Act 2004. Civil partners are treated in exactly the same way as spouses, so that a transfer from one civil partner to the other gives rise to no gain and no loss.

Civil partnerships are a totally different concept to trading partnerships: do not confuse them.

6 End of chapter activities

Activity 7.6

Eric had taxable trading profits of £25,650 and gains of £35,300 in 2005/06.

Task

Calculate Eric's capital gains tax liability for 2005/06.

Activity 7.7

Lorna disposed of assets as follows.

(i) On 1 January 2005 she sold her car at a loss of £10,700.

(ii) On 28 February 2005 she sold some shares at a loss of £6,300.

(iii) On 1 May 2005 she sold some shares (acquired August 2004) and realised a gain of £7,800. The shares were a business asset for taper relief purposes.

(iv) On 1 October 2005 she sold some shares at a loss of £2,000.

(v) On 1 December 2005 she sold a business asset (acquired July 2005) for £50,000, making a gain of £3,000.

(vi) On 1 April 2006 she sold some gilt-edged securities (acquired May 2005), making a gain of £10,000.

Task

What loss, if any, is available to be carried forward at the end of 2005/06?

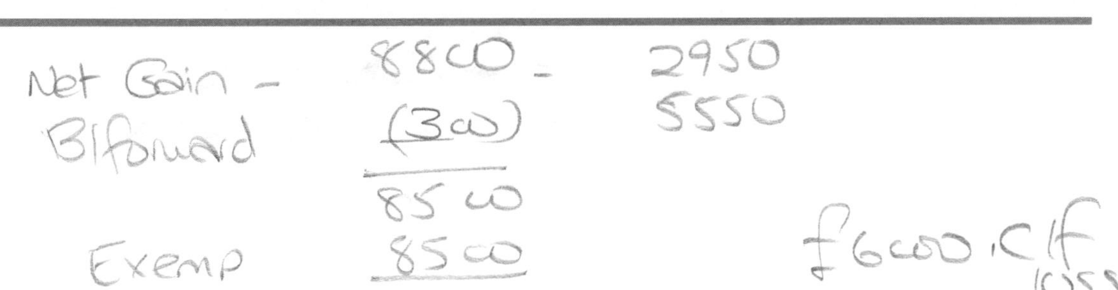

Key learning points

- ☑ An individual pays **CGT** on his **net chargeable gains** in a tax year.
- ☑ There is an **annual exemption** for an individual for each tax year.
- ☑ Taxable **gains are taxed as an extra slice of savings (excluding dividend) income.**
- ☑ A company pays **corporation tax** on its **net chargeable gains** in an accounting period.
- ☑ **Capital losses** are deducted against gains in the **same tax year or accounting period.**
- ☑ Excess losses are **carried forward.**
- ☑ An individual may **only set off brought forward losses to reduce his gains down to the amount of the annual exemption.**
- ☑ There needs to be three things for a capital gain to arise: **chargeable person, chargeable disposal, chargeable asset.**
- ☑ **Taper relief** reduces gains for individuals after 5 April 1998.
- ☑ Taper relief is applied to an individual's net gains **before the set off of current and brought forward capital losses.**
- ☑ The **annual exemption is deducted after the application of taper relief.**
- ☑ Disposals between **spouses** are on a **no gain/ no loss** basis.

Quick quiz

1 CGT is payable by individuals at ..... %, ... % and ......%. Fill in the blanks

2 Companies are taxable on net chargeable gains in a tax year. TRUE or FALSE?

3 Tom made a chargeable gain (no taper relief) of £8,000 and an allowable loss of £(5,000) in 2005/06.

His loss carried forward to 2006/07 is:

A Nil
B £(100)
C £(4,900)
D £(5,000)

4 Mark acquired a business asset on 1 July 2003. He sold the asset on 1 May 2005. His gain was £4,000.

What is the gain after taper relief?

A Nil
B £1,000
C £2,000
D £4,000

5 How are disposals between a husband and wife who are living together treated for CGT?

Answers to quick quiz

1 CGT is payable at **10**%, **20**% and **40**%.

2 FALSE. A company is taxed on its net chargeable gains in an **accounting period**.

3 A A current year loss must be set against a current year gain even though this brings the gain below the annual exemption.

4 C The ownership period runs from 1 July 2003 to 30 April 2005 = 1 complete year, so the taper relief % is 50%.

5 Disposals between spouses who are living together give rise to no gain and no loss.

Activity checklist

This checklist shows which performance criteria, range statement or knowledge and understanding point is covered by each activity in this chapter. Tick off each activity as you complete it.

Activity		
7.1	☐	This activity deals with Knowledge and Understanding point 14: rates of tax payable on gains on business assets disposed of by individuals.
7.2	☐	This activity deals with Knowledge and Understanding point 14: rates of tax payable on gains on business assets disposed of by individuals.
7.3	☐	This activity deals with Performance Criteria 18.3.A: Identify and value correctly any chargeable assets that have been disposed of.
7.4	☐	This activity deals with Performance Criteria 18.3.D: apply reliefs, deferrals and exemptions correctly.
7.5	☐	This activity deals with Performance Criteria 18.3.D: apply reliefs, deferrals and exemptions correctly.
7.6	☐	This activity deals with Knowledge and Understanding point 14: rates of tax payable on gains on business assets disposed of by individuals.
7.7	☐	This activity deals with Performance Criteria 18.3.A and 18.3.D: identify and correctly value any chargeable assets that have been disposed of; apply reliefs, deferrals and exemptions correctly.

chapter 8

The computation of gains and losses

Contents

Performance criteria

18.3 A Identify and value correctly any chargeable assets that have been disposed of

18.3 C Calculate chargeable gains and allowable losses

Range statement

18.3 Chargeable assets that have been: sold, gifted, lost, destroyed

Knowledge and understanding

11 Identification of business assets disposed of including part disposals (Element 18.3)

12 Calculation of gains and losses on disposals of business assets including indexation allowance (Element 18.3)

1 The basic computation

1.1 Proforma

A chargeable gain (or an allowable loss) is generally calculated as follows.

	£
Disposal consideration (or market value)	45,000
Less incidental costs of disposal	(400)
Net proceeds	44,600
Less allowable costs	(21,000)
Unindexed gain	23,600
Less indexation allowance (if available)	(8,500)
Indexed gain	15,100

For individuals, taper relief may then apply.

1.2 Costs

Incidental costs of disposal may include:

- valuation fees (but not the cost of an appeal against the Revenue's valuation)
- estate agency fees
- advertising costs
- legal costs

These costs should be deducted separately from any other allowable costs (because they do not qualify for any indexation allowance if it was available on that disposal).

Allowable costs include:

- the original cost of acquisition
- incidental costs of acquisition
- enhancement expenditure

Incidental costs of acquisition may include the types of cost listed above as incidental costs of disposal, but acquisition costs do qualify for indexation allowance (from the month of acquisition) if it is available on the disposal.

1.3 Enhancement expenditure

Enhancement expenditure is capital expenditure which enhances the value of the asset and is reflected in the state or nature of the asset at the time of disposal, or expenditure incurred in establishing, preserving or defending title to, or a right over, the asset. Excluded from this category are:

- costs of repairs and maintenance
- costs of insurance
- any expenditure deductible for income tax purposes
- any expenditure met by public funds (for example council grants)

Enhancement expenditure may qualify for indexation allowance from the month in which it becomes due and payable.

1.4 Disposal consideration

Usually the disposal consideration is the proceeds of sale of the asset, but a disposal is deemed to take place at market value:

(a) where the disposal is **not a bargain at arm's length**
(b) where the disposal is made for a **consideration which cannot be valued**
(c) where the disposal is by way of a **gift**

Activity 8.1

D Ltd bought a plot of land for £100,000, and spent £6,000 on clearing it. However, by the time D Ltd sold the land (at a large profit) it had become overgrown, and was in the same state as it would have been if the work had not been done. Is the £6,000 deductible as enhancement expenditure?

2 The indexation allowance

2.1 Introduction

Indexation was introduced in March 1982. The purpose of having an indexation allowance was to remove the inflationary element of a gain from taxation. You will not have to deal with assets acquired before April 1982 in your examination.

Individuals are entitled to an indexation allowance until April 1998, but not thereafter.

The above rule does not apply to companies. Companies are entitled to an indexation allowance until the date of disposal of an asset.

Example: indexation allowance

John bought a shop for use in his business on 2 January 1987 and sold it on 19 November 2005.

Indexation allowance will be available for the period January 1987 to April 1998 only.

2.2 Calculation of indexation allowance

To calculate an indexation allowance, you need an indexation factor calculated from the month the asset was acquired to the date the asset was sold or, for individuals, to April 1998, if earlier. You will be given this indexation factor in the examination. You will not be expected to calculate it.

The indexation factor is multiplied by the cost of the asset or other expenditure to calculate the indexation allowance.

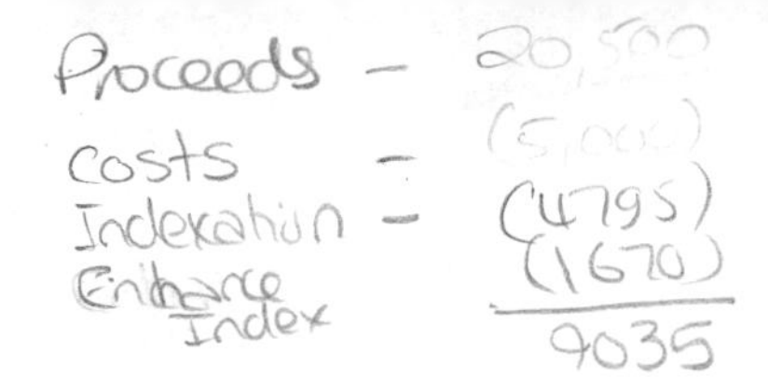

Activity 8.2

A business asset is acquired by an individual on 15 February 1983 at a cost of £5,000. Enhancement expenditure of £2,000 is incurred on 10 April 1984. The asset is sold for £20,500 on 20 December 2005. Calculate the indexation allowance. Assume indexation factors February 1983 to April 1998 = 0.959; April 1984 to April 1998 = 0.835.

Activity 8.3

Z Ltd acquired a freehold factory in July 2001 for £100,000. It sold the factory for £180,000 in August 2005. What is the indexed gain on sale? Assume an indexation factor July 2001 – August 2005 = 0.098.

2.3 Indexation and losses

The indexation allowance cannot create or increase an allowable loss. If there is a gain before the indexation allowance, the allowance can reduce that gain to zero, but no further. If there is a loss before the indexation allowance, there is no indexation allowance.

Activity 8.4

Simon bought a business asset for £97,000 in August 1994 and sold it for £24,000 in April 2005. What is the allowable loss? Assume an indexation factor August 1994 – April 1998 = 0.124.

3 Connected persons

A transaction between 'connected persons' is treated as one between parties to a transaction otherwise than by way of a bargain made at arm's length. The effect of this is that the acquisition and disposal are deemed to take place for a consideration equal to the market value of the asset, rather than the actual price paid.

If a loss results, it can be set only against gains arising in the same or future years from disposals to the same connected person and the loss can only be set off if he or she is still connected with the person sustaining the loss.

An individual is connected with:

- his spouse
- his relatives (brothers, sisters, ancestors and lineal descendants)
- the relatives of his spouse
- the spouses of his and his spouse's relatives

From 5 December 2005 the term 'spouse' includes civil partners.

A company is connected with:

- a person who (alone or with persons connected with him) controls it
- another company under common control

Companies are dealt with in detail later in this text.

4 Part disposals

4.1 General rule

The disposal of part of a chargeable asset is a chargeable event. The chargeable gain (or allowable loss) is computed by deducting from the disposal value a fraction of the original cost of the whole asset.

The fraction is:

$$\frac{A}{A+B} = \frac{\text{value of the part disposed of}}{\text{value of the part disposed of} + \text{market value of the remainder}}$$

A is the proceeds (for arm's length disposals) *before* deducting incidental costs of disposal.

The part disposal fraction should not be applied indiscriminately. Any expenditure incurred wholly in respect of a particular part of an asset should be treated as an allowable deduction in full for that part and not apportioned. An example of this is incidental selling expenses, which are wholly attributable to the part disposed of.

Activity 8.5

Mr Smith owns a business asset which originally cost him £27,000 in March 1984. He sold a quarter interest in the asset in July 2005 for £18,000. The market value of the three-quarter share remaining is estimated to be £36,000. What is the chargeable gain after taper relief? Assume an indexation factor March 1984 – April 1998 = 0.858.

Activity 8.6

Louisa bought a plot of land for use in her business for £150,000 in January 2001. In August 2005, she sold part of the land for £187,000, which was net of legal fees on the sale of £3,000. At that time, the value of the remaining land was £327,000. What expenditure could she deduct in computing her chargeable gain?

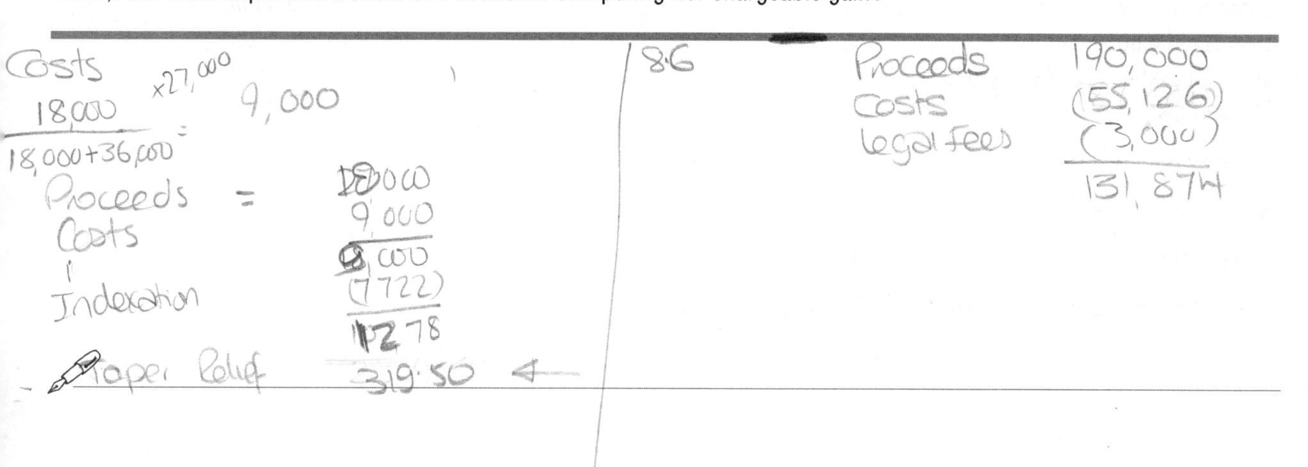

5 Chattels

5.1 Gains on chattels

A **chattel** is tangible movable property.

A **wasting asset** is an asset with an estimated remaining useful life of 50 years or less.

Plant and machinery, whose predictable useful life is always deemed to be less than 50 years, is therefore an example of a wasting chattel (unless it is immovable, in which case it will be wasting but not a chattel).

Wasting chattels are exempt from CGT (so that there are no chargeable gains and no allowable losses). There is one exception to this, but this is not assessable in Unit 18.

Activity 8.7

ABC Ltd bought a racehorse for use at client events in 1999 for £3,000. The racehorse was sold in June 2005 for £10,000. Calculate any chargeable gain arising.

If a chattel is not exempt under the wasting chattels rule, any gain arising on its disposal will still be exempt from CGT if the asset is sold for gross proceeds of £6,000 or less.

If sale proceeds exceed £6,000, any gain is limited to a maximum of 5/3 × (gross proceeds – £6,000).

Example

Greenacre Ltd purchased a painting for its boardroom on 1 June 2001 for £3,000. The painting was sold on 21 June 2005 for £7,200 (which was net of auctioneer's commission of 10%). What was the chargeable gain? Assume an indexation factor June 2001 – June 2005 = 0.083.

Solution

Calculate the gain as usual:

	£
Proceeds	7,200
Less: cost	(3,000)
Unindexed gain	4,200
Less: indexation £3,000 × 0.083	(249)
Indexed gain	3,951

The maximum gain is:

5/3 (8,000* – 6,000) = £3,333

*This is the gross proceeds £7,200 × 100/90

The chargeable gain is the lower of £3,951 and £3,333, ie £3,333.

Activity 8.8

A Ltd purchased a Chippendale chair on 1 June 1987 for £800. On 10 October 2005 it sold the chair at auction for £6,300 (which was net of the auctioneer's 10% commission). What was the chargeable gain?

Assume indexation factor = 0.871

5.2 Losses on chattels

Where a chattel, not exempt under the wasting chattels rule is sold for less than £6,000 and a loss arises, the allowable loss is restricted by assuming that the chattel had been sold for £6,000. Any incidental costs of disposal can be deducted from the gross proceeds of £6,000.

This rule cannot turn a loss into a gain, only reduce the loss, perhaps to zero.

Activity 8.9

E Ltd purchased a rare first edition on 1 July 2002 for £8,000 which it sold in October 2005 at auction for £2,700 (which was net of 10% commission). Compute the loss. Assume an indexation factor July 2002 to October 2005 = 0.084.

6 End of chapter activity

Activity 8.10

Hardup Ltd made the following disposals in the year ended 31 March 2006.

(a) On 12 May 2005 it sold an office block for £120,000. The company had bought the offices for £65,000 on 1 July 1990.

(b) On 18 June 2005 it sold a plot of land for £69,000. It had bought it for £20,000 on 1 April 1983 and had spent £4,000 on defending its title to the land in July 1987.

(c) On 25 June 2005 the company exchanged contracts for the sale of a workshop for £173,000. Completion took place on 24 July 2005. It had bought the workshop for £65,000 on 16 October 1985.

(d) Painting which hung in the boardroom. Acquired July 1999 for £3,000. Sold for £7,500 in October 2005.

(e) Vase which was in the reception area. Acquired May 2001 for £8,500. Sold for £5,000 in December 2005.

Task

Compute Hardup Ltd's capital gains for the year end 31.3.06.

Indexation factors:

April 1983 – June 2005	1.241
October 1985 – July 2005	0.989
July 1987 – June 2005	0.853
July 1990 – May 2005	0.496
October 1985 – June 2005	0.976
July 1999 to October 2005	0.155
May 2001 to December 2005	0.097

Key learning points

- ☑ A chargeable gain is the **proceeds** less **cost** and **indexation allowance** (if any).
- ☑ **Enhancement expenditure** is deductible if it is reflected in **the state and nature of an asset** at the date of disposal.
- ☑ **Indexation allowance** runs from the **date of acquisition** to the **date of disposal** (for **companies**) or **April 1998** (for **individuals**).
- ☑ Indexation allowance **cannot create or increase a loss.**
- ☑ In some cases, **market value** is used in a CGT computation.
- ☑ Disposals between **connected persons** are at market value.
- ☑ If a **loss arises on a disposal to a connected person** it can only **be set against gains arising on disposals to the same connected person.**
- ☑ On a **part disposal**, the **cost must be apportioned** between the **part disposed of** and the **part retained**.
- ☑ If a **chattel** is sold for **up to £6,000**, there is **no chargeable gain** and any **loss is restricted**.
- ☑ If sale proceeds on the disposal of a chattel exceed £6,000, **any gain is limited to a maximum of $^5/_3$ (gross proceeds – £6,000)**
- ☑ **Gains on most wasting chattels** are **exempt** and **losses** are **not allowable.**

Quick quiz

1 Lemon Ltd buys a factory. It paints the outside of the factory and builds an extension. The extension is destroyed by fire and is not replaced. It pays legal fees on defending a legal action about the ownership of the land.

Which of the additional expenditure will be allowable on a sale of the factory?

A legal fees only
B legal fees and extension only
C extension and painting only
D all of it

2 How does the calculation of the indexation allowance differ for companies and individuals?

3 10 acres of land are sold for £30,000 out of 25 acres. The original cost was £18,000. The costs of sale were £4,000. The rest of the land is valued at £60,000. What is the allowable expenditure?

Answers to quick quiz

1 A Painting – not allowable because not capital in nature
Extension – not allowable as not reflected in the state of the asset at disposal
Legal fees – allowable as incurred in defending title to asset

2 Indexation runs to the date of disposal for companies. For individuals it stops at April 1998.

3 $\frac{30,000}{30,000 + 60,000} \times$ £18,000 = £6,000 + £4,000 (costs of disposal) = £10,000

Activity checklist

This checklist shows which performance criteria, range statement or knowledge and understanding point is covered by each activity in this chapter. Tick off each activity as you complete it.

Activity		
8.1	☐	This activity deals with Performance Criteria 18.3.C: calculate chargeable gains and allowable losses.
8.2	☐	This activity deals with Knowledge and Understanding point 12: calculation of gains and losses on disposals of business assets including indexation allowance.
8.3	☐	This activity deals with Performance Criteria 18.3.C: calculate chargeable gains and allowable losses.
8.4	☐	This activity deals with Performance Criteria 18.3.C : calculate chargeable gains and allowable losses.
8.5	☐	This activity deals with Performance Criteria 18.3.C calculate chargeable gains and allowable losses.
8.6	☐	This activity deals with Performance Criteria 18.3.C: calculate chargeable gains and allowable losses.
8.7	☐	This activity deals with Performance Criteria 18.3 A: identity and value correctly any chargeable assets that have been disposed of.
8.8	☐	This activity deals with Performance Criteria 18.3.C: calculate chargeable gains and allowable losses.
8.9	☐	This activity deals with Performance Criteria 18.3.C: calculate chargeable gains and allowable losses.
8.10	☐	This activity deals with Performance Criteria 18.3.C: calculate chargeable gains and allowable losses.

chapter 9

Shares and securities

Contents

Performance criteria

18.3 A Identify and value correctly any chargeable assets that have been disposed of

18.3 B Identify shares disposed of by companies

18.3 C Calculate chargeable gains and allowable losses

Range statement

18.3 Chargeable assets that have been: sold, gifted, lost, destroyed

Knowledge and understanding

11 Identification of business assets disposed of including part disposals (Element 18.3)

12 Calculation of gains and losses on disposals of business assets including indexation allowance (Element 18.3)

1 The matching rules for companies

1.1 The problem

Quoted and unquoted shares and securities present special problems when attempting to compute gains or losses on disposal. For instance, suppose that a company buys some quoted shares in X plc as follows.

Date	*Number of shares*	*Cost*
		£
5 May 1993	100	150
17 January 2000	100	375

On 15 June 2005, it sells 120 of its shares for £1,450. To determine its chargeable gain, we need to be able to work out which shares out of the two original holdings were actually sold.

1.2 The solution

We therefore need **matching rules**. These **allow us to decide which shares have been sold and so work out what the allowable cost on disposal should be.**

In what follows, we will use 'shares' to refer to both shares and securities.

The **matching of shares** sold by a company is in the following order.

(a) Shares acquired on the **same day**
(b) Shares acquired in the **previous nine days**, taking earlier acquisitions first
(c) Shares from the **FA 1985 pool** (see below)

Where shares are disposed of within nine days of acquisition, **no indexation allowance is available** even if the acquisition and the disposal fall in different months. Acquisitions matched with disposals under the nine day rule never enter the FA 1985 pool (see below).

2 The FA 1985 pool

2.1 Introduction

For companies we treat shares as a 'pool' which grows as new shares are acquired and shrinks as they are sold. **The FA 1985 pool** (so called because it was introduced by rules in the Finance Act 1985) **comprises the following shares of the same class in the same company.**

- **Shares held by a company on 1 April 1985 and acquired by that company on or after 1 April 1982.**
- **Shares acquired by that company on or after 1 April 1985.**

Note that the FA 1985 pool only contains shares acquired on or after 1 April 1982. You will not be required to deal with shares purchased before this date in the examination so they are not considered here.

In making computations which use the FA 1985 pool, we must keep track of:

(a) the **number** of shares;
(b) the **cost** of the shares ignoring indexation;
(b) the **indexed cost** of the shares.

Each FA 1985 **pool is started by aggregating the cost and number of shares acquired between 1 April 1982 and 1 April 1985** inclusive. In order to calculate the indexed cost of these shares, an indexation allowance, computed from the relevant date of acquisition of the shares to April 1985, is added to the cost.

Example: the FA 1985 pool

Oliver Ltd bought 1,000 shares in Judith plc for £2,750 in August 1984 and another 1,000 for £3,250 in December 1984. Assume indexation factors: August 1984 – April 1985 = 0.055; December 1984 – April 1985 = 0.043. The FA 1985 pool at 1 April 1985 is as follows.

Solution

	No of shares	*Cost*	*Indexed cost*
		£	£
August 1984	1,000	2,750	2,750
December 1984	1,000	3,250	3,250
	2,000	6,000	6,000
Indexation allowance			
0.055 × £2,750			151
0.043 × £3,250			140
Indexed cost of the pool at 1 April 1985			6,291

2.2 Operative events

Disposals and acquisitions of shares which affect the indexed value of the FA 1985 pool are termed **'operative events'**. **Prior to reflecting each such operative event within the FA 1985 share pool, a further indexation allowance (described as an indexed rise) must be computed up to the date of the operative event concerned from the date of the last such operative event** (or from April 1985 if the operative event in question is the first one).

If there are several operative events between 1 April 1985 and the date of a disposal, the indexation procedure described above will have to be performed several times over.

Activity 9.1

Following on from the above example, assume that Oliver Ltd acquired 2,000 more shares on 10 July 1986 at a cost of £4,000. Recalculate the value of the FA 1985 pool on 10 July 1986 following the acquisition.

Assume an indexation factor April 1985 – July 1986 = 0.028.

2.3 Disposals from the FA 1985 pool

In the case of a disposal, following the calculation of the indexed rise to the date of disposal, the cost and the indexed cost attributable to the shares disposed of are deducted from the amounts within the FA 1985 pool. The proportions of the cost and indexed cost to take out of the pool should be computed using the same A/(A + B) fraction that is used for any other part disposal. However, we are not usually given the value of the remaining shares (B in the fraction). We then just use numbers of shares.

The indexation allowance is the indexed cost taken out of the pool minus the cost taken out. As usual, the indexation allowance cannot create or increase a loss.

Activity 9.2

Continuing the above exercise, suppose that Oliver Ltd sold 3,000 shares on 10 July 2005 for £17,000. Compute the gain, and the value of the FA 1985 pool following the disposal.

Assume an indexation factor July 1986 – July 2005 = 0.949.

3 The matching rules for individuals

3.1 Introduction

For individuals, the pooling of shares ceased for acquisitions on or after 6 April 1998. This means the time of each post April 1998 acquisition can be recorded enabling the length of ownership for each share to be calculated for tapering purposes.

From an exam point of view it is important that you identify shares acquired post 6 April 1998 and that you deal with them individually.

3.2 Matching rules

Share disposals for individuals are matched with acquisitions in the following order.

(a) Same day acquisitions.

(b) Acquisitions within the following 30 days.

(c) Previous acquisitions after 5 April 1998 identifying the most recent acquisition first (a LIFO basis).

(d) Any shares in the FA 1985 pool at 5 April 1998 (the FA 1985 pool runs from 6 April 1982 (instead of 1 April 1982) to 5 April 1998 for individuals).

Example

Sue acquired the following shares in X plc.

	No of shares
1.4.90	10,000
1.9.98	5,000
10.11.00	7,000
30.12.05	2,000

On 11.12.05 Sue sold 12,000 shares. With which acquisitions is Sue's share disposal matched?

Solution

Sue will initially match the disposal with the 2,000 shares bought on 30.12.05 (next 30 days). She will then match with the other post April 1998 acquisitions on a LIFO basis, so the 7,000 shares bought on 10.11.00 and 3,000 of the shares bought on 1.9.98 are deemed to be sold. 2,000 of the shares acquired on 1.9.98 and the FA 1985 pool shares remain.

3.3 FA 1985 pool for individuals

For all FA 1985 pools held by an individual at 5 April 1998 indexation allowance to April 1998 is calculated and then effectively the pool is closed.

Activity 9.3

Ron acquired the following shares in First Ltd:

Date of acquisition	*No of shares*	*Cost*
		£
9.11.90	10,000	25,000
4.8.04	3,000	11,400
15.7.05	5,000	19,000

He disposed of 18,000 shares on 10 July 2005 for £72,000. The shares are business assets for the purposes of taper relief. Calculate the chargeable gain arising after taper relief but before the deduction of the annual exemption.

Assume an indexation factor November 1990 – April 1998 = 0.251.

4 Bonus and rights issues

4.1 Bonus issues (scrip issues)

When a company issues bonus shares all that happens is that the size of the original holding is increased. Since bonus shares are issued at no cost there is no need to adjust the original cost. Instead the number of shares purchased at particular times are increased by the bonus. The normal matching rules will then be applied.

Example: bonus issues

The following transactions by an individual in the ordinary shares of X plc would be matched as shown below

6.4.86	Purchase of 600 shares
6.4.90	Purchase of 600 shares
6.4.04	Purchase of 1,000 shares
6.10.04	Bonus issue of one for four
6.12.05	Sale of 1,500 shares

(a) Post 6.4.98 acquisition

		No of shares
6.4.04	Purchase	1,000
6.10.04	Bonus	250
		1,250
6.12.05	Sold	(1,250)

(b) FA 1985 pool

		No of shares
6.4.86	Purchase	600
6.4.90	Purchase	600
		1,200
6.10.04	Bonus	300
		1,500
6.12.05	Sold	(250)
Number of shares remaining in FA 1985 pool		1,250

4.2 Rights issues

The difference between a bonus issue and a rights issue is that in a rights issue the new shares are paid for and this results in an adjustment to the original cost. As with bonus issues, rights shares derived from shares in the 1985 pool go into that holding and for individuals, those derived from post 5.4.98 holdings attach to those holdings. You should add the number and cost of each of right issue to each holding as appropriate.

The length of the period of ownership for taper relief purposes depends on the date of acquisition of the original holding **not** the date of acquisition of the rights shares.

Example

Bal had the following transactions in shares in STT Ltd:

12.8.97	Bought 5,000 shares for £5,000.
19.10.03	Took up rights issue of 1 for 5 at £2.50 per share.
12.7.04	Bought 1,000 shares for £1,500.
14.8.05	Sold 7,000 shares for £14,000.

Compute the gain arising on the disposal in 2005. Assume indexation factor: August 1997 – April 1998 = 0.026

For an individual, your first step should, always be to identify shares acquired after 6.4.98:

Post 6.4.98 acquisition (12.7.04)

Disposal proceeds	£
(1,000/7,000 x £14,000)	2,000
Less: cost	(1,500)
Gain	500

As the shares had been held for one year 50% taper relief is due.

Gain after taper relief = £250

FA 1985 Pool

	Number	*Cost*	*Indexed cost*
12.8.97	5,000	5,000	5,000
Index to April 1998			
5,000 x 0.026			130
	5,000	5,000	5,130
Rights issue	1,000	2,500	2,500
	6,000	7,500	7,630

The Rights Shares were all derived from the FA 1985 pool shares so they must all be put in this pool.

	£
Disposal Proceeds (6,000/7,000 x £14,000)	12,000
Less: cost	(7,500)
Indexation	(130)
	4,370

Taper relief is based on the length of ownership of the original shares (not the rights shares)

Gain after taper relief (25% x £4,370) = £1,093

Total gains £1,593

Activity 9.4

Simon had the following transactions in S Ltd.

1.10.95	Bought 10,000 shares for £15,000
11.9.02	Bought 2,000 shares for £5,000
1.2.04	Took up rights issue 1 for 2 at £2.75 per share
14.10.05	Sold 5,000 shares for £15,000

Compute the gain arising in October 2005, after taper relief (if applicable). The shares have always been a business asset for taper relief purposes. Indexation factor October 1995 – April 1998 = 0.085.

For companies, you will always need to index the value of the FA1985 pool to the date of the rights issue. Add the number and cost of the rights issue shares after you have added the indexation to the pool. Rights issues made to individuals before 6.4.98 should be dealt with in the FA 1985 pool in a similar way.

Activity 9.5

J Ltd had the following transactions in the shares of T plc.

July 1985	Purchased 1,000 shares for £3,000
May 1986	Took up one for four rights issue at £4.20 per share
October 2005	Sold the shares for £10,000

Compute the chargeable gain or allowable loss arising on the sale in October 2005.

Indexation factors: May 1986 – October 2005 = 0.949; July 1985 – May 1986 = 0.027.

5 End of chapter activities

Activity 9.6

Frances sold her ordinary shares in The Hastings Hardening Company Ltd on 17 May 2005 for £24,000. She had bought ordinary shares in the company on the following dates.

	No of shares	*Cost*
		£
19 September 1985	2,000	1,700
12 December 2003	2,000	5,500
17 January 2005	2,000	6,000

Task

Calculate, before the annual exemption but after taper relief, the capital gain for 2005/06. The shares are a business asset for taper relief purposes.

Indexation factor: September 1985 – April 1998 = 0.704.

Activity 9.7

Lorus Ltd acquired the following shares in Henna plc:

	No of shares	*Cost*
		£
11 July 1988	1,000	5,000
19 September 1999	2,000	18,000
28 July 2005	1,500	15,000

Lorus Ltd sold 4,000 shares for £44,000 on 3 August 2005.

Task

Calculate the capital gain arising on the disposal.

Indexation factors: July 1988 – September 1999 = 0.558; September 1999 – August 2005 = 0.145.

Key learning points

- ☑ We need **special rules for matching** shares sold with shares purchased.
- ☑ There are **different rules** for **companies** and for **individuals**.
- ☑ The **FA 1985 pool** for companies contains shares acquired between **1.4.82** and **nine days before the date of the current disposal.**
- ☑ **Indexation allowance for companies** is given to the **date of disposal.**
- ☑ Shares acquired **after 5 April 1998** by an individual are matched on a **last in first out** (LIFO) basis
- ☑ The **FA 1985 pool** for individuals contains shares acquired between **6.4.82** and **5.4.98.**
- ☑ **Bonus and rights issues** are attached to the **holding to which they relate**.

Quick quiz

1 Disposals by companies are generally identified in the following order:

.... acquisitions

Previous............ days acquisitions

Shares in the .... pool

2 What shares are included in the FA 1985 pool for companies?

3 Disposals by individuals are identified in the following order:

.... acquisitions

Next .... days acquisitions

Acquisitions after .... on a .... basis

Shares in the .... pool

4 What shares are included in the FA 1985 pool for individuals?

5 What is the difference between a bonus and a rights issue?

Answers to quick quiz

1 **Same day** acquisitions
Previous **nine** days acquisitions
Shares in the **FA 1985** pool

2 Shares held by a company on 1 April 1985 and acquired by that company on or after 1 April 1982 and shares acquired by that company on or after 1 April 1985.

3 **Same day** acquisitions
Next **30** days acquisitions
Acquisitions after **5.4.98** on a **LIFO** basis
Shares in the **FA 1985** pool

4 Shares acquired by an individual on or after 6 April 1982 held at 5 April 1998.

5 In a rights issue the new shares are paid for. In a bonus issue there is no payment for the issue of the shares.

Activity checklist

This checklist shows which performance criteria, range statement or knowledge and understanding point is covered by each activity in this chapter. Tick off each activity as you complete it.

Activity		
9.1	☐	This activity deals with Performance Criteria 18.3.C: calculate chargeable gains and allowable losses.
9.2	☐	This activity deals with Performance Criteria 18.3.C: calculate chargeable gains and allowable losses.
9.3	☐	This activity deals with Performance Criteria 18.3.A : identify and value correctly any chargeable assets that have been disposed of
9.4	☐	This activity deals with Performance Criteria 18.3.A and 18.3.C : identify and value correctly any chargeable assets that have been disposed of; calculate chargeable gains and allowable losses.
9.5	☐	This activity deals with Performance Criteria 18.3.B: identify shares disposed of by companies.
9.6	☐	This activity deals with Performance Criteria 18.3.A and 18.3.C : identify and value correctly any chargeable assets that have been disposed of; calculate chargeable gains and allowable losses.
9.7	☐	This activity deals with Performance Criteria 18.3.B: identify shares disposed of by companies.

chapter 10

Deferral reliefs

Contents

Performance criteria

18.3 D Apply reliefs, deferrals and exemptions correctly

Range statement

18.3 Reliefs: rollover relief, relief for gifts

Knowledge and understanding

13 Capital gains exemptions and reliefs on business assets including rollover relief and taper relief (Element 18.3)

1 Gift relief

1.1 Introduction

If an individual gives away a business asset (see below), an election can be made by the 31 January which is nearly six years after the end of the tax year of the transfer, **for the transferor's gain to be reduced to nil.**

If an election is made the transferee is deemed to acquire the asset for market value at the date of transfer less the transferor's deferred gain (no taper relief given). The transferee will qualify for further indexation allowance (if available) on that reduced base cost from the date of the transfer. The transferee will start a new period for taper relief from the date of his acquisition.

Activity 10.1

Tim makes a gain of £50,000 on the gift of an asset to Sue. The market value of the asset on the date of the gift was £120,000 and Sue and Tim elected for Tim's gain to be reduced to £Nil under the gift relief provisions.

At what value is Sue deemed to acquire the gift?

Activity 10.2

On 6 December 2005 Angelo gave to his son Michael a freehold shop valued at £200,000 and claimed gift relief. Angelo had originally purchased the shop from which he had run his business in July 2000 for £30,000. Michael continued to run a business from the shop premises but decided to sell the shop in May 2007 for £195,000. Compute Michael's chargeable gains on sale. Assume the rules of CGT in 2005/06 continue to apply in May 2007.

1.2 Qualifying assets

Transfers of business assets include transfers of :

(a) **Assets used in a trade, profession or vocation carried on**:

  (i) by the donor, or
  (ii) by the donor's personal company

A **'personal company'** is one in which not less than 5% of the voting rights are controlled by the individual disposing of the shares.

(b) **Shares and securities in trading companies**, where:

  (i) the shares or securities are **not listed on a recognised stock exchange** (but they may be on the AIM); or

  (ii) the company concerned is the donor's **personal company**

Activity 10.3

20 years ago, Rupert formed a company with £1,000 in share capital. The company used this money to buy a painting, but has since had no transactions. The painting is now worth £60,000. Rupert wishes to give all of the shares in the company to his daughter, claiming gift relief. Why will gift relief be unavailable?

2 Rollover relief

2.1 Introduction

A gain may be 'rolled over' (deferred) where it arises on the disposal of a business asset which is replaced. This is **rollover relief**. A claim cannot specify that only part of a gain is to be rolled over.

2.2 Conditions

All the following conditions must be met.

- **The old asset sold and the new asset bought are both used only in the trade** or trades carried on **by the person claiming rollover relief**.
- **The old asset and the new asset must both be qualifying assets. Qualifying assets include:.**
  - (i) Land and buildings (including parts of buildings) occupied as well as used only for the purpose of the trade
  - (ii) Fixed (that is, immovable) plant and machinery
  - (iii) Goodwill (until 31.3.02 only for companies)
- **Reinvestment of the proceeds of the old asset takes place in a period beginning one year before and ending three years after the date of the disposal.**
- **The new asset is brought into use in the trade on its acquisition** (not necessarily immediately, but not after any significant and unnecessary delay).

The new asset can be for use in a different trade from the old asset.

2.3 Method of relief

Deferral is obtained by carrying forward the chargeable gain and deducting it from the cost of the new asset. To obtain full relief, the whole of the consideration for the disposal must be reinvested.

The new asset will have a CGT 'cost' of its purchase price less the gain rolled over into its acquisition.

Example

Barry bought a shop for use in his business in January 2003 for £50,000. He sold the shop in March 2006 for £250,000. In the same month he bought larger retail premises for £500,000.

The gain arising on the disposal of the shop, £200,000, (£250,000 - £50,000) may be fully deferred as the full disposal proceeds have been reinvested in the larger retail premises. The base cost of the larger retail premises is £500,000 - £200,000 = £300,000

Activity 10.4

A freehold factory was purchased by Zoë for business use in August 1999. It was sold in December 2005 for £70,000, giving rise to a gain of £17,950. A replacement factory was purchased in June 2006 for £80,000. Compute the base cost of the replacement factory, taking into account any possible rollover gain from the disposal in December 2005. Ignore taper relief.

Rollover relief applies to the untapered gain. When the replacement asset is sold taper relief on that sale will only be given by reference to the holding period for that asset (assuming further rollover relief is not claimed on this disposal). **Effectively, taper relief on the rolled over gain, for the period of ownership of the original asset, is lost.**

Example

The gain rolled over in the previous example was the gain of £200,000 before taper relief. If Barry disposes of the larger freehold premises in July 2006 no taper relief will be due as the larger premises have not been held for one year.

Activity 10.5

Karen is a sole trader who bought a business asset for £204,579 on 5 November 1998 and sold it on 31 December 2005 for £491,400. A replacement business asset was acquired on 1 November 2005 at a cost of £546,000. The new asset was sold on 3 September 2007 for £914,550. Karen made a claim for rollover relief on the first asset sale but not on the second asset sale.

Calculate the taxable gains for each asset disposal.

Asset one
Proceeds 491,400
Cost 204579
286,821
no T.R.

Asset Two
Proceeds 914,550
Cost (546,000 - 286,821) 259,179
655,371
T.Relief 50% chargeable 327,686

2.4 Partial reinvestment of proceeds

If the proceeds of the sale of an asset are not fully reinvested in a new qualifying asset within the appropriate time period, an amount of the gain equal to the proceeds not reinvested is immediately chargeable. The balance of the gain can be rolled over.

For example, Jemina realised a gain of £700,000 on the disposal of land used in her business. The land was sold for £1,000,000. A factory was bought for £800,000 in the following month. The proceeds not reinvested are £200,000 so this amount of the gain is immediately chargeable. £500,000 of the gain can be rolled over and set against the base cost of the factory. This means the base cost of the factory is £300,000.

3 End of chapter activities

Activity 10.6

Alistair bought 1,000 shares in DEF Ltd, an unquoted trading company, for £10,000 in July 2002. He gave them to his brother Edward in September 2004 when they were worth £25,000. Edward sold the shares for £35,000 in October 2005.

Task

(a) Calculate Edward's gain on sale after taper relief if gift relief was claimed on the gift to Edward.
(b) Calculate the gains arising if gift relief is not claimed.

Activity 10.7

Louis plc bought a freehold factory for £150,000 in July 1999. It sold it for £200,000 in October 2002. It had acquired another factory in June 2002 at a cost of £250,000. Louis plc sold the second factory for £275,000 in May 2005.

Task

Calculate the gain on sale of the second factory, assuming all reliefs available were claimed.

Assume indexation factors: July 1999 to October 2002 = 0.078; June 2002 to May 2005 = 0.077.

Key learning points

- ☑ **Gift relief** is available to **defer gains on the gift of business assets.**
- ☑ The **gain on the gift reduces the base cost** of the asset **for the transferee**.
- ☑ The **transferee** will **start a new period of ownership** for taper relief.
- ☑ **Assets used in a trade by the donor or his personal company** and **unquoted share in a personal company** are all business assets qualifying for gift relief.
- ☑ When **certain types of assets used in a business** are sold and **other such assets bought**, it is possible to **defer (roll-over) the gains on the assets sold**.
- ☑ **If proceeds of sale are not fully reinvested an amount of the gain equal to the proceeds not reinvested is immediately chargeable.** The remainder of the gain may be rolled over.
- ☑ The **rolled over gain** will **reduce the base cost of the new asset**.
- ☑ The new asset must be acquired in the period commencing **one year before and ending three years after the disposal**.

Quick quiz

1 What is a personal company for gift relief?

2 Graham buys a shop for use in his business in May 1997 for £100,000. He gives it to his son, Neil, in March 2006 when it is worth £150,000. The indexation factor between May 1997 and April 1998 was 0.036. What is the base cost for Neil?

3 In order to qualify for rollover relief, reinvestment must normally take place within .... year(s) before and .... year(s) after the disposal of the original asset.

4 Rollover relief may be available to defer a gain arising on the disposal of unlisted shares. True/ False?

5 What effect does gift relief or rollover relief have on taper relief?

Answers to quick quiz

1 A personal company is one in which an individual controls not less than 5% of the voting rights.

2

	£
Market value	150,000
Less: cost	(100,000)
	50,000
Less: indexation allowance 0.036 x £100,000	(3,600)
Gain	46,400

Base cost for Neil £(150,000 – 46,400) = £103,600

3 In order to qualify for rollover relief, reinvestment must normally take place within **one year** before and **three years** after the disposal of the original asset.

4 FALSE. Shares are not a qualifying assets for rollover relief purposes.

5 The taper relief period will commence when the 'new' asset is acquired . This means the taper relief period that had been built up on the old asset is lost.

Activity checklist

This checklist shows which performance criteria, range statement or knowledge and understanding point is covered by each activity in this chapter. Tick off each activity as you complete it.

Activity		
10.1	☐	This activity deals with Performance Criteria 18.3.D: apply reliefs, deferrals and exemptions correctly.
10.2	☐	This activity deals with Performance Criteria 18.3.D: apply reliefs, deferrals and exemptions correctly.
10.3	☐	This activity deals with Performance Criteria 18.3.D: apply reliefs, deferrals and exemptions correctly.
10.4	☐	This activity deals with Knowledge and Understanding point 13: capital gains tax exemptions and reliefs on business assets including rollover relief.
10.5	☐	This activity deals with Knowledge and Understanding point 13: capital gains tax exemptions and reliefs on business assets including rollover relief.
10.6	☐	This activity deals with Performance Criteria 18.3.D: apply reliefs, deferrals and exemptions correctly.
10.7	☐	This activity deals with Knowledge and Understanding point 13: capital gains tax exemptions and reliefs on business assets including rollover relief.

PART C

Corporation tax

chapter 11

An outline of corporation tax

Contents

Performance criteria

18.4 A Enter adjusted trading profits and losses, capital allowances, investment income and capital gains in the Corporation Tax computation

18.4 C Calculate Corporation Tax due, taking account of marginal relief

Range statement

There are no additional contextual requirements in this element relevant to this chapter.

Knowledge and understanding

15 The computation of profit for Corporation Tax purposes including income, capital gains and charges (Element 18.4)

16 Calculation of Corporation Tax payable by starting, small, large and marginal companies including those with associated companies (Element 18.4)

1 The scope of corporation tax

1.1 Introduction

Corporation tax is paid by companies. It is charged on the profits (including chargeable gains) arising in each accounting period. Corporation tax is not charged on dividends received from companies resident in the UK.

1.2 Proforma corporation tax computation

The profits chargeable to corporation tax (PCTCT) for an accounting period are derived as follows.

	£
Taxable trading profits (known as Schedule D Case I)	**X**
Interest (Known as Schedule D Case III)	**X**
Other income (Known as Schedule D Case VI)	**X**
Rental income (Known as Schedule A)	**X**
Chargeable gains	**X**
Total profits	**X**
Less charges on income (Gift Aid donation)	**(X)**
Profits chargeable to corporation tax (PCTCT) for an accounting period	**X**

It would be of great help in the examination if you could learn the above proforma to calculate PCTCT. Then when answering a corporation tax question you could immediately reproduce the proforma and insert the appropriate numbers into the proforma as you are given the information in the question. We will look at the various items in this proforma as we work through this chapter.

Do note that the Schedules and Cases still apply for corporation tax and should be learnt. However because you are more familiar with the income tax terms we will use similar, more descriptive, income tax, terminology in this text.

1.3 Accounting periods

Corporation tax is chargeable in respect of **accounting periods** and it is important to understand the difference between an accounting period and a period of account. A period of account is any period for which a company prepares accounts; usually this will be 12 months in length but it may be longer or shorter than this. An accounting period starts when a company commences to trade or otherwise becomes liable to corporation tax, or immediately after the previous accounting period finishes. An accounting period finishes on the earliest of:

- 12 months after its start
- the end of the company's period of account
- the commencement of the company's winding up
- the company's ceasing to be resident in the UK
- the company's ceasing to be liable to corporation tax

An accounting period cannot exceed 12 months in length.

If a company has a long period of account, exceeding 12 months, it is split into two accounting periods: the first 12 months and the remainder.

Companies' taxable profits are always computed for accounting periods. There are no basis period rules, there is no personal allowance and there is no taper relief or annual exemption for capital gains.

1.4 Allocating profits of a long period of account

Allocate profits of a long period of account to accounting periods using the following rules:

(a) **Taxable trading profits** before capital allowances is apportioned on a **time basis**.

(b) **Capital allowances** and balancing charges are **calculated for each accounting period.**

(c) **Interest is allocated to the period in which it accrues.**

(d) **Rental income** and other income is apportioned on a time basis.

(e) **Chargeable gains** are taken into account for the accounting **period in which they are realised.**

(f) **Charges on income** (see below) are deducted from the profits of the accounting **period in which they are paid**.

Now try the above allocation in the following activity.

Activity 11.1

Xenon Ltd makes up an 18 month set of accounts to 30 June 2006 with the following results.

	£
Taxable trading profits	180,000
Interest	
18 months @ £500 accruing per month	9,000
Capital gain (1 May 2006 disposal)	250,000
Less: Charge on income (paid 31.12.04)	(50,000)
	389,000

There are no capital allowances claimed in the period. What are the profits chargeable to corporation tax for each of the accounting periods based on the above accounts?

2 Profits chargeable to corporation tax

2.1 Taxable trading profits

The taxable trading profits of companies are derived from the net profit figure in the accounts, adjusted as follows.

	£	£
Net profit per accounts		X
Add expenditure not allowed for taxation purposes		X
		X
Less: income not taxable as trading income	X	
expenditure not charged in the accounts but allowable for the purposes of taxation	X	
capital allowances	X	
		X
Taxable trading profits		X

The adjustment of profits computation shown above broadly follows that for computing business profits subject to income tax.

When adjusting profits as supplied in a profit and loss account confusion can arise as regards whether figures are net or gross. Properly drawn up company accounts should normally include all income gross. However, some questions mention 'net' figures. Read the question carefully.

The calculation of capital allowances follows income tax principles. For companies, there is never any reduction of allowances to take account of any private use of an asset. The director or employee suffers a taxable benefit instead.

2.2 Charges on income

One-off and regular charitable gifts of money qualify for tax relief under the **gift aid scheme as a charge on income.** The amount paid is deducted in computing PCTCT.

For corporation tax purposes Gift Aid donations are the **only** charge on income you will meet. The amount paid must be added back in computing taxable trading profits but then the amount paid is deducted in calculating PCTCT.

There is a confusing difference between income tax and corporation tax computations. Royalties are a charge in income for income tax purposes, but they are not a charge for corporation tax purposes. Patent royalties that are paid/ received for trade purposes are included in taxable trading profits on an accruals basis. Royalties paid/ received for non-trade purposes are included in other income. Conversely, gift aid donations are not charges on income for income tax purposes.

Donations to charities which are incurred wholly and exclusively for the purposes of the trade are deductions from taxable trading profits instead of charges on income.

2.3 Rental income

A company with rental income is treated as running a property letting business. All the rents and expenses for all properties are pooled, to give a single profit or loss known as a Schedule A profit or loss. Rental income is taxed on an **accruals basis**. You will not be expected to calculate rental income (assessable under Unit 19). However, you may be given a figure for a profit or loss from property and be required to deal with it in the corporation tax computation as appropriate.

2.4 Income received/paid net of tax

Companies receive patent royalties from individuals net of 22% tax. This means that the payer withholds 22% tax and pays it over to the Revenue on the company's behalf.

Income which suffers a deduction of tax at source is included within the corporation tax computation at its gross equivalent. For example £4,875 of patent royalties interest received net of tax would need to be grossed up by multiplying by 100/78 to include £6,250 within either taxable trading profits or other income.

Patent royalties paid by a company to an individual are paid net of 22% tax. Interest paid to individuals is paid net of 20% tax.

The way in which relief is given for the tax suffered at source is covered later in this text. Essentially, if tax suffered on income received net exceeds tax deducted from patent royalties and interest paid net, the difference is subtracted in calculating the mainstream corporation tax due.

Patent royalties and interest which relate to the trade are included in taxable trading profits normally on an accruals basis. Patent royalties which do not relate to the trade are taxed as other income. Non-trading interest is taxed is dealt with separately (see below).

2.5 Interest received gross

UK companies receive interest gross from banks and building societies. Interest on most gilts is received gross.

Interest received from other UK companies is also received gross. This means debenture interest received from another UK company will be received gross.

2.6 Chargeable gains

Companies do not pay capital gains tax. Instead their chargeable gains are included in the profits chargeable to corporation tax. A company's capital gains or allowable losses are computed in a similar way to individuals (see earlier in this text) but with a few major differences:

(a) Indexation allowance calculations may include periods of ownership after 6 April 1998. **Indexation is calculated to the month of disposal of an asset.**

(b) **The FA 1985 pool for shares does not close at 5 April 1998: it runs to the month of disposal of the shares**. This means that different matching rules are needed (see earlier in this text)

(c) The **taper relief does not apply**

(d) No **annual exemption is available**

Activity 11.2

A company had the following results in the year ended 31 March 2006.

	£
Trading profits	85,000
Bank deposit interest income	6,000
Building society interest income	1,500
Debenture interest income	3,200
Capital gains	2,950
Gift Aid donation paid	15,200

All interest received was on non-trading investments.

What were the company's profits chargeable to corporation tax?

2.7 Dividends from UK companies

Dividends received from other UK companies are not included in profits chargeable to corporation tax.

They are, however, taken into account in determining the rate of corporation tax payable (see below).

Activity 11.3

The following is a summary of the profit and loss account of A Ltd for the year to 31 March 2006.

	£	£
Gross profit on trading		180,000
Bank deposit interest		700
Dividends from UK companies (net)		3,600
Building society interest received		292
Less: trade expenses (all allowable)	62,000	
gift aid donation paid	1,100	
		(63,100)
		121,492

The capital allowances for the period total £5,500. There was also a capital gain of £13,867.

Compute the profits chargeable to corporation tax.

3 Charge to corporation tax

3.1 Introduction

The rates of corporation tax are fixed for financial years. A financial year runs from 1 April to the following 31 March and is identified by the calendar year in which it begins. For example, the year ended 31 March 2006 is the Financial year 2005 (FY 2005). This should not be confused with a tax year, which runs from 6 April to the following 5 April.

The full rate of corporation tax is 30%.

Activity 11.4

A company had profits chargeable to corporation tax of £2,000,000 in the year ended 31 March 2006. What was the corporation tax payable?

3.2 The small companies rate (SCR)

The SCR of corporation tax applies to the profits chargeable to corporation tax of UK companies whose 'profits' are not more than £300,000.

The SCR is 19%.

'Profits' means profits chargeable to corporation tax plus the grossed-up amount of dividends received from UK companies. The grossed-up amount of UK dividends is the dividend received grossed up by multiplying by 100/90.

The grossed-up amount of UK dividends may be referred to as 'Franked Investment Income' (FII).

Activity 11.5

B Ltd had the following results for the year ended 31 March 2006.

	£
Taxable trading profits	42,000
Dividend received 1 May 2005	9,000

Compute the corporation tax payable.

3.3 The starting rate

A starting rate of corporation tax of 0% applies to companies with 'profits' of up to £10,000. This rate may need to be adjusted if any PCTCT is distributed to non corporate shareholders.

Activity 11.6

Dexter Limited has the following income for the year ended 31 March 2006.

(a) PCTCT of £9,500, and
(b) Dividend received of £270.

Calculate the corporation tax liability for the year. Assume all profits were retained in the year.

3.4 Marginal relief

3.4.1 Small companies marginal relief

Small companies marginal relief applies where the 'profits' of an accounting period of a UK resident company are over £300,000 but under £1,500,000. We first calculate the corporation tax at the full rate and then deduct:

(M – P) × I/P × marginal relief fraction

where M = upper limit (currently £1,500,000)
P = 'profits' (see above Paragraph)
I = PCTCT

The marginal relief fraction is 11/400.

You will be given the marginal relief formula in the examination.

Activity 11.7

Lenox Ltd has the following results for the year ended 31 March 2006.

	£
PCTCT	296,000
Dividend received 1 December 2005	12,600

Calculate the corporation tax liability.

In your exam you may need to be aware that there is a **marginal rate of tax of 32.75%** that applies to PCTCT between the small companies' limits.

This is calculated as follows:

	£		£
Upper limit	1,500,000	@ 30%	450,000
Lower limit	(300,000)	@ 19%	(57,000)
Difference	1,200,000		393,000

$$\frac{393,000}{1,200,000} = 32.75\%$$

Effectively the band of profits (here £1,200,000) falling between the upper and lower limits is taxed at a rate of 32.75%

PCTCT 296,000
DIVS 14,000
310,000

Corp Tax = 296 × 30% 88,800
less small comp Relief
(1500000 − 310,000) × 296/310 × 11/400 = 31247
57553

BPP PROFESSIONAL EDUCATION

Example

A Ltd has PCTCT of £350,000 for the year ended 31.3.06. Its corporation tax liability is

	£
£350,000 × 30%	105,000
Less: small companies' marginal relief	
11/400 (1,500,000 – 350,000)	(31,625)
	73,375

This is the same as calculating tax at 19% × £300,000 + 32.75% × £50,000 = £57,000 + £16,375 = £73,375.

Consequently tax is charged at an effective rate of 32.75% on PCTCT that exceeds the small companies' lower limit.

Note that although there is an effective corporation tax charge of 32.75%, this rate of tax is never used in actually calculating corporation tax. The rate is just an effective marginal rate that you must be aware of.

3.4.2 Starting rate marginal relief

For companies with 'profits' between £10,001 and £50,000, the small companies rate less a starting rate marginal relief applies. The formula for calculating this marginal relief is the same as that given above except that 'M' is the upper limit for starting rate purposes (£50,000). However the fraction used here is 19/400. The small companies' rate only applies in full when 'profits' exceed £50,000.

Activity 11.8

Armstrong Ltd has the following income for its year ended 31 March 2006:

		£
(a)	PCTCT	29,500
(b)	Dividend received	2,700

Calculate the corporation tax liability. Assume no dividends were paid in the year.

The effective marginal rate of tax when PCTCT falls between the starting rate limits is 23.75%. Again, this is an effective marginal rate of tax that you need to be aware of but it is a rate that is never actually used in working out the CT charge. It is calculated as:

£		£
50,000	@ 19%	9,500
(10,000)	@ 0%	Nil
40,000		9,500

$$\frac{9,500}{40,000} = 23.75\ \%$$

PCTCT falling into the band (here £40,000) suffers tax at an effective rate of 23.75%.

3.5 Changes in the rate – Accounting periods straddling 31 March

If there is a change in the corporation tax rate, and a company's accounting period does not fall entirely within one financial year, the profits of the accounting period are apportioned to the two financial years on a time basis. Note that the profits as a whole are apportioned. We do not look at components of the profit individually, unlike apportionment of profits of a long period of account to two accounting periods.

The 'profits' falling into each financial year determines the rate of corporation tax that applies to the PCTCT of that year. This could be the full rate, the small companies' rate or the starting rate, and marginal relief could be available.

Activity 11.9

Frances Ltd makes up accounts to 31 December each year. For the year ended 31 December 2006 its profit and loss account was as follows.

	£
PCTCT	40,000
Dividends plus tax credits	2,500
'Profits'	42,500

Calculate the corporation tax liability for the year assuming that the small companies' rate for FY 2006 is 20% and the marginal relief fraction is 1/40 but the limits are unchanged.

The corporation tax rate and limits have remained unchanged from FY 2002 to FY 2005.

3.6 Associated companies

The expression **'associated companies'** in tax has no connection with financial accounting. For tax purposes a company is associated with another company if either controls the other or if both are under the control of the same person or persons (individuals, partnerships or companies).

If a company has one or more 'associated companies', then the profit limits for starting rate and small companies rate purposes are divided by the number of associated companies + 1 (for the company itself).

Companies which have only been associated for part of an accounting period are deemed to have been associated for the whole period for the purpose of determining the profit limits.

An associated company is ignored for these purposes if it has not carried on any trade or business at any time in the accounting period (or the part of the period during which it was associated). This means that you should ignore dormant companies.

3.7 Short accounting periods

The profit limits are reduced proportionately if an accounting period lasts for less than 12 months.

Activity 11.10

For the nine months to 31 January 2006 a company with two other associated companies had PCTCT of £78,000 and no dividends received. Compute the corporation tax payable.

4 Additional corporation tax for small companies

Special rules apply where a company with an underlying tax rate of less than 19% makes a distribution to a non-corporate shareholder on or after 1 April 2004. In such cases a minimum CT rate of 19% must be applied to any PCTCT distributed to non-corporate shareholders.

The **underlying rate of corporation tax** is calculated as $\frac{\text{CT} \times 100}{\text{PCTCT}}$. CT is after starting rate marginal relief.

Here is an example where all PCTCT is distributed to non-corporate shareholders.

Example

Assume that PCTCT for an accounting period are £9,000. These profits are distributed by way of a dividend to individuals. The tax computation would be:

Step 1:	Work out CT using normal rules:		
	PCTCT £9,000 @ 0%	=	£nil
	Corporation Tax due	=	£nil
Step 2:	Calculate the underlying rate		
	The underlying rate:		
	(tax/PCTCT × 100) = 0.000/9,000×100	=	0%
Step 3:	Tax PCTCT up to the amount of the non corporate distribution at 19%		
	Non corporate distribution £9,000 @ 19%	=	£1,710
Step 4:	Tax remaining PCTCT at the underlying rate		
	Remaining PCTCT		Nil
	Total CT due		£1,710

78000 x19%

The following is an example where PCTCT is partly distributed to non-corporate shareholders.

Example

Assume that the PCTCT for an accounting period is £38,000. The distributions made during the accounting period totalled £33,000 of which £3,000 were paid to a company. The tax calculation will be:

			£
***Step 1*:**	Work out CT using normal rules:		
	PCTCT	£38,000 @ 19% =	7,220
	Less Starting rate marginal relief	£(50,000 – 38,000) × 19/400 =	(570)
	Corporation tax due on PCTCT		6,650
***Step 2*:**	Calculate the underlying rate		
	The underlying rate is	6,650/38,000 × 100 =17.5%	
***Step 3*:**	Tax PCTCT up to the amount of the non corporate distribution at 19%		
		£30,000 @ 19% =	5,700
***Step 4*:**	Tax remaining PCTCT at the underlying rate		
	(£38,000 – £30,000) @ 17.5%	£8,000 @ 17.5% =	1,400
	Total CT due		7,100

5 End of chapter activity

Activity 11.11

Tree Ltd, a company with no associated companies, had the following results for the eighteen months to 31 December 2005:

	£
Taxable trading profits	180,000
Chargeable gain – realised 1.6.05	172,000
Gift aid donation – paid 30.9.05	5,000
Gift aid donation – paid 30.9.04	22,000
Interest	36,000
Dividend received 30.3.05	27,000

The interest accrued evenly over the period

Task

Compute the corporation tax liability in respect of the profits arising in the eighteen months to 31 December 2005.

Key learning points

- ☑ Companies pay **corporation tax** on their profits for each **accounting period**.
- ☑ The **usual length** of an accounting period is **12 months**, but it may be **shorter**.
- ☑ If a company has a **period of account longer than 12 months**, the **first 12 months** will be **one accounting period** and the **remainder** a **second accounting period**.
- ☑ **Profits chargeable to corporation tax** are **income** plus **gains** minus **charges**.
- ☑ All **UK rental activities** are treated as a **single source of income** taxable as **rental income** on an accruals basis.
- ☑ A **gift aid donation** is a **charge** on income for corporation tax purposes.
- ☑ **Tax rates** are set for **financial years**.
- ☑ Companies pay **corporation tax** at the **starting rate**, **small companies rate** or **full rate**.
- ☑ **Marginal relief** is available for some companies depending on their '**profits**' (chargeable profits plus grossed up dividends received).
- ☑ Adjustments are required for **associated companies** and **short accounting periods**.
- ☑ There is a **minimum corporation tax charge of 19% when small companies distribute their PCTCT to individual shareholders**.

Quick quiz

1 Trading profits (before capital allowances) of a long period of account are apportioned .... Fill in the blank.

2 S Ltd, a company with one associated company, had profits chargeable to corporation tax of £8,500 for its six month accounting period to 31 March 2006. No distributions were made in the period.

Its corporation tax liability for the period will be:

A £Nil
B £831
C £1,425
D £1,615

3 VAC Ltd, a company with no associated companies, has profits chargeable to corporation tax for the year to 31 March 2006 of £25,000. No dividends were paid in the year.

What is the marginal rate of corporation tax paid by the company on its profits between £10,000 and £25,000?

A 19%
B 23.75%
C 30%
D 32.75%

4 For the year to 31 March 2006, M Ltd, a company with one associated company, has the following results:

	£
PCTCT	110,000
Dividend received from UK company	45,000

What is M Ltd's corporation tax liability for the year?

A £20,900
B £21,388
C £21,845
D £36,845

Answers to quick quiz

1 Trading profits (before capital allowances) of a long period of account are apportioned **on a time basis**.

2 C

Starting rate upper limit = $\frac{50,000}{2} \times \frac{6}{12}$ = £12,500

Starting rate lower limit = $\frac{10,000}{2} \times \frac{6}{12}$ = £2,500

	£
Starting rate marginal relief applies: £8,500 × 19%	1,615
Less 19/400 (£12,500 – £8,500)	(190)
	1,425

3 B

The marginal rate of corporation tax on profits between the starting rate upper and lower limits is 23.75%.

4 C

Small companies' limits

Lower limit = $\frac{£300,000}{2}$ = £150,000

Upper limit = $\frac{£1,500,000}{2}$ = £750,000

'Profits' £110,000 + £45,000 × $^{100}/_{90}$ = £160,000

∴ Small companies' marginal relief applies

	£
£110,000 × 30%	33,000
$^{11}/_{400}(750,000 - 160,000) \times \frac{110,000}{160,000}$	(11,155)
	21,845

Activity checklist

This checklist shows which performance criteria, range statement or knowledge and understanding point is covered by each activity in this chapter. Tick off each activity as you complete it.

Activity		
11.1	☐	This activity deals with Knowledge and Understanding point 15: the computation of profit for Corporation Tax purposes including income, capital gains and charges.
11.2	☐	This activity deals with Performance Criteria 18.4.A: enter adjusted trading profits and losses, capital allowances, investment income and capital gains in the corporation tax computation.
11.3	☐	This activity deals with Performance Criteria 18.4.A: enter adjusted trading profits and losses, capital allowances, investment income and capital gains in the corporation tax computation.
11.4	☐	This activity deals with Performance Criteria 18.4.C: calculate corporation tax payable, taking account of marginal relief.
11.5	☐	This activity deals with Performance Criteria 18.4.C: calculate corporation tax payable, taking account of marginal relief.
11.6	☐	This activity deals with Performance Criteria 18.4.C: calculate corporation tax payable, taking account of marginal relief.
11.7	☐	This activity deals with Performance Criteria 18.4.C: calculate corporation tax payable, taking account of marginal relief.
11.8	☐	This activity deals with Performance Criteria 18.4.C: calculate corporation tax payable, taking account of marginal relief.
11.9	☐	This activity deals with Performance Criteria 18.4.C: calculate corporation tax payable, taking account of marginal relief.
11.10	☐	This activity deals with Performance Criteria 18.4.C: calculate corporation tax payable, taking account of marginal relief.
11.11	☐	This activity deals with Performance Criteria 18.4.C: calculate corporation tax payable, taking account of marginal relief.

chapter 12

Corporation tax losses

Contents

Performance criteria

18.4 B Set-off and deduct loss reliefs and charges correctly

Range statement

18.4 Loss reliefs relating to: trade losses, non trade losses

Knowledge and understanding

17 Set-off of trading losses incurred by companies (Element 18.4)

1 Reliefs for losses

1.1 Trading losses

The following reliefs are available for trading losses incurred by a company.

(a) **Set-off against current profits**
(b) **Carry back against earlier profits**
(c) **Carry forward against future trading profits**

A claim must be made for reliefs (a) and (b). The reliefs are given in the order shown.

Relief (c) is given automatically for any loss for which the other reliefs are not claimed.

1.2 Capital losses

Capital losses can only be set against capital gains in the same or future accounting periods, never against income. Capital losses must be set against the first available gains.

1.3 Rental income losses

Rental income losses are first set off against non-rental income and gains of the company for the current period.

Any excess is then carried forward as if a rental income loss arising in the later accounting period for offset against future income (of all descriptions).

Activity 12.1

A plc had the following results in the three years to 31.3.06. Show its PCTCT in each year.

		Year ended	
	31.3.04	*31.3.05*	*31.3.06*
	£	£	£
Taxable trading profits/(loss)	20,000	24,000	20,000
Capital gain/(loss)	(8,000)	2,000	7,000

2 Loss relief against future income: s 393(1) ICTA 1988

A company **must set off a trading loss not otherwise relieved against income from the same trade in future accounting periods**. Relief is given against the first available profits. This relief is given automatically, there is no need to make a claim for it.

Activity 12.2

A Ltd has the following results for the three years to 31 March 2006.

		Year ended	
	31.3.04	*31.3.05*	*31.3.06*
	£	£	£
Taxable trading profit/(loss)	(8,550)	3,000	6,000
Rental income	0	1,000	1,000

Calculate the profits chargeable to corporation tax for all three years showing any losses available to carry forward at 1 April 2006.

3 Loss relief against total profits: s 393A(1) ICTA 1988

A company may claim to set a trading loss incurred in an accounting period against total profits (before deducting charges) of the same accounting period. Any charges (gift aid donations) that become unrelieved remain unrelieved.

Such a loss may then be carried back and set against total profits (before deducting charges) of an accounting period falling wholly or partly within the 12 months of the start of the period in which the loss was incurred.

If a period falls partly outside the 12 months, loss relief is limited to the proportion of the period's profits (before charges) equal to the proportion of the period which falls within the 12 months.

Any possible s 393A(1) claim for the period of the loss must be made before any excess loss can be carried back to a previous period.

Any carry-back is to more recent periods before earlier periods. Relief for earlier losses is given before relief for later losses.

A claim for relief against current or prior period profits must be made within two years of the end of the accounting period in which the loss arose. Any claim must be for the whole loss (to the extent that profits are available to relieve it). The loss can however be reduced by not claiming full capital allowances, so that higher capital allowances are given (on higher tax written down values) in future years. Any loss remaining unrelieved may be carried forward under s 393(1) to set against future profits of the same trade.

Activity 12.3

Helix Ltd has the following results.

		Year ended	
	30.9.04	*30.9.05*	*30.9.06*
	£	£	£
Taxable trading profit/(loss)	10,500	10,000	(35,000)
Bank interest	500	500	500
Chargeable gains	0	0	4,000
Charges on income:			
Gift Aid donation	250	250	250

Show the PCTCT for all the years affected assuming that s 393A(1) loss relief is claimed. Assume the provisions of FA 2005 continue to apply. Show the amount of loss of remaining to carry forward at 1.10.06.

4 Choosing loss reliefs

Several alternative loss reliefs may be available. In making a choice consider:

- **The rate at which relief will be obtained:**

  (i) 30% at the full rate (FY 2005)
  (ii) 19% at the small companies' rate (FY 2005)
  (iii) 0% at the starting rate (FY 2005)
  (iv) 23.75% if the starting rate marginal relief applies (FY 2005)
  (v) 32.75% if the small companies' marginal relief applies (FY 2005)

  We previously outlined how the 23.75% and 32.75% marginal rates are calculated. Remember these are just marginal rates of tax; they are never actually used in computing a company's corporation tax.

- If the carry back of a loss takes profits below the starting rate upper limit, consider whether the minimum rate of 19 % needs to be applied in respect of any non-corporate distribution.
- **How quickly relief will be obtained**: s 393A(1) relief is quicker than s 393(1) relief.
- **The extent to which relief for gift aid donations might be lost.**

When choosing between loss relief claims ALWAYS consider the rate of tax 'saved' by the loss first.

If in the current period the loss 'saves' 19% tax but if carried forward saves 30% tax then a carry forward is the better choice (even though the timing of loss relief is later).

If the tax saved now is 30% and in the future is the same (30%) THEN consider timing (in this example a current claim is better timing wise).

So, first - rate of tax saved, second - timing.

Activity 12.4

M Ltd has had the following results.

	Year ended 31 March		
	2004	*2005*	*2006*
	£	£	£
Taxable trading profits/(loss)	2,000	(1,000,000)	200,000
Chargeable gains	35,000	750,000	0
Gift aid donations paid	30,000	20,000	20,000

Recommend appropriate loss relief claims, and compute the mainstream corporation tax for all years based on your recommendations. Assume that future years' profits will be similar to those of the year ended 31 March 2006. The company did not make any distributions in any of the above three years.

Assume that tax rates and allowances for FY 2005 apply to all years.

5 End of chapter activity

Activity 12.5

Daley plc has had the following results since it started to trade.

	Year ended 31.12.03	*Six months ended 30.6.04*	*Year ended 30.6.05*
	£	£	£
Taxable trading profits/(loss)	109,000	85,000	(200,000)
Interest	11,000	12,000	14,000
Chargeable gains/ (allowable losses)	(5,000)	2,000	(1,000)
Gift aid donation	Nil	3,000	1,000

Reliefs are always claimed as early as possible. There are no associated companies.

Task

Compute the corporation tax liability for all three periods, and show all amounts to be carried forward at 30 June 2005. Assume that tax rates and allowances for FY 2005 apply to all years.

Key learning points

- ☑ **Reliefs for losses** depend on the **type of loss** involved.
- ☑ **Capital losses** can only be set against **capital gains** of the **same or future accounting periods**.
- ☑ **Rental income losses** are first set-off against **other income and gains** of the **current period** and any **excess is carried forward** as a **rental income loss**.
- ☑ **Trading losses** can be **carried forward** against **future taxable trading profits of the same trade**.
- ☑ **S393A relief** is given against **total profits before charges**. Gift aid donations remain unrelieved.
- ☑ **S393A relief** may be given against **current period profits** and **against profits of the previous 12 months** (or, **previous 36 months** if the **trade is ceasing**).
- ☑ A claim for **current period S393A relief can be made without a claim for carryback**.
- ☑ However, if a **loss is to be carried back** a claim for **current period relief must have been made first**.
- ☑ When **selecting a loss relief**, firstly consider the **rate at which relief is obtained** and, secondly, the **timing of the relief**.

Quick quiz

1 Against what profits may trading losses carried forward be set against?

2 On 1 April 2005 MB Ltd had trading losses of £50,000 brought forward:

MB Ltd's results for the year to 31 March 2006 were:

	£
Taxable trading profits	40,000
Rental income	25,000
Capital gain	2,000

What amount, if any, of the trading loss remains to be carried forward at 31 March 2006?

A £10,000
B £5,000
C £3,000
D £Nil

3 CR Ltd has the following results for the two years to 31 March 2006:

	Year ended	
	31.3.05	*31.3.06*
	£	£
Taxable trading profits (loss)	170,000	(320,000)
Interest	5,000	50,000
Capital gain (loss)	(20,000)	12,000
Gift aid payment	5,000	5,000

What amount of trading losses remain to be carried forward at 1.4.06 assuming that all possible s 393A ICTA 1988 claims are made?

A £83,000
B £95,000
C £100,000
D £105,000

4 Which is the first thing to think about when selecting a loss relief – the rate at which the relief is obtained or the timing of the relief?

Answers to quick quiz

1 Profits from the same trade.

2 A The trading loss can be set only against the taxable trading profits of £40,000. The balance of the loss must be carried forward for relief against future taxable trading profits.

3 B

	Year ended	
	31.3.05	*31.3.06*
	£	£
Taxable trading	170,000	–
Interest	5,000	50,000
	175,000	50,000
Less: s 393A loss	(175,000)	(50,000)
	–	–

Loss £320,000 – £50,000 – £175,000 = £95,000

Capital losses are carried forward to set against future capital gains. There are capital losses of £8,000 remaining to be carried forward at 1.4.06.

S393A losses are deducted before gift aid donations in both the year of the loss and in previous years.

4 Rate of relief, then timing.

Activity checklist

This checklist shows which performance criteria is covered by each activity in this chapter. Tick off each activity as you complete it.

Activity		
12.1	☐	This activity deals with Performance Criteria 18.4.B: Set-off and deduct loss reliefs and charges correctly.
12.2	☐	This activity deals with Performance Criteria 18.4.B: Set-off and deduct loss reliefs and charges correctly.
12.3	☐	This activity deals with Performance Criteria 18.4.B: Set-off and deduct loss reliefs and charges correctly.
12.4	☐	This activity deals with Performance Criteria 18.4.B: Set-off and deduct loss reliefs and charges correctly.
12.5	☐	This activity deals with Performance Criteria 18.4.B: Set-off and deduct loss reliefs and charges correctly.

PART D

National Insurance

chapter 13

National insurance

Contents

Performance criteria

18.4 E Identify the National Insurance Contributions payable by employers

18.2 F Identify the National Insurance Contributions payable by self-employed individuals

Range statement

18.2 Clients: sole traders, partnerships

Knowledge and understanding

18 Calculation of National Insurance Contributions payable by self employed persons and employers of not contracted out employees (Elements 18.2 & 18.4)

1 National insurance for employers

1.1 Introduction

Four classes of national insurance contribution (NIC) exist, as set out below.

(a) **Class 1**. This is divided into:

 (i) **Primary**, paid by employees
 (ii) **Secondary, Class 1A and Class 1B** paid by employers

(b) **Class 2**. Paid by the self-employed

(c) **Class 3**. Voluntary contributions (paid to maintain rights to certain state benefits)

(d) **Class 4.** Paid by the self-employed

Class 1 Primary, Class 1B and Class 3 contributions are outside the scope of your syllabus.

1.2 Class 1 secondary contributions

The National Insurance Contributions Office (NICO), which is part of the Revenue, examines employers' records and procedures to ensure that the correct amounts of NICs are collected.

Employers pay NICs related to the employee's earnings. Employers' contributions are deductible trading expenses.

'Earnings' broadly comprise gross pay, excluding benefits which cannot be turned into cash by surrender (eg holidays). No deduction is made for employee pension contributions deducted from the employee's pay.

An employer's contribution to an employee's approved personal pension or an approved occupational pension scheme is excluded from the definition of 'earnings'.

There are a number of exclusions from NIC 'earnings' including:

(a) Payment of personal incidental expenses up to £5 (UK)/£10 (non-UK) a night for every night the employee is away from home.

(b) Relocation expenses (although expenses exceeding £8,000 are subject to class 1A NICs as described below).

(c) An expense with a business purpose. For example, if an employee is reimbursed for business travel or for staying in a hotel on the employer's business this is not normally 'earnings'. However, if an employee is reimbursed for his own home telephone charges the reimbursed cost of private calls (and all reimbursed rental) is earnings.

(d) Where an employer reimburses an employee using his own car for business mileage, the earnings element is the excess of the mileage rate paid over the HMRC 'up to 10,000 business miles' 'approved mileage rate'(currently 40p). This applies even where business mileage exceeds 10,000 pa.

(e) In general, non cash vouchers (eg book tokens, high street store vouchers) are subject to NICs. However, the following are exempt.

- Childcare vouchers for children up to 16 years old of up to £50 per week
- Vouchers for the use of sports and recreational facilities (where tax exempt)
- Vouchers for meals on the employer's premises
- Other meal vouchers to a maximum of 15p per day
- Transport vouchers where the employee earns less than £8,500 a year.

1.3 Rates of contribution

The rates of contribution for 2005/06, and the income bands to which they apply, are set out in the Rates and Allowances Tables in this text.

Employers pay secondary contributions of 12.8% on earnings above the earnings threshold of £4,895 or the equivalent monthly or weekly limit. There is no upper limit.

There is a lower earnings limit of £4,264 (or the equivalent monthly or weekly limit). The significance of the lower earnings limit (LEL) is that 'nil rate contributions' will be credited where the employee's earnings are between the LEL and the earnings threshold. These 'nil rate contributions' frank the employee's record and so create an entitlement to certain state benefits.

There are different rules for employees who are contracted out of the State Second Pension but these are not in your syllabus.

NICs are calculated in relation to an earnings period. This is the period to which earnings paid to an employee are deemed to relate. Where earnings are paid at regular intervals, the earnings period will generally be equated with the payment interval, for example a week or a month. An earnings period cannot usually be less than seven days long.

NIC for employees is calculated on a non-cumulative basis, so only the earnings in the earnings period are considered. The monthly earnings threshold is the annual limit divided by 12.

Activity 13.1

Sally works for Red plc. She is paid £2,750 per month. Show the secondary class 1 contributions paid by Red plc for 2005/06.

Activity 13.2

Mark works for Black plc. He is paid the following in one week in 2005/06.

	£
Wages	200
Business travel reimbursed	20
Bonus paid in Marks & Spencer plc vouchers	50
Relocation expenses	2,000

Show the secondary contributions payable by Black plc for the week.

1.4 Class 1A contributions

Employers must pay Class 1A NIC in respect of most taxable benefits for example, private medical insurance. However, benefits are exempt if they are:

- Within class 1, or
- Provided for employees earning at a rate of less than £8,500 a year

In addition childcare provided on the employer's premises are exempt. Other employer provided childcare provision, for example, where the employer contracts for places in commercial nurseries, are exempt from Class 1A NICs to the extent of £50 per week. However, if an employer provides cash to meet or reimburse childcare expenses the cash is 'earnings' for employer Class 1 NIC purposes. There is also exemption for certain other minor benefits (eg small private use of employer's assets).

Class 1A contributions are paid at 12.8% of the taxable value of the benefit. There is no earnings threshold.

Class 1A contributions are collected annually in arrears, and are due by 19 July following the tax year.

Activity 13.3

Nitin's employer provides him with a company car throughout 2005/06.

The taxable value of the benefit arising is £10,000.

Calculate the Class 1A national insurance contributions that will be payable by Nitin's employer.

2 National insurance for the self employed

2.1 Class 2 contributions

The self employed (sole traders and partners) **pay NICs in two ways. Class 2 contributions are payable at a flat rate.** It is possible, however, to be excepted from payment of Class 2 contributions (or to get contributions already paid repaid) if annual profits are less than £4,345. **The Class 2 rate for 2005/06 is £2.10 a week.**

Self employed people must register with the HMRC for Class 2 contributions within three months of the end of the month in which they start self employment. People who fail to register may incur a £100 penalty.

2.2 Class 4 contributions

Additionally, **the self employed pay Class 4 NICs, based on the level of the individual's business profits.**

Main rate Class 4 NICs are calculated by applying a fixed percentage (8% for 2005/06) to the individual's profits between the lower limit (£4,895 for 2005/06) and the upper limit (£32,760 for 2005/06). Additional rate contributions are 1% (for 2005/06) on profits above that upper limit.

Activity 13.4

A sole trader had profits of £14,100 for 2005/06. Show his Class 4 NIC liability.

Activity 13.5

An individual's trade profits were £35,000. Show the Class 4 NICs due.

For Class 4 NIC purposes, business profits are the taxable trading profits, less:

(a) **Trading losses**
(b) **Trade charges on income**

Class 4 NICs are collected by the Revenue. They are paid **at the same time as the associated income tax liability**. This will be covered later in this text. Interest is charged on overdue contributions.

3 End of chapter activity

Activity 13.6

(a) Arnold is employed by Julius Ltd. In 2005/06, his remuneration package consists of the following.

Salary	£2,500
Company car – taxable benefit	£5,000
Childcare vouchers	£2,250
Private medical insurance – taxable benefit	£750

Task

Show the national insurance contributions payable by Julius Ltd for 2005/06.

(b) Marcia is a self-employed florist. In 2005/06, her profits are £38,000.

Task

Show the total national insurance contributions payable by Marcia.

Key learning points

- ☑ **Class 1 secondary national insurance contributions** are paid by employers.
- ☑ Employers pay NICs related to the **employee's earnings**.
- ☑ '**Earnings**' broadly comprise **gross pay** excluding benefits which cannot be turned into cash.
- ☑ There are a number of **exemptions**, for example **relocation expenses, business travel.**
- ☑ Secondary contributions are payable at **12.8%** above the **earnings threshold**.
- ☑ NICs are calculated in relation to **earnings periods**, for example **weekly** or **monthly**.
- ☑ **Class 1A contributions** are payable on **benefits** provided to employees.
- ☑ **Self employed individuals** pay **Class 2** and **Class 4** contributions.
- ☑ **Class 2** contributions are **£2.10 per week**.
- ☑ **Class 4** contributions are payable at **8%** between **upper and lower limits**.
- ☑ **Additional class 4** contributions are payable at **1%** above the **upper limit**.

Quick quiz

1 Which, if either, of the following types of expenses incurred by a company are allowable when calculating taxable trading profits?

   1 Secondary Class 1 NICs incurred in respect of staff working in the business.

   2 The cost of staff entertainment

   A 1 only
   B 2 only
   C Both 1 and 2 are allowable
   D Neither 1 nor 2 are allowable

2 On what are Class 1A contributions paid?

3 How are Class 4 NICs calculated?

Answers to quick quiz

1 C Both types of expense are allowable.

2 Class 1A NICs are paid by an employer on taxable benefits.

3 The main rate is a fixed percentage of an individual's trading profits between an upper and lower limit. The additional rate applies above the upper limit.

Activity checklist

This checklist shows which performance criteria, range statement or knowledge and understanding point is covered by each activity in this chapter. Tick off each activity as you complete it.

Activity		
13.1	☐	This activity deals with Performance Criteria 18.4.E: identify the National Insurance Contributions paid by employers
13.2	☐	This activity deals with Performance Criteria 18.4.E: identify the National Insurance Contributions paid by employers
13.3	☐	This activity deals with Performance Criteria 18.4.E: identify the National Insurance Contributions paid by employers
13.4	☐	This activity deals with Performance Criteria 18.2.F: identify the National Insurance Contributions paid by self-employed individuals
13.5	☐	This activity deals with Performance Criteria 18.2.F: identify the National Insurance Contributions paid by self-employed individuals
13.6	☐	This activity deals with Knowledge and Understanding point 18: calculation of national insurance contributions payable by self-employed persons and employers of not contracted out employees.

PART E

Administration

chapter 14

Administration of income tax and CGT

Contents

Performance criteria

18.2 E Identify the due dates of payment of Income Tax by unincorporated businesses, including payments on account

18.2 G Complete correctly the self employed and partnership supplementary pages for the tax return for individuals, together with relevant claims and elections and submit them within statutory time limits.

18.1 D, 18.3 E

Ensure that computations and submissions are made in accordance with current tax law and take account of current Revenue Practice.

18.1 G, 18.2 J, 18.3 H, 18.4 J

Maintain client confidentiality at all times

18.1 F, 18.2 I, 18.3 G

Give timely and constructive advice on the maintenance of accounts and the recording of information relevant to tax returns

Range statement

18.2 Clients: sole traders, partnerships

Knowledge and understanding

19 Self assessment including payment of tax and filing of returns for unincorporated businesses and companies (Elements 18.2 & 18.4)

1 The administration of taxation

The **Treasury** formally imposes and collects taxation. The management of the Treasury is the responsibility of the Chancellor of the Exchequer. The Treasury appoint the **Commissioners** for Her Majesty's Revenue and Customs (HMRC), a body of civil servants. The Commissioners administer income tax, capital gains tax and corporation tax as well as other taxes including value added tax, and excise duties. Before April 2005 the Inland Revenue and HM Customs and Excise were separate entities but they have now been merged. Throughout this text we will call HMRC 'The Revenue'.

For income tax purposes, the UK has historically been divided into **tax districts**. These are being merged into larger areas, with separate offices in each **area** being responsible for different aspects of the Revenue's work. Each area is headed by an **area director**.

The Revenue tax staff were historically described as '**Inspectors**' and '**Collectors**', although these terms are now less commonly used. The legislation now commonly refers to an '**officer of Revenue and Customs**' rather than an 'inspector' when setting out the Revenue's powers. They are responsible for supervising the self-assessment system and agreeing tax liabilities. Collectors may be referred to a **receivables management officers**, and are local officers who are responsible for following up amounts of unpaid tax referred to then by the **Accounts Office**.

The structure of Revenue offices is also being changed. **Taxpayer service offices** are being set up to do routine checking, computation *and* collection work, while **Taxpayer district offices** investigate selected accounts and enforce the payment of tax. **Taxpayer assistance offices** handle enquiries and arrange specialist help for taxpayers.

The **General Commissioners** (not to be confused with the Commissioners for HMRC) are appointed by the Lord Chancellor to hear **appeals** against Revenue decisions. They are part-time and unpaid. They are appointed for a local area (a **division**). They appoint a clerk who is often a lawyer or accountant and who is paid for his services by the Revenue.

The **Special Commissioners** are also appointed by the Lord Chancellor. They are full-time paid professionals. They generally hear the more complex appeals.

Many taxpayers arrange for their accountants to prepare and submit their tax returns. The taxpayer is still the person responsible for submitting the return and for paying whatever tax becomes due: the accountant is only acting as the taxpayer's agent.

2 Notification of chargeability

Individuals who are chargeable to tax for any tax year and who have not received a notice to file a return are, in general, required to give notice of chargeability to the Revenue within six months from the end of the year ie by 5 October 2006 for 2005/06.

The maximum mitigable penalty where notice of chargeability is not given is 100% of the tax assessed which is not paid on or before 31 January following the tax year.

3 Tax returns and keeping records

3.1 Tax returns

An individual's tax return comprises a Tax Form, together with supplementary pages for particular sources of income.

3.2 Time limit for submission of tax returns

The **filing due date for filing a tax return is the later of:**

- **31 January following the end of the tax year which the return covers.**
- **three months after the notice to file the return was issued.**

If an individual wishes the Revenue to prepare the self-assessment on their behalf, earlier deadlines apply. The filing date is normally the later of:

- **30 September following the tax year; eg for 2005/06, by 30 September 2006.**
- **two months after notice to file the return was issued.**

However, some individuals are issued with a four page short tax return. In this case the Revenue will calculate the tax as there is no space on the form for the self-assessment, although they do not guarantee to calculate the tax before the due date of 31 January unless the return is filed before 30 September.

3.3 Penalties for late filing

3.3.1 Individual returns

The maximum penalties for delivering a tax return after the filing due date are:

(a)	**Return up to 6 months late:**	**£100**
(b)	**Return more than 6 months but not more than 12 months late:**	**£200**
(c)	**Return more than 12 months late:**	**£200 + 100% of the tax liability**

In addition, the General or Special Commissioners can direct that a maximum penalty of £60 per day be imposed where failure to deliver a tax return continues after notice of the direction has been given to the taxpayer. In this case the additional £100 penalty, imposed under (b) if the return is more than six months late, is not charged.

The fixed penalties of £100/£200 can be set aside by the Commissioners if they are satisfied that the taxpayer had a reasonable excuse for not delivering the return. If the tax liability shown on the return is less than the fixed penalties, the fixed penalty is reduced to the amount of the tax liability. The tax geared penalty is mitigable by the Revenue or the Commissioners.

3.3.2 Reasonable excuse

A taxpayer only has a reasonable excuse for a late filing if a default occurred because of a factor outside his control. This might be non-receipt of the return by the taxpayer, serious illness of the taxpayer or a close relative, or destruction of records through fire and flood. Illness is only accepted as a reasonable excuse if the taxpayer was taking timeous steps to complete the return, and if the return is filed as soon as possible after the illness etc.

3.3.3 Returns rejected as incomplete

If a return, filed before the filing date, is rejected by the Revenue as incomplete later than 14 days before the filing deadline of 31 January, a late filing penalty will not be charged if the return is completed and returned within 14 days of the rejection. This only applies if the omission from the return was a genuine error. It does not apply if a return was deliberately filed as incomplete in the hope of extending the time limit.

3.4 Standard accounting information

'Three line' accounts (ie income less expenses equals profit) only need be included on the tax return of businesses with a turnover (or gross rents from property) of less than £15,000 pa. This is not as helpful as it might appear, as underlying records must still be kept for tax purposes (disallowable items etc) when producing three line accounts.

Large businesses with a turnover of at least £5 million which have used figures rounded to the nearest £1,000 in producing their published accounts can compute their profits to the nearest £1,000 for tax purposes.

The tax return requires trading results to be presented in a standard format. Although there is no requirement to submit accounts with the return, accounts may be filed. If accounts accompany the return, the Revenue's power to raise a discovery assessment (see below) is restricted.

3.5 Keeping of records

All taxpayers must keep and retain all records required to enable them to make and deliver a correct tax return.

Records must be retained until the later of:

(a) (i) **5 years after the 31 January following the tax year where the taxpayer is in business** (as a sole trader or partner or letting property)

(ii) **1 year after the 31 January following the tax year otherwise**

(b) provided notice to deliver a return is given before the date in (a):

(i) **the time after which enquiries by the Revenue into the return can no longer be commenced**

(ii) **the date any such enquiries have been completed**

Where a person receives a notice to deliver a tax return after the normal record keeping period has expired, he must keep all records in his possession at that time until no enquiries can be raised in respect of the return or until such enquiries have been completed.

The maximum (mitigable) penalty for each failure to keep and retain records is £3,000 per tax year/accounting period.

Record keeping failures are taken into account in considering the mitigation of other penalties. Where the record keeping failure is taken into account in this way, a penalty will normally only be sought in serious and exceptional cases where, for example, records have been destroyed deliberately to obstruct an enquiry or there has been a history of serious record keeping failures.

4 Self-assessment and claims

4.1 Self-assessment

Every personal tax return must be accompanied by a self-assessment.

A self assessment is a calculation of the amount of taxable income and gains after deducting reliefs and allowances, and a calculation of the income tax and CGT payable after taking into account tax deducted at source and tax credits.

The self-assessment calculation may either be made by the taxpayer or the Revenue. If a return is filed within certain time limits (normally, 30 September following the tax year to which it relates, see above) the Revenue will make a self-assessment on the taxpayer's behalf on the basis of the information contained in the return and send a copy of the assessment to the taxpayer. These assessments, even though raised by the Revenue, are treated as self-assessments.

If the taxpayer files a return after the above deadline but without completing the self-assessment, the Revenue will not normally reject the return as incomplete. However the Revenue are not then bound to complete the self-assessment in time to notify the taxpayer of the tax falling due on the normal due date (generally the following 31 January), and it is the taxpayer's responsibility to estimate and pay his tax on time.

Within nine months of receiving a tax return, the Revenue can amend a taxpayer's self-assessment to correct any obvious errors or mistakes; whether errors of principle, arithmetical mistakes or otherwise. The taxpayer does have the right to reject any corrections of obvious errors made by the Revenue.

Within 12 months of the due filing date (*not* the actual filing date), the taxpayer can give notice to the Revenue to amend his tax return and self-assessment. Such amendments by taxpayers are not confined to the correction of obvious errors.

The same rules apply to corrections and amendments of partnership statements and stand alone claims (see below).

4.2 Claims

4.2.1 General rules

All claims and elections which can be made in a tax return must be made in this manner if a return has been issued. A claim for any relief, allowance or repayment of tax must normally be quantified at the time it is made.

Certain claims have a time limit that is longer than the time limit for filing or amending a tax return. A claim may therefore be made after the time limit for amending the tax return has expired. Claims not made on the tax return are referred to as **'stand alone' claims**.

4.2.2 Claims involving more than one year

Self-assessment is intended to avoid the need to reopen earlier years, so relief should be given for the year of the claim. This rule can best be explained by considering a claim to carry back a trading loss to an earlier year of assessment:

(a) the claim for relief is treated as made in relation to the year in which the loss was actually incurred;

(b) the amount of any tax repayment due is calculated in terms of tax of the earlier year to which the loss is being carried back; and

(c) any tax repayment etc is treated as relating to the later year in which the loss was actually incurred.

4.2.3 Error or mistake claims

An error or mistake claim may be made for errors in a return or partnership statement where tax would otherwise be overcharged. The claim may not be made where the tax liability was computed in accordance with practice prevailing at the time the return or statement was made.

An error or mistake claim may not be made in respect of a claim. If a taxpayer makes an error or mistake in a claim, he may make a supplementary claim within the time limits allowed for the original claim.

The taxpayer may appeal to the Special Commissioners against any refusal of an error or mistake claim.

5 Payment of tax, interest and penalties

5.1 Payments of tax

The self-assessment system may result in the taxpayer making three payments of income tax:

Date	Payment
31 January in the tax year	**1st payment on account**
31 July after the tax year	**2nd payment on account**
31 January after the tax year	**Final payment to settle the remaining liability**

Payments on account are usually required where the income tax due in the previous year exceeded the amount of income tax deducted at source; this excess is known as **'the relevant amount'**. Income tax deducted at source includes tax suffered, PAYE deductions and tax credits on dividends.

The payments on account are each equal to 50% of the relevant amount for the previous year.

Activity 14.1

Gordon paid tax for 2005/06 as follows:

		£
Total amount of income tax assessed		9,200
This included:	Tax deducted under PAYE	1,700
	Tax deducted on savings income	1,500
He also paid:	Capital gains tax	4,800

How much are the payments on account for 2006/07?

Payments on account are not required if the relevant amount falls below a de minimis limit of £500. Also, payments on account are not required from taxpayers who paid 80% or more of their tax liability for the previous year through PAYE or other deduction at source arrangements.

If the previous year's liability increases following an amendment to a self-assessment, or the raising of a discovery assessment, an adjustment is made to the payments on account due.

Payments on account are normally fixed by reference to the previous year's tax liability but if a taxpayer expects his liability to be lower than this **he may claim to reduce his payments on account to:**

(a) a **stated amount**, or
(b) **nil**.

The claim must state the reason why he believes his tax liability will be lower, or nil.

If the taxpayer's eventual liability is higher than he estimated he will have reduced the payments on account too far. Although the payments on account will not be adjusted, the taxpayer will suffer an interest charge on late payment.

A penalty of the difference between the reduced payment on account and the correct payment on account may be levied if the reduction was claimed fraudulently or negligently.

The balance of any income tax together with all CGT due for a year, is normally payable on or before the 31 January following the year.

Activity 14.2

Giles made payments on account for 2005/06 of £6,500 each on 31 January 2006 and 31 July 2006, based on his 2004/05 liability. He then calculates his total income tax for 2005/06 at £18,000 of which £2,750 was deducted at source. In addition he calculated that his CGT liability for disposals in 2005/06 is £5,120.

What is the final payment due for 2005/06?

In one case the due date for the final payment is later than 31 January following the end of the year. **If a taxpayer has notified chargeability by 5 October but the notice to file a tax return is not issued before 31 October, then the due date for the payment is three months after the issue of the notice.**

Tax charged in an amended self-assessment is usually payable on the later of:

(a) the normal due date, generally 31 January following the end of the tax year; and
(b) the day following 30 days after the making of the revised self-assessment.

Tax charged on a discovery assessment is due thirty days after the issue of the assessment.

5.2 Surcharges

Surcharges are normally imposed in respect of amounts paid late:

Paid		*Surcharge*
(a)	within 28 days of due date:	none
(b)	more than 28 days but not more than six months after the due date:	5%
(c)	more than six months after the due date:	10%

Surcharges apply to:

(a) balancing payments of income tax and any CGT under self-assessment or a determination
(b) tax due on the amendment of a self-assessment
(c) tax due on a discovery assessment

The surcharge rules do not apply to late payments on account.

No surcharge will be applied where the late paid tax liability has attracted a tax-geared penalty on the failure to notify chargeability to tax, or the failure to submit a return, or on the making of an incorrect return (including a partnership return).

5.3 Interest

Interest is chargeable on late payment of both payments on account and balancing payments. In both cases interest runs from the due date until the day before the actual date of payment.

Interest is charged from 31 January following the tax year (or the normal due date for the balancing payment, in the rare event that this is later), even if this is before the due date for payment on:

(a) tax payable following an amendment to a self-assessment;
(b) tax payable in a discovery assessment; and
(c) tax postponed under an appeal which becomes payable.

Since a determination (see below) is treated as if it were a self-assessment, interest runs from 31 January following the tax year.

If a taxpayer claims to reduce his payments on account and there is still a final payment to be made, interest is normally charged on the payments on account as if each of those payments had been the lower of:

(a) the reduced amount, plus 50% of the final income tax liability; and
(b) the amount which would have been payable had no claim for reduction been made.

Activity 14.3

Herbert's payments on account for 2005/06 based on his income tax liability for 2004/05 were £4,500 each. However, when he submitted his 2004/05 income tax return in January 2006, he made a claim to reduce the payments on account for 2005/06 to £3,500 each. The first payment on account was made on 29 January 2006, and the second on 12 August 2006.

Herbert filed his 2005/06 tax return in December 2006. The return showed that his tax liabilities for 2005/06 (before deducting payments on account) were income tax: £10,000, capital gains tax: £2,500. Herbert paid the balance of tax due of £5,500 on 19 February 2007.

For what periods and in respect of what amounts will Herbert be charged interest?

Where interest has been charged on late payments on account but the final balancing settlement for the year produces a repayment, all or part of the original interest is remitted.

5.4 Repayment of tax and repayment supplement

Tax is repaid when claimed unless a greater payment of tax is due in the following 30 days, in which case it is set-off against that payment.

Interest is paid on overpayments of:

(a) payments on account
(b) final payments of income tax and CGT, including tax deducted at source or tax credits on dividends
(c) penalties and surcharges

Repayment supplement runs from the original date of payment (even if this was prior to the due date), until the day before the date the repayment is made. Income tax deducted at source and tax credits are treated as if they were paid on the 31 January following the tax year concerned.

6 Enquiries, determinations and discovery assessments

6.1 Enquiries into returns

The Revenue have a limited period within which to commence enquiries into a return or amendment. The officer must give written notice of their intention by:

(a) the **first anniversary of the due filing date (not the actual filing date)**; or

(b) **if the return is filed after the due filing date, the quarter day following the first anniversary of the actual filing date. The quarter days are 31 January, 30 April, 31 July and 31 October**.

If the taxpayer amended the return after the due filing date, the enquiry 'window' extends to the quarter day following the first anniversary of the date the amendment was filed. Where the enquiry was not raised within the limit which would have applied had no amendment been filed, the enquiry is restricted to matters contained in the amendment.

Enquiries may be made into partnership returns (or amendments) upon which a partnership statement is based within the same time limits. A notice to enquire into a partnership return is deemed to incorporate a notice, to enquire into each individual partner's return.

Enquiries may also be made into stand alone claims, provided notice is given by the later of:

(a) The quarter day following the first anniversary of the making or amending of the claim
(b) 31 January next but one following the tax year, if the claim relates to a tax year
(c) the first anniversary of the end of the period to which a claim relates if it relates to a period other than a tax year

The procedures for enquiries into claims mirror those for enquiries into returns.

The Revenue do not have to have, or give, any reason for raising an enquiry. In particular the taxpayer will not be advised whether he has been selected at random for an audit. Enquiries may be full enquiries, or may be limited to 'aspect' enquiries.

In the course of the enquiries **the Revenue may require the taxpayer to produce documents, accounts or any other information required. The taxpayer can appeal to the Commissioners.**

During the course of the enquiries the Revenue may amend a self-assessment if it appears that insufficient tax has been charged and an immediate amendment is necessary to prevent a loss to the Crown. This might apply if, for example, there is a possibility that the taxpayer will emigrate.

If a return is under enquiry the Revenue may postpone any repayment due as shown in the return until the enquiry is complete. The Revenue have discretion to make a provisional repayment but there is no facility to appeal if the repayment is withheld.

At any time during the course of an enquiry, the taxpayer may apply to the Commissioners to require the Revenue to notify the taxpayer within a specified period that the enquiries are complete, unless they can demonstrate that they have reasonable grounds for continuing the enquiry.

If both sides agree, disputes concerning a point of law can be resolved through litigation without having to wait until the whole enquiry is complete.

The Revenue must issue a notice that the enquiries are complete, and make any resulting amendments to the self-assessment, partnership statement or claim.

If the taxpayer is not satisfied with the amendments he may, within 30 days, appeal to the Commissioners.

Once an enquiry is complete the Revenue cannot make further enquiries. The Revenue may, in limited circumstances, raise a discovery assessment if they believe that there has been a loss of tax (see below).

The majority of investigation cases are handled by local inspectors, but serious cases are dealt with by the Special Compliance Office.

Where an irregularity is detected, unless it appears to be of a very serious nature, the first overture will often be made by the local inspector writing to the taxpayer or his agent suggesting that he has reason to doubt that full and correct returns have been made and inviting the taxpayer's comments. Correspondence will be followed by interviews at which the inspector will try to collect further evidence, and the taxpayer's accountant may be asked to prepare a detailed report showing the estimated tax unpaid.

The Revenue use various methods to attempt to calculate undisclosed income. Gross profit margins either for previous periods or for similar businesses are standardly used. As a last resort, some indication can be derived from the taxpayer's personal assets. A growth in these, taken together with an assumed level of personal expenditure, can point to an unexplained source, presumably undisclosed income. A sensible taxpayer will co-operate with the Revenue as any resistance on his part at this stage will count heavily against him in the final assessment or penalties.

6.2 The Revenue's powers

The Revenue's powers include the following.

(a) **The power to call for documents of taxpayers and others**. The Revenue may require any person to produce any documents which may contain information relevant to any taxpayer's tax liability. The Revenue may also require the taxpayer to provide written answers about questions of fact. The Inspector must give the person holding the documents reasons for applying for the right to demand documents, unless the commissioner is satisfied that giving reasons would prejudice the assessment or collection of tax.

(b) **The power to call for papers of tax accountants**. The Revenue is not normally empowered to demand documents from the taxpayer's accountant. but if he has either:

   (i) been convicted of an offence in relation to tax
   (ii) been penalised for assisting in making an incorrect return

   the Revenue can, in certain circumstances, demand documents relating to the taxpayer's affairs. A tax accountant is anyone (including a barrister or solicitor) who helps a taxpayer to prepare or deliver documents for tax purposes.

(c) **The power of entry with a warrant to obtain documents**. Where there are reasonable grounds for suspecting that an offence involving fraud in connection with tax has been, is being or is about to be committed and that evidence is to be found on certain premises, a warrant can be obtained authorising the Revenue to search the premises and remove anything which they has reasonable cause to suppose may be required as evidence.

(d) **The power to obtain information about interest and dividends**. The Revenue can require details from banks and building societies.

6.3 Determinations

The Revenue may only raise enquiries if a return has been submitted.

If notice has been served on a taxpayer to submit a return but the return is not submitted by the due filing date, the Revenue may make a determination of the tax due. Such a determination must be made to the best of their information and belief, and is then treated as if it were a self-assessment. This enables the Revenue to seek payment of tax, including payments on account for the following year and to charge interest.

6.4 Discovery assessments

If the Revenue discover that profits have been omitted from assessment, that any assessment has become insufficient, or that any relief given is, or has become excessive, an assessment may be raised to recover the tax lost.

If the tax lost results from an error in the taxpayer's return but the return was made in accordance with prevailing practice at the time, no discovery assessment may be made.

A discovery assessment may only be raised where a return has been made if:

(a) there has been fraudulent or negligent conduct by the taxpayer or his agent

(b) at the time that enquiries into the return were completed, or could no longer be made, the Revenue did not have information to make them aware of the loss of tax

These rules do not prevent the Revenue from raising assessments in cases of genuine discoveries, but prevent assessments from being raised due to the Revenue's failure to make timely use of information or to a change of opinion on information made available.

6.5 Appeals and postponement of payment of tax

A taxpayer may appeal against an amendment to a self-assessment or partnership statement, or an amendment to or disallowance of a claim, following an enquiry, or against an assessment which is not a self-assessment, such as a discovery assessment.

The appeal must normally be made within 30 days of the amendment or self-assessment.

The notice of appeal must state the **grounds** of appeal. These may be stated in general terms. At the hearing the Commissioners may allow the appellant to put forward grounds not stated in his notice if they are satisfied that his omission was not wilful or unreasonable.

In some cases it may be possible to agree the point at issue by negotiation with the Revenue, in which case the appeal may be settled by agreement. If the appeal cannot be agreed, it will be heard by the General or Special Commissioners.

An appeal does not relieve the taxpayer of liability to pay tax on the normal due date unless he obtains a 'determination' of the Commissioners or agreement of the Inspector that payment of all or some of the tax may be postponed pending determination of the appeal. The amount not postponed is due 30 days after the determination or agreement is issued, if that is later than the normal due date.

If any part of the postponed tax becomes due a notice of the amount payable is issued and the amount is payable 30 days after the issue of the notice. Interest, however, is still payable from the normal due date.

7 Client confidentiality

Whenever you prepare accounts or returns on behalf of a client you should remember that you are bound by the ethical guideline of client confidentiality. This means that you should not discuss a client's affairs with third parties without the client's permission. You should also take care not to leave documents relating to a client's affairs in public places such as on trains or in restaurants.

8 End of chapter activity

Activity 14.4

Tim is a medical consultant. His total tax liability for 2004/05 was £16,800. Of this £7,200 was paid under the PAYE system, £800 was withheld at source from bank interest and £200 was suffered on dividends received during the year.

Tim's total tax liability for 2005/06 was £22,000. £7,100 of this was paid under PAYE system, £900 was withheld at source from bank interest and there was a £250 tax credit on dividends.

Tim did not make any claim in respect of his payments on account for 2005/06. The Revenue issued a 2005/06 tax return to Tim on 5 May 2006.

Task

State what payments Tim was required to make in respect of his 2005/06 tax liability and the due dates for the payment of these amounts.

Key learning points

- ☑ The **tax return** is due for filing by **31 January following the end of the tax year**.
- ☑ However, if the taxpayer wants the **Revenue to calculate tax**, he must normally file it by **30 September following the end of the tax year.**
- ☑ **Two payments on account** of income tax are due on **31 January in the tax year** and **31 July following the end of the tax year.**
- ☑ Payments on account are based on the **previous year's tax bill**.
- ☑ On **31 January following the end of the tax year**, the **balance** of any income tax is due.
- ☑ **CGT** is due to be paid on **31 January following the end of the tax year.**
- ☑ There is an extensive regime of **penalties**, **surcharges** and **interest**.
- ☑ The Revenue have extensive, but not unlimited, **powers to enquire into returns**.

Quick quiz

1 Julia is sent her 2005/06 tax return on 6 August 2006. The return is not a short tax return.

By what date must she file the tax return if she does not want to calculate her tax liability?

A 30 September 2006
B 5 October 2006
C 5 November 2006
D 31 January 2007

2 What penalty is due if a tax return is delivered 4 months late?

3 Christopher had a tax liability of £6,000 for 2004/05. In 2005/06, his tax liability was £10,000.

How is Christopher's tax liability for 2005/06 paid?

4 Oliver should have made a balancing payment of £10,000 on 31 January 2006. He actually paid it on 31 May 2006.

What surcharge is due?

Answers to quick quiz

1 B later of 30 September 2006 and 2 months after the issue of the tax return.

2 £100

3 Two payments of £3,000 each on 31 January 2006 and 31 July 2006, balance of £4,000 on 31 January 2007.

4 5% x £10,000 = £500

Activity checklist

This checklist shows which performance criteria is covered by each activity in this chapter. Tick off each activity as you complete it.

Activity		
14.1	☐	This activity deals with Performance Criteria 18.2.E: identify the due dates of payment of Income Tax by unincorporated businesses, including payments on account
14.2	☐	This activity deals with Performance Criteria 18.2.E: identify the due dates of payment of Income Tax by unincorporated businesses, including payments on account
14.3	☐	This activity deals with Performance Criteria 18.2.E: identify the due dates of payment of Income Tax by unincorporated businesses, including payments on account
14.4	☐	This activity deals with Performance Criteria 18.2.E: identify the due dates of payment of Income Tax by unincorporated businesses, including payments on account

chapter 15

Payment of tax by companies

Contents

Performance criteria

18.4 D Identify and set off income tax deductions and credits

18.4 F Identify the amount of Corporation Tax payable and the due dates of payment, including payments on account

18.4 G Complete corporation tax returns correctly and submit them, together with relevant claims and elections within statutory time limits

18.4 I Give timely and constructive advice to clients on the maintenance of accounts and the recording of information relevant to tax returns

Range statement

There are no additional contextual requirements in this element relevant to this chapter.

Knowledge and understanding

19 Self assessment including payment of tax and filing of returns for unincorporated businesses and companies (Elements 18.2 & 18.4)

1 Returns under the corporation tax self assessment system

1.1 Returns

A company's tax return (CT600) must include a self assessment of any tax payable.

A copy of the CTSA return form (CT 600) is included in the appendix to this text.

An obligation to file a return arises only when the company receives a notice requiring a return. A return is required for each accounting period ending during or at the end of the period specified in the notice requiring a return.

A company that does not receive a notice requiring a return must, if it is chargeable to tax, **notify the Revenue within twelve months of the end of the accounting period**. Failure to do so results in a maximum penalty equal to the tax unpaid twelve months after the end of the accounting period.

A return for each of the company's accounting periods is due on or before the filing date. This is the later of:

(a) **12 months after the end of the accounting period**

(b) **if the accounting period ends in a period of account which is not more than 18 months long, 12 months from the end of the period of account**

(c) **if the accounting ends in a period of account which is more than 18 months long, 30 months from the start of the period of account; and**

(d) **three months from the date on which the notice requiring the return was made.**

Activity 15.1

A Ltd prepares accounts for the eighteen months to 30 June 2005. A notice requiring a return for the year ended 30 June 2005 was issued to A Ltd on 1 September 2005. State the periods for which A Ltd must file a tax return and the filing dates.

1.2 Penalties

There is a £100 penalty for a failure to submit a return on time, rising to £200 if the delay exceeds three months. These penalties become £500 and £1,000 respectively when a return was late (or never submitted) for each of the preceding two accounting periods.

An additional tax geared penalty is applied if a return is more than six months late. The penalty is 10% of the tax unpaid six months after the return was due if the total delay is up to 12 months, but 20% of that tax if the return is over 12 months late.

There is a tax geared penalty for a fraudulent or negligent return and for failing to correct an innocent error without unreasonable delay. The maximum penalty is equal to the tax that would have been lost had the return been accepted as

correct. The Revenue can mitigate (reduce) this penalty. If a company is liable to more than one tax geared penalty, the total penalty is limited to the maximum single penalty that could be charged.

A company may amend a return within twelve months of the filing date. The Revenue may correct obvious errors in a return or amendment within nine months of the day it was filed. The company may amend its return so as to reject the correction. If the time limit for amendments has expired, the company may reject the correction by giving notice within three months.

Wherever possible claims must be made on a tax return or on an amendment to it and must be quantified at the time the return is made.

Activity 15.2

AB Ltd prepares accounts to 30 September each year. Its corporation tax return for the year to 30 September 2003 was filed on time. The return for the year to 30 September 2004 was filed on 1 December 2005 and the return for the year end 30 September 2005 was filed on 1 November 2006. In all cases a notice requiring a return was issued within three months of the end of the period of account concerned.

What fixed penalty is due in respect of the late filing of the return for the period to 30 September 2005?

A £100
B £200
C £500
D £1,000

1.3 Records

Companies must keep records until the latest of:

(a) six years from the end of the accounting period
(b) the date any enquiries are completed
(c) the date after which enquiries may not be commenced

All business records and accounts, including contracts and receipts, must be kept.

If a return is demanded more than six years after the end of the accounting period, any records which the company still has must be kept until the later of the end of any enquiry and the expiry of the right to start an enquiry.

Failure to keep records can lead to a penalty of up to £3,000 for each accounting period affected. However, this penalty does not apply when the only records which have not been kept are ones which could only have been needed for the purposes of claims, elections or notices not included in the return.

The Revenue do not generally insist on original records being kept but original records relating to payments made net of tax must be preserved.

1.4 Enquiries

The Revenue may enquire into a return or an amendment, provided that they give written notice that they are going to enquire by a year after the later of:

(a) the filing date

(b) the 31 January, 30 April, 31 July or 31 October next following the actual date of delivery of the return or amendment

Only one enquiry may be made in respect of any one return or amendment.

If a notice of an enquiry has been given, the Revenue may demand that the company produce documents. Documents relating to an appeal need not be produced and the company may appeal against a notice requiring documents to be produced.

If the Revenue demand documents, but the company does not produce them, there is a penalty of £50. There is also a daily penalty, which applies for each day from the day after the imposition of the £50 penalty until the documents are produced.

The Revenue may amend a self assessment at any time during an enquiry if they believe there might otherwise be a loss of tax. The company may appeal against such an amendment

An enquiry ends when the Revenue give notice that it has been completed and notify what they believe to be the correct amount of tax payable. Before that time, the company may ask the Commissioners to order the Revenue to notify the completion of its enquiry by a specified date. Such a direction will be given unless the Revenue can demonstrate that they have reasonable grounds for continuing the enquiry.

The company has 30 days from the end of an enquiry to amend its self assessment in accordance with the Revenue's conclusions. If the Revenue are not satisfied with the company's amendments, they have a further 30 days to amend the self assessment. The company then has another 30 days in which it may appeal against the Revenue's amendments.

Activity 15.3

V Ltd filed its corporation tax return for the year to 30 June 2005 on 30 September 2006. A notice requiring the return was issued on 1 October 2005. What is the latest date by which the Revenue must give notice if they wish to enquire into the return?

A 30 June 2006
B 30 June 2007
C 31 October 2006
D 31 October 2007

1.5 Determinations and discovery assessments

If a return is not delivered by the filing date, the Revenue may issue a determination of the tax payable. There is no appeal against this but it is automatically replaced by any self assessment made by the company by the later of five years from the filing date and 12 months from the determination.

If the Revenue believe that not enough tax has been assessed they can make a discovery assessment. When a tax return has been delivered this power is limited:

(a) No discovery assessment can be made on account of an error as to the basis on which the tax liability ought to be computed, if the basis generally prevailing at the time when the return was made was applied.

(b) A discovery assessment can only be made if either:

 (i) the loss of tax is due to fraudulent or negligent conduct

 (ii) the Revenue could not reasonably be expected to have been aware of the loss, given the information so far supplied to them, when their right to start an enquiry expired or when they notified the company that an enquiry had finished

2 Payment of tax and interest

2.1 Tax payable by small/medium sized companies

Corporation tax is due for payment by small and medium sized companies **nine months after the end of the accounting period**.

2.2 Tax payable by large companies

Large companies must pay their corporation tax in instalments. **Broadly, a large company is any company that pays corporation tax at the full rate** (profits exceed £1,500,000 where there are no associated companies).

Instalments are due on the 14th day of the month, starting in the seventh month. Provided that the accounting period is twelve months long subsequent instalments are due in the tenth month during the accounting period and in the first and fourth months after the end of the accounting period. If an accounting period is less than twelve months long subsequent instalments are due at three monthly intervals but with the final payment being due in the fourth month of the next accounting period.

Example

X Ltd is a large company with a 31 December accounting year end. Instalments of corporation tax will be due to be paid by X Ltd on:

- 14 July and 14 October in the accounting period;
- 14 January and 14 April after the accounting period ends

Thus for the year ended 31 December 2005 instalment payments are due on 14 July 2005, 14 October 2005, 14 January 2006 and 14 April 2006.

Activity 15.4

S Ltd, a large company, has a corporation tax liability of £700,000 in respect of its accounting year 31 March 2006.

On which date will the company be required to pay the FINAL QUARTERLY instalment of the liability?

A 14 October 2005

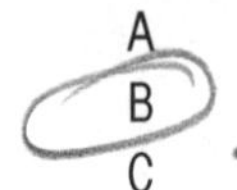

B 14 July 2006

C 31 July 2006

D 1 January 2007

2.3 Calculation of instalments

Instalments are based on the estimated corporation tax liability for the current period (not the previous period). This means that it will be extremely important for companies to forecast their tax liabilities accurately. Large companies whose directors are poor at estimating may find their company's incurring significant interest charges. The amount of each instalment is computed by:

(a) working out $3 \times CT/n$ where CT is the amount of the estimated corporation tax liability payable in instalments for the period and n is the number of months in the period;

(b) allocating the smaller of that amount and the total estimated corporation tax liability to the first instalment;

(c) repeating the process for later instalments until the amount allocated is equal to the corporation tax liability. This gives four equal instalments for 12 month accounting periods and also caters for periods which end earlier than expected.

The company is therefore required to estimate its corporation tax liability before the end of the accounting period, and must revise its estimate each quarter.

Activity 15.5

A company has a CT liability of £880,000 for the eight month period to 30 September 2005. Accounts had previously always been prepared to 31 January. Show when the CT liability is due for payment.

A company is not required to pay instalments in the first year that it is 'large', unless its profits exceed £10 million. The £10 million limit is reduced proportionately if there are associated companies. For this purpose only, a company will be regarded as an associated company where it was an associated company at the START of an accounting period. (This differs from the normal approach in CT where being an associated company for any part of the AP affects the thresholds of both companies for the whole of the AP.)

There is a de minimis limit in that any company whose liability for its accounting period does not exceed £10,000 need not pay by instalments.

2.4 Interest

Interest runs from the due date on over/underpaid instalments. The position is looked at cumulatively after the due date for each instalment. The Revenue calculate the interest position after the company submits its corporation tax return.

Example

X plc prepared accounts to 31.12.05. The company has always prepared accounts to 31 December each year. It paid CT instalments of:

Date	*Amount*
	£m
14.7.05	3.5
14.10.05	8.5
14.01.06	4.5
14.4.06	4.5
	21.0

X plc's CT return showed a CT liability of £22m. The £1m balance was paid on 1.10.06. £22m should have been paid in instalments. The under(over) payments were:

Date	*Paid*	*Correct*	*Under(over) paid*
	£m	£m	£m
14.7.05	3.5	5.5	2
14.10.05	8.5	5.5	
	12.0	11.0	(1)
14.1.06	4.5	5.5	
	16.5	16.5	–
14.4.06	4.5	5.5	
	21.0	22.0	1

Interest would be charged (received) as follows.

14.7.05 – 13.10.05	Interest charged on £2m
14.10.05 – 13.1.06	Interest received on £1m
14.1.06 – 13.4.06	No interest
14.4.06 – 30.9.06	Interest charged on £1m

2.5 Incorrect instalments

There are penalties if a company deliberately and flagrantly fails to pay instalments of sufficient size. After a company has filed its return or the Revenue has determined its liability, the Revenue may wish to establish the reason for inadequate instalment payments. It can do this by asking the company to produce relevant information or records (presumably to decide if a penalty applies). The failure to supply these will lead to an initial fixed penalty which may also be followed by a daily penalty which may continue until the information/records are produced.

Companies can have instalments repaid if they later conclude they ought not to have been paid.

3 Income tax suffered or withheld

A paying company is not required to withhold income tax on payments of:

(a) annual interest
(b) royalties
(c) annuities
(d) annual payments

if it reasonably believes that the **recipient is chargeable to corporation tax on the payment**.

Thus such payments made by one UK company to another UK company are paid gross.

However such payments made to individuals, partnerships etc (ie non companies) are made under deduction of income tax at 20% (eg debenture interest) or 22% (eg patent royalties).

When the company pays interest or patent royalties it deducts the gross amount in its corporation tax computation. For items paid net (such as debenture interest and patent royalties paid to non corporate recipients), **it acts as an agent for the Revenue and retains income tax at 20% (interest) or 22% (patents) on the gross amount for payment to the Revenue.** The *net* amount is then payable to the payees (for example the individual debenture holders).

Companies may receive some income which has suffered 22% income tax at source. The cash income plus the income tax suffered, that is the gross figure, forms part of a company's income. The **income tax suffered is deductible from the corporation tax liability**.

Activity 15.6

In its accounting period to 31 March 2006 SB Ltd:

1 Received patent royalties of £7,800 from an individual
2 Paid £5,000 of debenture interest to another UK resident company

The amounts shown are the amounts paid and received by the company. What is the net amount of income tax suffered that SB Ltd may deduct in calculating its corporation tax payable for the period?

A £2,200
B £1,716
C £790
D £616

4 Company return forms

A copy of two of the pages of the corporation tax self assessment return form (CT 600) are included in practice activity 47 in this text. You may be asked to complete these pages as part of your examination and you should start to familiarise yourself with them now.

The examiner has said that you will not have to deal with any other pages of the CT 600 return in your examination.

Activity 15.7

(a) Hogg Ltd prepares accounts for the year to 31 December 2005. Its profits chargeable to corporation tax for the year will be £1,750,000. The company has always paid corporation tax at the full rate.

Task

State the amounts and due dates for the payment of corporation tax by Hogg Ltd in respect of the year to 31 December 2005.

(b) In 2007 Hogg Ltd changes its accounting date to 31 October 2007. Assume that the liability for the ten months to 31 October 2007 is expected to be £600,000.

Task

State the due dates for and the amount of instalments of corporation tax that Hogg Ltd will be required to pay in respect of this period.

Key learning points

- ☑ In general, **returns must be filed within 12 months** of the end of an accounting period.
- ☑ The Revenue have **power to enquire into returns**.
- ☑ **Small and medium sized companies** pay corporation tax **nine months after the end of an accounting period**.
- ☑ **Large companies** pay corporation tax in **four quarterly instalments.**
- ☑ **Interest** is payable on **overpaid and underpaid tax**.
- ☑ A paying company is only required to **withhold income tax** on **payments other than to companies**.
- ☑ Any **net income tax suffered** by a company can be **deducted** from the corporation tax liability.

Quick quiz

1 Fairfield Ltd has profits chargeable to corporation tax of £800,000 for its year ended 31 March 2006. It has two wholly owned subsidiaries. If corporation tax is always paid as it falls due, the corporation tax payable on 1 January 2007 will be:

A £Nil
B £60,000
C £240,000
D £800,000

2 Eaton Ltd has profits chargeable to corporation tax of £2,400,000 for its year ended 31 December 2005. The first instalment of the corporation tax liability for this year will be due on:

Due date
A 14 April 2005
B 14 April 2006
C 14 July 2005
D 1 October 2006

3 M Ltd, a large company, has an estimated corporation tax liability of £240,000 in respect of its accounting year 31 March 2006.

What will be the amount of each of the company's quarterly instalments?

A £Nil
B £52,800
C £60,000
D £240,000

4 VW Ltd prepares accounts to 30 June each year. Its corporation tax return for the year to 30 June 2003 was filed on time. The return for the year to 30 June 2004 was filed on 1 November 2005 and the return for the year end 30 June 2005 was filed on 1 December 2006. In all cases a notice requiring a return was issued within three months of the end of the period of account concerned.

What fixed penalty is due in respect of the late filing of the return for the period to 30 June 2004?

Answers to quick quiz

1 A

PCTCT	£800,000
UL = £1,500,000 ÷ 3 = £500,000	
	£
Gross Corporation Tax (£800,000 × 30%)	240,000
Instalments (100%)	(240,000)
Due 1 January 2007	NIL

A company that pays corporation tax at the full rate of 30% must pay its corporation tax liability in quarterly instalments starting in the seventh month of the accounting period.

2 C Eaton Ltd is a large company paying corporation tax at the full rate of 30%.

The first instalment is paid in the seventh month of the accounting period.

3 C ¼ × £240,000 = £60,000

4 The return is more than three months late but it is only the second late filing of a return so the fixed penalty is £200.

Activity checklist

This checklist shows which performance criteria, range statement or knowledge and understanding point is covered by each activity in this chapter. Tick off each activity as you complete it.

Activity

Activity		
15.1	☐	This activity deals with Performance Criteria 18.4 G: complete corporation tax returns correctly and submit them, together with relevant claims and elections within statutory time limits
15.2	☐	This activity deals with Performance Criteria 18.4 I: give timely and constructive advice to clients on the maintenance of accounts and the recording of information relevant to tax returns
15.3	☐	This activity deals with Performance Criteria 18.4 I: give timely and constructive advice to clients on the maintenance of accounts and the recording of information relevant to tax returns
15.4	☐	This activity deals with Performance Criteria 18.4.F: identify the amount of Corporation Tax payable and the due dates of payment, including payments on account
15.5	☐	This activity deals with Performance Criteria 18.4 F: identify the amount of Corporation Tax payable and the due dates of payment, including payments on account
15.6	☐	This activity deals with Performance Criteria 18.4 D: identify and set off income tax deductions and credits
15.7	☐	This activity deals with Performance Criteria 18.4 F: identify the amount of Corporation Tax payable and the due dates of payment, including payments on account

PART F

Answers to activities

Chapter 1: Introduction to business taxation

Activity 1.1

	Non-savings income	*Savings (excl dividend) income*	*Dividend income*	*Total*
	£	£	£	£
Business profits	16,000	0	0	
Building society interest	0	6,000	0	
Dividends	0	0	8,750	
STI	16,000	6,000	8,750	30,750
Less: Personal allowance	(4,895)			
Taxable income	11,105	6,000	8,750	25,855

Activity 1.2

	£
£2,090 × 10%	209
£30,310 × 22%	6,668
£17,600 × 40%	7,040
£50,000	13,917

Chapter 2: Computing trading income

Activity 2.1

Supplementary work and marketing (drainage; obtaining planning permission)

A profit motive

The manner of acquisition (extra land was bought)

Activity 2.2

Expenditure on the tyres is revenue rather than capital expenditure. This means it is deductible in computing taxable trading profits. The expenditure is revenue expenditure rather than capital because it is a cost of remedying the normal wear and tear associated with the tractor.

Activity 2.3

	£
Healing (70%)	560

The private portion of the above bill must be added back in computing taxable trading profits.

Activity 2.4

	£
Entertaining Customers	7,300
	7,300

Activity 2.5

£230 + £700 = £930

Activity 2.6

C £9,000 + £16,000 + £8,000 = £33,000

Activity 2.7

	£
Add back loan to customer	1,400
Deduct decrease in general bad debt provision	(3,100)
Net deduction	1,700

Activity 2.8

	£	£
Profit per accounts		12,710
Add: Depreciation	1,500	
Provision against a fall in raw material prices	5,000	
Entertainment expenses	750	
Patent royalties (to treat as a charge)	1,200	
Legal expenses (relate to a capital item)	250	
		8,700
		21,410
Less rental income received (to tax as property income)		(860)
Adjusted trading profit		20,550

Activity 2.9

	Explanation	£	£
Profit per account			5,640
Add: salary – paid to Brillo	1	260	
rent	1	210	
light and heat	1	57	
motor expenses	1	48	
stockroom extension	3	101	
increase in general provision	1	200	
donations	2	10	
entertaining	4	90	
gifts	5	70	
depreciation	3	600	
goods withdrawn at selling price	2	400	
			2,046
			7,686
Less: profit on sale of plant	3	240	
profit on sale of investment	3	1,032	
bank interest received	6	54	
			(1,326)
Adjusted trading profit before capital allowances			6,360

The explanations are set out on the following page.

Explanations for treating items as disallowable/not taxable under trading profits.

1 Appropriation of profit

2 Not expenditure laid out wholly and exclusively for the purpose of trade

3 Capital items. The profit on these items may be subject to capital gains tax. It is not subject to income tax, so it is not part of taxable trading profits.

4 Entertaining expenses specifically disallowed

5 Gifts of drink specifically disallowed

6 Non-trading income. The bank interest will be taxed as savings (excl. dividend) income

Chapter 3: Capital allowances

Activity 3.1

No: its principal purpose is to provide a permanent wall.

Activity 3.2

(a) **No**: they would be part of the **setting**.

(b) **Yes**: they would **perform a specific function**.

Activity 3.3

	£
WDV b/f	20,000
Less: disposal proceeds	(12,000)
	8,000
WDA @ 25%	(2,000)
WDV c/f	6,000

Activity 3.4

	Pool	*Allowances*
	£	£
WDV b/f	123,000	
Disposals (**limited to cost**)	(27,000)	
	96,000	
WDA 25%	(24,000)	24,000
WDV c/f	72,000	

Activity 3.5

	£
WDV b/f	60,000
WDA @ 25% × 6/12	(7,500)
WDV c/f	52,500

As the period is a six month period writing down allowances are computed as 25% × $^{6}/_{12}$.

Activity 3.6

	FYA @ 40% £	Pool £	Allowances £
WDV b/f		48,000	
WDA @ 25% × $^{6}/_{12}$		(6,000)	6,000
		42,000	
Addition	20,000		
FYA @ 40%	(8,000)		8,000
		12,000	
WDV c/f		54,000	14,000

WDA is pro-rated in a short period but the FYA are not.

As GWC is a medium sized enterprise FYA are available at the rate of 40%.

Activity 3.7

The capital allowances are as follows.

	FYA @ 40% £	FYA @ 100%	Pool £	Allowances £
1.3.02 – 31.7.03				
Additions (£13,000 + £9,603)	22,603			
FYA 40%	(9,041)			9,041
			13,562	
Year ended 31.7.04				
Disposals			(4,000)	
			9,562	
WDA 25%			(2,391)	2,391
			7,171	
Addition (1.6.04)	6,000			
FYA 50%	(3,000)			3,000
			3,000	5,391
			10,171	
Year ended 31.7.05				
WDA 25%			(2,543)	2,543
			7,628	
Addition (31.12.04)		10,000		
FYA 100%		(10,000)		10,000
			0	
WDV c/f			7,628	
				12,543

Note: **First year allowances are not pro-rated in a long period of account.**

Activity 3.8

	Car £	*Allowances* £
1.7.02 – 31.12.02		
Purchase price	15,500	
WDA 25% × 6/12 of £15,500 = £1,938,		
Limited to £3,000 × 6/12 = £1,500	(1,500)	1,500
	14,000	
Year ended 31.12.03		
WDA 25% of £14,000 = £3,500,		
Limited to £3,000	(3,000)	3,000
	11,000	
Year ended 31.12.04		
WDA 25% of £11,000	(2,750)	2,750
	8,250	
Year ended 31.12.05		
Proceeds	(4,000)	
Balancing allowance	4,250	4,250

Note that a balancing allowance arises in the period the car is sold.

Activity 3.9

(a)

	£
Year ended 30.4.02	
Purchase Price	12,000
WDA 25%	(3,000)
	9,000
Year ended 30.4.03	
WDA 25%	(2,250)
	6,750
Year ended 30.4.04	
WDA 25%	(1,688)
	5,062
Year ended 30.4.05	
WDA 25%	(1,266)
	3,796
Year ended 30.4.06	
Disposal proceeds	(300)
Balancing allowance	3,496

(b) If the asset is still in use at 30 April 2006, a WDA of 25% × £3,796 = £949 would be claimable in the year to 30 April 2006. The tax written down value of £3,796 – £949 = £2,847 would be added to the general pool at the beginning of the next period of account. The disposal proceeds of £200 would be deducted from the general pool in that period's capital allowances computation.

Activity 3.10

Only the sports pavilion will qualify.

Activity 3.11

The showrooms and offices are non-qualifying parts of the building. As the cost of the non qualifying parts, £600,000, is more than 25% of the total expenditure on the building, industrial buildings allowances are not available on it. The cost of the land is not qualifying expenditure.

Therefore, the qualifying expenditure for industrial buildings allowance purposes is £1,500,000 (£2,100,000 – £600,000)

Activity 3.12

The building was in industrial use at the end of the accounting period so an industrial buildings allowance of 4% of cost per annum is available. The allowance in the nine months to 30.9.05 is, therefore, 9/12 × £600,000 × 4% = £18,000

Activity 3.13

Frankie

	£
Cost 1.10.01	100,000
Y/e 31.12.01 to y/e 31.12.04 WDA 4 × 4%	(16,000)
Residue before sale	84,000
Y/e 31.12.05 Proceeds (limited to cost)	(100,000)
Balancing charge	(16,000)

Holly

	£
Residue before sale	84,000
Balancing charge	16,000
Residue after sale	100,000

The tax life of the building ends on 1.10.01 + 25 years = 30.9.2026

The date of Holly's purchase is 1.9.05

The unexpired life is therefore 21 years 1 month (253 months)

	£
Y/e 30.9.05 WDA £100,000 × 12/253	4,743
Next 20 accounting periods at £4,743 a year	94,860
Y/e 30.9.26 (balance)	397
	100,000

Activity 3.14

		FYA @ 40%	*General Pool*	*Expensive car (60%)*	*Allowances*
		£	£	£	£
WDV b/f			8,000		
Year ended 31.12.03					
14.9.03	Machinery sold		(700)		
			7,300		
16.9.03	Addition – car (no FYA available)		4,000		
			11,300		
	WDA 25%		(2,825)		2,825
1.12.03	Machinery	7,693			
	FYA @ 40%	(3,077)			3,077
			4,616		
	WDV c/f		13,091		
	Total allowances				5,902
Year ended 31.12.04					
5.7.04	Mercedes			22,000	
21.3.04	Plant sold (restricted to cost)		(2,000)		
22.3.04	Car sold		(3,200)		
			7,891		
	WDA @ 25%		(1,973)		1,973
	WDV c/f		5,918		
	WDA restricted			(3,000) × 60%	1,800
	WDV c/f			19,000	
	Total allowances				3,773

		FYA @ 50%	FYA @ 40%	Pool	Expensive car (60%)	Allowances
Y/e 31.12.05		£	£	£	£	£
WDV b/f				5,918	19,000	
5.2.05	Car (no FYA)			3,000		
30.6.05	Plant sold			(2,602)		
				6,316		
	WDA 25%			(1,579)		1,579
				4,737		
15.6.05	Mercedes sold				(4,000)	
	Balancing allowance				15,000 × 60%	9,000
15.6.05	Volvo				18,000	
	WDA restricted				(3,000) × 60%	1,800
4.2.05	Machine on HP	4,000				
	FYA @ 50%	(2,000)				2,000
				2,000		
30.6.05	Plant		3,000			
	FYA @ 40%		(1,200)	1,800		1,200
	WDV c/f			8,537	15,000	
	Total allowances					15,579

Tutorial Notes:

1 It is important that you adopt the above columnar layout in your examination. This should ensure that you achieve good marks on this task.

2 The private use of an asset by an **employee** does not lead to a restriction in the capital allowances available.

Activity 3.15

Cuckold Ltd should acquire factory (i), as shown in the working below.

Factory (ii) is clearly unattractive since, with its tax life expired, industrial buildings allowances cannot be claimed. Factories (iii) and (iv) have greater total allowances available than factory (i) but the annual allowance is much smaller.

Working: industrial buildings allowances on alternative factories

	Factory (i)	*Factory (ii)*	*Factory (iii)*	*Factory (iv)*
Residue after sale*	£100,000	£80,000	£150,000	£120,000
Remaining tax life**	1 year	0	23 years	17 years
Allowances available	£100,000	0	£150,000	£120,000
in y/e 31.3.2007	1 year = £100,000		23 years = £6,522	17 years = £7,059

* The residue after sale is the lower of the price paid by the new purchaser and the original cost.

** The tax life of an industrial building begins when it is first brought into use and ends 25 years later

Chapter 4: Basis of assessment for unincorporated businesses

Activity 4.1

Jameel's basis period for 2005/06 is the year ended 30 June 2005.

Activity 4.2

2005/06	1.7.05 – 5.4.06 9/12 × £10,000	£7,500
2006/07	1.7.05 – 30.6.06	£10,000
2007/08	1.7.06 – 30.6.07	£15,000
2008/09	1.7.07 – 30.6.08	£18,000

As there is a 12 month period of account ending in the second tax year, this is the basis period for the second tax year.

Activity 4.3

2004/05	Year ended 30.9.04	£10,000
2005/06	Year ended 30.9.05	£7,000
2006/07	1.10.05 – 31.12.06 £(6,000 + 2,000)	£8,000

Activity 4.4

Year	Basis period	Working	*Taxable profits* £
2000/01	1.9.00 – 5.4.01	£8,000 × 7/8	7,000
2001/02	1.9.00 – 31.8.01	£8,000 + (£15,000 × 4/12)	13,000
2002/03	1.5.01 – 30.4.02		15,000
2003/04	1.5.02 – 30.4.03		9,000
2004/05	1.5.03 – 30.4.04		10,500
2005/06	1.5.04 – 30.6.05	£(16,000 + 950 – 12,000)	4,950
			59,450

The overlap profits are the profits from 1 September 2000 to 5 April 2001 (taxed in 2000/01 and in 2001/02) and those from 1 May 2001 to 31 August 2001 (taxed in 2001/02 and 2002/03).

	£
1.9.00 – 5.4.01 £8,000 × 7/8	7,000
1.5.01 – 31.8.01 £15,000 × 4/12	5,000
Total overlap profits	12,000

Activity 4.5

(a)

	£
2003/04	
(1.5.03 – 5.4.04) £24,000 + (3/12 × £40,000)	34,000
2004/05	
Y/e 31.12.04	40,000
2005/06	
Y/e 31.12.05	60,000

(b) Overlap profits

3 m/e 5.4.04 (taxed in 2003/04 and 2004/05) £10,000

(c) The result of rather complicated tax rules is that when a business starts, certain profits may be taxed in more than one tax year. Profits that have been taxed twice in this way are known as **'overlap profits'**. When a business ceases trading overlap profits may be deducted from profits that would otherwise be taxed in the final tax year of the business.

Over the entire life of a business taxable profits will equal actual profits.

Chapter 5: Trading losses

Activity 5.1

£18,000 – £14,000 (s 380 claim) = £4,000

Activity 5.2

The year of the loss is 2005/06. The loss for 2005/06 is £25,000

	2004/05	*2005/06*
	£	£
Income	18,000	18,000
Less s 380 relief	(7,000)	(18,000)
STI	11,000	0
Less personal allowance	(4,745)	(4,895)
Taxable income	6,255	0

In 2005/06, £4,895 of the loss has been wasted because that amount of income would have been covered by the personal allowance. If Janet claims s 380 relief, there is nothing she can do about this waste of loss relief. However, Janet might have been best advised to claim relief in 2004/05 before making a claim in 2005/06. This would have had the effect of moving the taxable income to 2005/06 so wasting less personal allowance.

Activity 5.3

MEMORANDUM

To: Tax manager
From : A. Technician
Subject: Losses

Shula has incurred a trading loss of £10,000 in 2005/06.

The alternative methods by which she may obtain relief for this loss are:

(a) Under s380 against total income of £8,000 in 2004/05. This disadvantage of this is that the benefit of personal allowance is wasted in 2004/05 but tax is otherwise mainly saved at 22%

(b) Under s380 against rental income of £21,000 in 2005/06.

(c) Adopt method (a) and then deal with the remaining loss using method (b), but the personal allowance is wasted in 2004/05.

(d) Under s385 against future taxable trading profits, ie in 2006/07 onwards. The disadvantage of this is that tax will not be saved until sometime in the future when profits are made

Chapter 6: Partnerships

Activity 6.1

	Total	*Jameel*	*Pratish*
1.4.05 – 31.12.05	£	£	£
(9/12 × £100,000)	75,000	50,000	25,000
1.1.06 – 31.3.06			
(3/12 × £100,000)	25,000	20,000	5,000
Taxable trading profits	100,000	70,000	30,000

Activity 6.2

	Total	*Kumar*	*Bal*
	£	£	£
Salaries	80,000	40,000	40,000
Profits (£130,000 – £80,000)	50,000	30,000	20,000
	130,000	70,000	60,000

Activity 6.3

	Total	*Shuan*	*Matthew*
	£	£	£
Interest on capital	5,400	1,200	4,200
Salaries	80,000	40,000	40,000
Profits	94,600	70,950	23,650
	180,000	112,150	67,850

Activity 6.4

	Total	*Jameel*	*Shammina*
1.1.05 – 30.6.05	£	£	£
Salary (× 6/12)	20,000	10,000	10,000
Profits	80,000	40,000	40,000
	100,000	50,000	50,000
1.7.05 – 31.12.05			
Salary (6/12 × £50,000/£30,000)	40,000	25,000	15,000
Profits (6/12 × £200,000) – £40,000	60,000	30,000	30,000
	100,000	55,000	45,000
Total y/e 31.12.05	200,000	105,000	95,000

Did you remember to time apportion the salary in each of the six month periods?

Activity 6.5

Year	*Basis period*	*Working*	*Taxable profits*
			£
2004/05	1.9.04 – 5.4.05	(£34,200 × 20%) × 4/12 + (£45,600 × 20%) × 3/12	4,560
2005/06	1.1.05 – 31.12.05	£45,600 × 20%	9,120

Activity 6.6

Tutorial note. Your first step with a partnership question should be to calculate profits for each period of account. Only after you have done this should you consider allocating the profits to tax years. Remember that the opening year rules apply when a partner joins a partnership. Similarly, when a partner leaves the closing year rules apply to the departing partner. All other partners are assessed on a continuing basis.

	Total	*A*	*B*	*C*
	£	£	£	£
Year ended 31.3.03				
Salaries	3,700	1,500	1,200	1,000
Balance	6,500	2,600	2,600	1,300
Total	10,200	4,100	3,800	2,300
Year ended 31.3.04				
April to June				
Salaries	925	375	300	250
Balance	4,275	1,710	1,710	855
Total	5,200	2,085	2,010	1,105
July to March				
Salaries	1,650		900	750
Balance	13,950		8,370	5,580
Total	15,600		9,270	6,330
Totals for the year	20,800	2,085	11,280	7,435
Year ended 31.3.05				
Salaries	2,200		1,200	1,000
Balance	10,400		6,240	4,160
Total	12,600		7,440	5,160
Year ending 31.3.06				
Salaries	2,200		1,200	1,000
Balance	15,800		9,480	6,320
Total	18,000		10,680	7,320

Taxable trading profits are as follows:	*A*	*B*	*C*
	£	£	£
Year 2002/03	4,100	3,800	2,300
2003/04	2,085	11,280	7,435
2004/05		7,440	5,160
2005/06		10,680	7,320

Chapter 7: Chargeable gains: an outline

Activity 7.1

(a) Carol's taxable income is as follows.

	£
Taxable trading profits	33,980
Less personal allowance	(4,895)
Taxable income	29,085

(b) The gains to be taxed are as follows.

	£
Net chargeable gains	18,400
Less annual exemption	(8,500)
Taxable gains	9,900

(c) The tax bands are allocated as follows.

	Total	*Income*	*Gains*
	£	£	£
Starting rate	2,090	2,090	0
Basic rate	30,310	26,995	3,315
Higher rate	6,585	0	6,585
		29,085	9,900

(d) The CGT payable is as follows.

	£
£3,315 × 20%	663
£6,585 × 40%	2,634
Total CGT payable	3,297

Activity 7.2

	£
Taxable trading profits	24,150
Less personal allowance	(4,895)
Taxable income	19,255
Remaining basic rate band (£32,400 - £19,255)	13,145
Capital gains	22,300
Less: annual exemption	(8,500)
Taxable gains	13,800
CGT:	
£13,145 × 20%	2,629
655 × 40%	262
13,800	2,891

Activity 7.3

No: motor cars are exempt assets.

Activity 7.4

The current year loss must be deducted in full from the gain before taper relief is applied:

	£
Gain	40,600
Loss	(1,300)
Net gain	39,300

The asset was owned for 7 years complete years after 5.4.98 so:

	£
Gain after taper relief (25%)	9,825
Less: Annual exemption	(8,500)
Taxable gain	1,325

Activity 7.5

	£
Gain	17,800
Loss	(6,000)
Current net gains	11,800
Less: brought forward loss	(3,300)
Gains before taper relief	8,500
Gains after taper relief (1 year ownership) £8,500 × 50%	4,250
Less: annual exemption	(8,500)
Taxable gains	Nil

Note that the benefit of the taper relief is effectively wasted since the brought forward loss reduces the gain down to the annual exemption amount but the taper is then applied to that amount reducing it further.

The loss carried forward is £6,700 (£10,000 – £3,300).

Activity 7.6

TAXABLE INCOME AND GAINS

	£
Taxable trading Profits	25,650
Less: Personal allowance	(4,895)
Taxable income	20,755

	£
Gains	35,300
Less annual exemption	(8,500)
Taxable gains	26,800

£11,645 (£32,400 – £20,755) of the gains fall within the basic rate band and are taxed at 20%. The remaining gains are taxed at 40%.

The capital gains tax liability is as follows.

	£
£11,645 × 20%	2,329
£15,155 × 40%	6,062
£26,800	8,391

Activity 7.7

Motor cars are exempt assets, so the loss brought forward from 2004/05 is £6,300.

The position for 2005/06 is as follows.

	£
Gains	
Shares (no taper relief)	7,800
Business asset (no taper relief)	3,000
	10,800
Less loss on shares	(2,000)
	8,800
Less loss brought forward	(300)
	8,500
Less annual exemption	(8,500)
Chargeable gains	0

Gilt-edged securities are exempt assets. Losses brought forward are (unlike current year losses) only used to bring net gains down to the annual exempt amount.

The loss carried forward at the end of 2005/06 is £(6,300 – 300) = £6,000.

Taper relief was not available on the shares or the business asset as neither had been held for a complete year.

Chapter 8: The computation of gains and losses

Activity 8.1

No: it is not reflected in the state or nature of the asset at the time of disposal.

Activity 8.2

For individuals the indexation allowance is available until April 1998 and is computed as follows.

	£
0.959 × £5,000	4,795
0.835 × £2,000	1,670
	6,465

Activity 8.3

For companies, indexation runs to the date of disposal of an asset.

	£
Proceeds	180,000
Less: cost	(100,000)
Unindexed gain	80,000
Less: indexation allowance	
0.098 × £100,000	(9,800)
Indexed gain	70,200

Activity 8.4

	£
Proceeds	24,000
Less cost	97,000
Allowable loss	(73,000)

Indexation cannot increase a loss.

Activity 8.5

The amount of the original cost attributable to the part sold is

$$\frac{18{,}000}{18{,}000+36{,}000} \times £27{,}000 = £9{,}000$$

	£
Proceeds	18,000
Less cost (see above)	(9,000)
Unindexed gain	9,000
Less indexation allowance 0.858 × £9,000	(7,722)
Indexed gain	1,278

The chargeable gain after taper relief is £319 (£1,278 × 25%)

Activity 8.6

Cost: £150,000 × 190/(190 + 327) = £55,126

Incidental costs of disposal: £3,000

Total: £58,126

Activity 8.7

The racehorse is a wasting chattel (estimated useful life of less than 50 years) so any gain arising is exempt.

Activity 8.8

	£
Proceeds	7,000
Less incidental costs of sale	(700)
Net proceeds	6,300
Less cost	(800)
Unindexed gain	5,500
Less indexation 0.871 × £800	(697)
Indexed gain	4,803

The maximum gain is 5/3 × £(7,000 – 6,000) = £1,667

The chargeable gain is the lower of £4,803 and £1,667, so it is £1,667.

Note: Taper relief is not available to companies. However, indexation is available to the date of disposal of an asset.

Activity 8.9

	£
Proceeds (assumed)	6,000
Less incidental costs of disposal (£2,700 x 10/90)	(300)
	5,700
Less cost	(8,000)
Allowable loss (indexation allowance cannot increase a loss)	(2,300)

Activity 8.10

CAPITAL GAINS COMPUTATION

	£
Office block (W1)	22,760
Plot of land (W2)	16,768
Workshop (W3)	44,560
Painting (W4)	2,500
Less: loss on vase (W5)	(2,500)
Taxable gains	84,088

Workings

1 *The office block*

	£
Proceeds	120,000
Less cost	(65,000)
Unindexed gain	55,000
Less indexation allowance £65,000 × 0.496	(32,240)
Indexed gain	22,760

2 *The plot of land*

	£
Proceeds	69,000
Less: cost	(20,000)
expenditure in July 1986	(4,000)
Unindexed gain	45,000
Less: indexation allowance	
1.241 × £20,000	(24,820)
0.853 × £4,000	(3,412)
Indexed gain	16,768

3 *The workshop*

	£
Proceeds	173,000
Less: cost	(65,000)
Unindexed gain	108,000
Less: indexation allowance 0.976 × £65,000	(63,440)
Indexed gain	44,560

4 *Painting*

	£
Proceeds	7,500
Less: cost	(3,000)
Unindexed gain	4,500
Less: indexation allowance 0.155 × £3,000	(465)
Indexed gain	4,035

Restricted to 5/3 × £(7,500 – 6,000) = £2,500

5 *Vase*

	£
Deemed proceeds	6,000
Less: cost	(8,500)
Allowable loss	(2,500)

Indexation does not increase an allowable loss.

Tutorial note 1. The date of disposal for chargeable gains purposes is the date that the disposal becomes unconditional. In this case the date of exchange, not the date of completion.

Tutorial note 2. Companies are entitled to the indexation allowance up to the date of the disposal of an asset.

Chapter 9: Shares and securities

Activity 9.1

	No of shares	Cost	Indexed cost
		£	£
Value at 1.4.85	2,000	6,000	6,291
Indexed rise			
£6,291 × 0.028			176
	2,000	6,000	6,467
Acquisition	2,000	4,000	4,000
Value at 10.7.86	4,000	10,000	10,467

Activity 9.2

	No of shares	Cost	Indexed cost
		£	£
Value at 10.7.86	4,000	10,000	10,467
Indexed rise			
£10,467 × 0.949			9,933
	4,000	10,000	20,400
Disposal	(3,000)		
Cost and indexed cost $\frac{3,000}{4,000}$ × £10,000 and £20,400		(7,500)	(15,300)
Value at 10.7.04	1,000	2,500	5,100

The gain is computed as follows:

	£
Proceeds	17,000
Less cost	(7,500)
Unindexed gain	9,500
Less indexation allowance £(15,300 – 7,500)	(7,800)
Indexed gain	1,700

Note that for companies indexation runs to the date of disposal of an asset.

Activity 9.3

Matching of shares

(a) Acquisition in 30 days after disposal:

	£
Proceeds $\frac{5,000}{18,000}$ × £72,000	20,000
Less cost	(19,000)
Gain	1,000

(b) Post 5.4.98 acquisitions

	£
Proceeds $\frac{3,000}{18,000} \times$ £72,000	12,000
Less cost	(11,400)
Gain	600

No taper relief is due since the period of ownership was only 11 months.

(c) FA 1985 pool

	Number of shares	*Cost* £	*Indexed cost* £
11.90 Acquisition	10,000	25,000	25,000
Index to 4.98 0.251 × £25,000			6,275
Pool closes at 5.4.98	10,000	25,000	31,275
7.05 sales	10,000	25,000	31,275

Gain

	£
Proceeds $\frac{10,000}{18,000} \times$ £72,000	40,000
Less cost	(25,000)
Unindexed gain	15,000
Less indexation from FA 1985 pool £(31,275 – 25,000)	(6,275)
Indexed gain	8,725

The gain after taper relief is £2,181 (25% × £8,725)

Total gains after taper relief £(1,000 + 600 + 2,181) £3,781

Activity 9.4

(a) *Post 5.4.98 holding*

	Number	*Cost* £
Shares acquired 11.9.02	2,000	5,000
Shares acquired 1.2.04 (rights) 1:2 @ £2.75	1,000	2,750
	3,000	7,750

Gain

	£
Proceeds $\frac{3,000}{5,000} \times$ £15,000	9,000
Less: cost	(7,750)
Gain	1,250

Taper relief (based on ownership of original holding 11.9.02 – 10.9.05)

25% (Three years: business asset) × £1,250 £312

(b) *FA 1985 pool*

	Number	*Cost*	*Indexed cost*
		£	£
1.10.95	10,000	15,000	15,000
IA to 4.98 £15,000 × 0.085			1,275
Pool at 5.4.98	10,000	15,000	16,275
Rights issues 1.2.04	5,000	13,750	13,750
	15,000	28,750	30,025
14.10.05 Sale	(2,000)	(3,833)	(4,003)
c/f	13,000	24,917	26,022

Gain

	£
Proceeds $\frac{2,000}{5,000} \times £15,000$	6,000
Less: cost	(3,833)
Unindexed gain	2,167
Less: indexation £(4,003 – 3,833)	(170)
Indexed gain	1,997
Taper relief (based on original holding 6.4.98 – 5.4.05)	
25% (Seven years: business asset) × £1,997	£499

(c) Total gains (after taper relief)

£(312 + 499) £811

Activity 9.5

The FA 1985 pool

	No of shares	*Cost*	*Indexed cost*
		£	£
July 1985	1,000	3,000	3,000
Indexed rise to May 1986 £3,000 × 0.027			81
May 1986 one for four rights	250	1,050	1,050
	1,250	4,050	4,131
Indexed rise to October 2005 £4,131 × 0.949			3,920
	1,250	4,050	8,051
Disposal in October 2005	(1,250)	(4,050)	(8,051)

	£
Proceeds	10,000
Less cost	(4,050)
Unindexed gain	5,950
Less indexation allowance £(8,051 – 4,050)	(4,001)
Indexed gain	1,949

Note that companies do not get taper relief but they get indexation to the date of disposal of an asset.

Activity 9.6

Post 6.4.98 acquisitions: match on a LIFO basis.

17.1.05

	£
Proceeds $\left(\frac{2,000}{6,000} \times £24,000\right)$	8,000
Less: cost	(6,000)
Chargeable gain	2,000

No taper relief as the shares have not been held for a complete year.

12.12.03

	£
Proceeds $\left(\frac{2,000}{6,000} \times £24,000\right)$	8,000
Less: cost	(5,500)
Chargeable gain	2,500

Chargeable gain after taper relief £1,250 (£2,500 × 50%)

The FA 1985 pool

	Shares	*Cost*	*Indexed cost*
		£	£
Acquisition 19.9.85	2,000	1,700	1,700
Indexation to April 1998 (Pool closes)			
£1,700 × 0.704			1,197
Value when pool closes (5.4.98)	2,000	1,700	2,897
Disposal 17.5.05	(2,000)	(1,700)	(2,897)
	0	0	0

	£
Proceeds $\frac{2,000}{6,000} \times £24,000$	8,000
Less cost	(1,700)
Unindexed gain	6,300
Less indexation allowance £(2,897 – 1,700)	(1,197)
Indexed gain	5,103

The chargeable gain after taper relief is £1,276 (£5,103 × 25%)

The total gains are £(2,000 + 1,250 + 1,276) = £4,526.

Activity 9.7

Previous nine days

	£
Proceeds $\frac{1,500}{4,000}$ × £44,000	16,500
Less: cost	(15,000)
Gain	1,500

No indexation allowance on disposals of shares acquired in previous nine days.

FA 1985 pool

		No of shares	*Cost*	*Indexed cost*
			£	£
11.7.88	Acquisition	1,000	5,000	5,000
19.9.99	Acquisition			
	Indexed rise £5,000 × 0.558			2,790
	Purchase	2,000	18,000	18,000
c/f		3,000	23,000	25,790
3.8.05	Disposal			
	Indexed rise £25,788 × 0.145			3,740
				29,530
	Sale	(2,500)	(19,167)	(24,608)
c/f		500	3,833	4,922

Gain

	£
Proceeds $\frac{2,500}{4,000}$ × £44,000	27,500
Less: cost	(19,167)
Unindexed gain	8,333
Less: indexation allowance (24,608 – 19,167)	(5,441)
Indexed gain	2,892

Chapter 10: Deferral reliefs

Activity 10.1

	£
Market value	120,000
Less: gain	(50,000)
Base cost	70,000

Activity 10.2

(a) *Angelo's CGT position (2005/06)*

	£
Proceeds	200,000
Less cost	(30,000)
Gain – subject to gift relief claim	170,000

(b) *Michael's CGT position (2006/07)*

	£
Proceeds	195,000
Less cost £(200,000 – 170,000)	(30,000)
Gain	165,000
Chargeable gain after taper relief (50%)	£82,500

Note. Michael acquired the asset on 6 December 2005 and sold it in May 2007. He therefore owned the asset for one complete year. 50% of the gain is taxable. Michael is not allowed to use any taper relief built up by Angelo.

Activity 10.3

The company is not a trading company

Activity 10.4

	£
Rollover gain	17,950
Cost of new factory	80,000
Less: rolled over gain	(17,950)
Base cost of new factory	62,050

Activity 10.5

31 December 2005 disposal

	£
Sale proceeds	491,400
Cost (5.11.1998)	(204,579)
Gain before taper relief	286,821

Since a replacement asset was purchased within the required time period, the gain before taper relief of £286,821 is rolled over against the cost of the new asset.

3 September 2007 disposal

	£	£
Sale proceeds		914,550
Cost (1 November 2005)	546,000	
Less: rollover relief	(286,821)	
		(259,179)
Gain		655,371

Ownership period is 1 November 2005 to 3 September 2007
= 1 complete year of ownership

Gain after taper relief	
Taxable gain (50%) for Karen	£327,686

Activity 10.6

(a) *Gain on gift*

	£
Market value of gift	25,000
Less: cost	(10,000)
Gift relief gain	15,000

This gain is reduced to £nil on gift relief claim

Gain on sale

	£
Proceeds	35,000
Less: cost (25,000 – 15,000)	(10,000)
Gift before taper relief	25,000

Taper relief period Sept 2004 – Sept 2005 = 1 year

£25,000 × 50% =	£12,500

(b)

	£	£
Gain on gift before taper relief (see (a))	15,000	
Gain after taper relief (25%)		3,750
Proceeds	35,000	
Less: cost	(25,000)	
Gain before taper relief	10,000	
Gain after taper relief £10,000 × 50%		5,000
		8,750

∴ Total gains are smaller if gift relief is not claimed

Activity 10.7

Gain on first factory

	£
Proceeds	200,000
Less: cost	(150,000)
Unindexed gain	50,000
Less: indexation allowance 0.078 × £150,000	(11,700)
Indexed Gain	38,300

This was all rolled over into the second factory because the **full proceeds** were 'reinvested' within the required time frame.

Gain on second factory

	£
Proceeds	275,000
Less: cost £(250,000 – 38,300)	(211,700)
Unindexed gain	63,300
Less: indexation allowance 0.077 × £211,700	(16,301)
Indexed gain	46,999

Tutorial note

If the second factory had been purchased for £190,000, £10,000 of the gain would have been immediately chargeable. The balance of the gain, £28,300 would have been rolled into the base cost of the second factory.

Chapter 11: An outline of corporation tax

Activity 11.1

The 18 month period of account is divided into:

Year ending 31 December 2005
6 months to 30 June 2006

Results are allocated:

	Y/e 31.12.05	*6m to 30.6.06*
	£	£
Taxable trading profits 12:6	120,000	60,000
Interest		
12 × £500	6,000	
6 × £500		3,000
Capital gain (1.5.06)		250,000
Less: Charge on income	(50,000)	
PCTCT (profits chargeable to corporation tax)	76,000	313,000

Activity 11.2

	£
Taxable trading profit	85,000
Interest £(6,000 + 1,500 + 3,200)	10,700
Chargeable gains	2,950
	98,650
Less charges	(15,200)
Profits chargeable to corporation tax	83,450

Activity 11.3

	£	£
Net profit per accounts		121,492
Less: Bank deposit interest	700	
dividends received	3,600	
building society interest	292	
		(4,592)
		116,900
Add: gift aid donation		1,100
		118,000
Less: capital allowances		(5,500)
PCTCT		112,500
Interest £(700 + 292)		992
Chargeable gain		13,867
		127,359
Less: charges paid: gift aid donation		(1,100)
Profits chargeable to corporation tax (PCTCT)		126,259

Activity 11.4

£2,000,000 × 30% = £600,000

Activity 11.5

	£
PCTCT	42,000
Dividend grossed up £9,000 × 100/90	10,000
'Profits' (below £300,000 limit)	52,000
Corporation tax payable	
£42,000 × 19%	£7,980

Activity 11.6

	£
PCTCT	9,500
Dividend grossed up £270 × 100/90	300
'Profits'	9,800
Corporation tax on PCTCT £9,500 × 0%	£ NIL

Activity 11.7

	£
PCTCT	296,000
Dividend grossed up £12,600 × 100/90	14,000
'Profits'	310,000

'Profits' are above £300,000 but below £1,500,000, so small companies' marginal relief applies.

	£
Corporation tax on PCTCT £296,000 × 30%	88,800
Less small companies' marginal relief	
£(1,500,000 – 310,000) × 296,000/310,000 × 11/400	(31,247)
	57,553

Activity 11.8

	£
PCTCT	29,500
Dividend grossed up £2,700 × 100/90	3,000
Profits	32,500

	£
Corporation tax at small companies rate:	
£29,500 × 19%	5,605
Less: starting rate marginal relief	
19/400 × ((£50,000 – £32,500) × £29,500/£32,500)	(755)
Corporation tax payable	4,850

Activity 11.9

	FY 2005 *3 months to* *31.3.06*	*FY 2006* *9 months to* *31.12.06*
	£	£
PCTCT (divided 3:9)	10,000	30,000
'Profits' (divided 3:9)	10,625	31,875
Lower limit for Starting rate		
FY 2005 £10,000 × 3/12	2,500	
FY 2006 £10,000 × 9/12		7,500
Upper limit for Starting rate		
FY 2005 £50,000 × 3/12	12,500	
FY 2006 £50,000 × 9/12		37,500
Tax on PCTCT		
FY 2005: £10,000 × 19%		1,900
Less: Starting rate marginal relief		
£(12,500 – 10,625) × 10,000/10,625 × 19/400		(84)
		1,816
FY 2006: £30,000 × 20%	6,000	
Less: starting rate marginal relief		
£(37,500 – 31,875) × 30,000/31,875 × 1/40	(132)	
		5,868
Corporation tax payable		7,684

Activity 11.10

(a) Division of the lower limit for the starting rate by the number of associated companies + 1

$£10,000 \times {}^{1}/_{3} = £3,333$

(b) Reduction in the lower limit for the starting rate as the accounting period is only nine months long

$£3,333 \times {}^{9}/_{12} = £2,500$

(c) Reduction in the upper limit for the starting rate

$£50,000 \times {}^{1}/_{3} \times {}^{9}/_{12} = £12,500$

(d) Reduction in the lower limit for SCR

$£300,000 \times {}^{1}/_{3} \times {}^{9}/_{12} = £75,000$

(e) Reduction in the upper limit for SCR

$£1,500,000 \times {}^{1}/_{3} \times {}^{9}/_{12} = £375,000$

(f) 'Profits' = £78,000

As 'profits' fall between the lower and upper limits for SCR purposes, the full rate less small companies' marginal relief applies:

(g) Corporation tax

	£
£78,000 × 30%	23,400
Less: small companies' marginal relief £(375,000 – 78,000) × 11/400	(8,168)
Corporation tax	15,232

Activity 11.11

Tutorial note. Long periods of account are always split into the first 12 months and the remainder. Taxable trading profits before capital allowances are time apportioned and interest is allocated on an accrued basis. In this case the interest accrues evenly, so can simply be time apportioned. Chargeable gains are allocated to the period they are realised and gift aid donations to the period in which they are paid. When there is a change in the rate of corporation tax it is important that you split the accounting period into financial years in order to calculate the corporation tax.

Tree Ltd

	Year to 30.6.05	*Six months to 31.12.05*
	£	£
Taxable trading profits (12/18: 6/18)	120,000	60,000
Chargeable gain	172,000	
Interest (12/18: 6/18)	24,000	12,000
Less: charge on income	(22,000)	(5,000)
Profits chargeable to corporation tax	294,000	67,000
Year to 30.6.05		
Corporation tax (W1)		
FY 04 and FY 05		
£294,000 × 30%	88,200	
Less 11/400 (1,500,000 – 324,000) × $\frac{294,000}{324,000}$	(29,346)	
	58,854	
Six months to 31.12.05 (W2)		
£67,000 × 19%		£12,730

Workings

1. Tax rate: year to 30.6.05

   The year to 30.6.05 falls into FY04 and FY05. As the rates of tax and marginal rate bands for both years are the same we do not need to split the profit between the financial years.

   As 'profits' are between the small companies' upper and lower limits in both financial years, small companies' marginal relief applies in both financial years. This can be calculated in one step as there has not been a change to the rates.

2. The six month period to 31.12.05 falls in the financial year 2005. As profits of £67,000 are above the starting rate upper limit of £25,000 and below the small companies rate lower limit of £150,000 for this period, the small companies rate applies.

Chapter 12: Corporation tax losses

Activity 12.1

		Year ended	
	31.3.04	*31.3.05*	*31.3.06*
	£	£	£
Taxable trading profits	20,000	24,000	20,000
Capital gain	–	–	1,000
PCTCT	20,000	24,000	21,000

Tutorial note. The capital loss must be carried forward to set against the gains in future periods. It cannot be set against taxable trading profits.

Activity 12.2

		Year ended	
	31.3.04	*31.3.05*	*31.3.06*
	£	£	£
Taxable trading profits	0	3,000	6,000
Less: s 393(1) loss relief		(3,000)	(5,550)
	0	0	450
Rental property income	0	1,000	1,000
PCTCT	0	1,000	1,450

Note that the trading loss carried forward is set only against the trading profit in future years. It cannot be set against the property income.

Loss memorandum

	£
Loss for y/e 31.3.04	8,550
Less s 393(1) relief y/e 31.3.05	(3,000)
Loss carried forward at 1.4.05	5,550
Less s 393(1) relief y/e 31.3.06	(5,550)
Loss carried forward at 1.4.06	0

Activity 12.3

The loss of the year to 30.9.06 is relieved under s 393A ICTA 1988 against current year profits and against profits of the previous twelve months.

	Year ended		
	30.9.04	*30.9.05*	*30.9.06*
	£	£	£
Taxable trading profits	10,500	10,000	0
Interest	500	500	500
Chargeable gains	0	0	4,000
	11,000	10,500	4,500
Less s 393A current period relief	0	0	(4,500)
	11,000	10,500	0
Less s 393A carryback relief	0	(10,500)	0
	11,000	0	0
Less: Non-trade charges	(250)	0	0
PCTCT	10,750	0	0
Unrelieved non-trade charges		250	250

S 393A (1) loss memorandum	£
Loss incurred in y/e 30.9.06	35,000
Less s 393A (1): y/e 30.9.06	(4,500)
y/e 30.9.05	(10,500)
Loss available to carry forward under s 393(1)	20,000

Activity 12.4

A s 393A(1) claim for the year ended 31 March 2005 will save tax partly in the small companies' marginal relief band, partly at the small companies rate and partly in the starting rate marginal relief band. It will waste the gift aid donation of £20,000.

PCTCT in the previous year is £7,000 (£35,000 + £2,000 – £30,000). This falls into the starting rate band lower limit so no corporation tax would have been due in this year and there is no point in making a loss claim.

If no current period s 393A(1) claim is made, £200,000 of the loss will save tax at the small companies rate and in the starting rate marginal relief band in the year ended 31 March 2006, with £20,000 of gift aid donations being wasted. The remaining £800,000 of the loss, would be carried forward to the year ended 31 March 2007 and later years to save tax at the small companies rate and in the starting rate marginal relief band.

To conclude a s 393A(1) claim should be made for the year of the loss but not in the previous year. £20,000 of gift aid donations would be wasted in the current year, but much of the loss would save tax at the small companies' marginal corporation tax rate and relief would be obtained quickly.

The final computations are as follows.

	Year ended 31 March		
	2004	*2005*	*2006*
	£	£	£
Taxable trading profits	2,000	0	200,000
Less s 393(1) relief	0	0	(200,000)
	2,000	0	0
Chargeable gains	35,000	750,000	0
	37,000	750,000	0
Less: s 393A current relief	0	(750,000)	0
	37,000	0	0
Less: gift aid	(30,000)	0	0
Profits chargeable to corporation tax	7,000	0	
MCT at 0%	0	0	0
Unrelieved gift aid donations	0	20,000	20,000

Activity 12.5

Profits chargeable to corporation tax

	Year ended 31.12.03	*6 months ended 30.6.04*	*Year ended 30.6.05*
	£	£	£
Taxable trading profits	109,000	85,000	0
Interest	11,000	12,000	14,000
Chargeable gains (losses are carried forward)	0	0	0
	120,000	97,000	14,000
Less s 393A(1) current period relief	–	–	(14,000)
	120,000	97,000	0
Less: s 393A carryback	(60,000)	(97,000)	0
	60,000	0	0
Less: gift aid donation	0	0	0
PCTCT	60,000	0	0
CT @ 19%	11,400	0	0
Unrelieved gift aid donation	0	3,000	1,000

Loss memorandum	£
Loss	200,000
Less s 393A(1) relief	(14,000)
Less s 393A(1) relief (6 months)	(97,000)
Less 6/12 × £120,000 (restricted)	(60,000)
Loss carried forward	29,000

A loss of £29,000 is available at 30 June 2005 to carry forward against future profits of the same trade. The loss carried back under s 393A ICTA 1988 can be carried back only to set against total profits of the previous 12 months.

There is also a capital loss of £4,000 to carry forward against future chargeable gains at 30.6.05. Note that capital losses cannot be carried back. The £5,000 capital loss in y/e 31.12.03 is offset to the extent of £2,000 in period ended 30.6.04 and the carried forward balance of £3,000 is added to the carried forward £1,000 capital loss of y/e 30.6.05 to total £4,000.

Chapter 13: National insurance

Activity 13.1

Earnings threshold £4,895 ÷ 12 = £408

Secondary contributions

£(2,750 – 408) = £2,342 × 12.8% = £299.78 × 12 = £3,597.36

Activity 13.2

'Earnings' £(200 + 50) = £250

Business travel reimbursed and relocation expenses are not treated as earnings.

Earnings threshold – £4,895 ÷ 52 = £94

£(250 – 94) = £156 × 12.8% = £19.97

Activity 13.3

£10,000 × 12.8% = £1,280

There is no earnings threshold in respect of Class 1A contributions.

Activity 13.4

	£
Profits	14,100
Less lower limit	(4,895)
	9,205

Class 4 NICs = 8% × £9,205 = £736.40 (main only)

Activity 13.5

	£
Profits (upper limit)	32,760
Less lower limit	(4,895)
	27,865

	£
Main rate Class 4 NICs 8% × £27,865	2,229.20
Additional rate class 4 NICs £(35,000 – 32,760) = £2,240 × 1%	22.40
	2,251.60

Activity 13.6

(a) *Class 1*

Earnings £2,500 per month

Monthly earnings threshold £4,895 ÷ 12 = £408

Secondary contributions

£(2,500 – 408) = £2,092 × 12.8% = £267.78 × 12 = £3,213.36

Class 1A

Car and medical insurance

£(5,000 + 750) = £5,750 × 12.8% = £736.00

Total contributions = £3,949.36

Childcare vouchers are less than £50 per week and so are not liable to Class 1 NICs, nor Class IA NICs

(b) *Class 2 contributions*

£2.10 × 52 = £109.20

Class 4 contributions

	£
Profits (upper limit)	32,760
Less: lower limit	(4,895)
	27,865

	£
Main rate Class 4 NICs	
8% × £27,865	2,229.20
Additional rate Class 4 NICs	
1% × (38,000 – 32,760)	52.40
Class 4 contributions	2,281.60
Total contributions (109.20 + 2,220.80)	£2,390.80

Chapter 14: Administration of income tax and CGT

Activity 14.1

	£
Total income tax	9,200
Less: tax credits (1,700 + 1,500)	(3,200)
	6,000

Payments on account for 2006/07:

31 January 2007:	Income tax £6,000 × 1/2	£3,000
31 July 2007:	As before, income tax	£3,000

There is no requirement to make payments on account of capital gains tax.

Activity 14.2

Income tax = £18,000 – £2,750 – £6,500 – £6,500 = £2,250

CGT = £5,120

Final payment due on 31 January 2007 for 2005/06 = £2,250 + £5,120 = £7,370

Activity 14.3

Herbert made an excessive claim to reduce his payments on account, and will therefore be charged interest on the reduction. The payments on account should have been £4,500 each based on the 2004/05 liability (not £5,000 each based on the 2005/06 liability). The balancing payment is £10,000 + 2,500 – 2 × 3,500 = £5,500. Interest will be charged as follows:

(a) first payment on account

- (i) on £3,500 – nil – paid on time
- (ii) on £1,000 from due date of 31 January 2006 to day before payment, 18 February 2007

(b) second payment on account

- (i) on £3,500 from due date of 31 July 2006 to day before payment, 11 August 2006
- (ii) on £1,000 from due date of 31 July 2006 to day before payment, 18 February 2007

(c) balancing payment

- (i) on £5,500 from due date of 31 January 2007 to day before payment, 18 February 2007

Activity 14.4

Tutorial note. Three payments of income tax may need to be made in respect of a tax year. Two payments of account are normally made on 31 January in the tax year and on the following 31 July. These are based on the prior year tax liability. A final balancing payment of the income tax due for a year is normally made on the 31 January following the year.

Tim's Payments on Account for 2005/06 were based on the excess of his 2004/05 tax liability over amounts deducted under the PAYE system, amounts deducted at source and tax credits on dividends:

	£
2004/05 tax liability	16,800
Less: PAYE	(7,200)
Tax deducted at source	(800)
Tax credit on dividends	(200)
Total payments on account for 2005/06	8,600

Two equal payments on account of £4,300 (£8,600 / 2) were required. The due dates for these payments were 31 January 2006 and 31 July 2006 respectively.

The final payment in respect of Tim's 2005/06 tax liability was due on 31 January 2007 and was calculated as follows:

	£
2005/06 tax liability	22,000
Less: PAYE	(7,100)
Tax deducted at source	(900)
Tax credit on dividends	(250)
	13,750
Less: Payments on account	(8,600)
Final payment due 31.1.07	5,150

Chapter 15: Payment of tax by companies

Activity 15.1

The company must file a return for the two accounting periods ending in the period specified in the notice requiring a return. The first accounting period is the twelve months to 31 December 2004 and the second is the six months to 30 June 2005. The filing date is twelve months after the end of the relevant period of account, 30 June 2006.

Activity 15.2

A The return is less than three months late and it is only the second late filing of a return so the fixed penalty is £100.

Activity 15.3

D Notice of an enquiry must be given by a year after the later of:

(a) the filing date, ie 30 June 2007

(b) the 31 January, 30 April, 31 July or 31 October following the actual delivery of the return, ie 31 October 2007

Thus 31 October 2007

Activity 15.4

B The instalments are due on the 14th of the month. For a twelve month accounting period the first instalment is due in the seventh month and thereafter instalments are due at three monthly intervals.

Take care: In this question you were asked for the due date of the **FINAL QUARTERLY INSTALMENT**. This is due in the fourth month after the end of the accounting period.

Activity 15.5

£880,000 must be paid in instalments.

The amount of each instalment is $3 \times \frac{£880,000}{8} = £330,000$

The due dates are:

	£
14 August 2005	330,000
14 November 2005	330,000
14 January 2006 (balance)	220,000

Activity 15.6

A Patent royalties received from individuals are received net of 22% tax:

$£7,800 \times \frac{22}{78} = £2,200.$

As the debenture interest was paid to another UK company, it would have been paid gross

Activity 15.7

Tutorial note. 'Large' companies must pay their CT liabilities in quarterly instalments.

(a) Hogg Ltd's corporation tax liability for the year is £1,750,000 × 30% = £525,000. The due dates for the payment of corporation tax by Hogg Ltd in respect of the year to 31.12.05 are:

		£
14 July 2005	1/4 × £525,000	131,250
14 October 2005	1/4 × £525,000	131,250
14 January 2006	1/4 × £525,000	131,250
14 April 2006	1/4 × £525,000	131,250
Total		525,000

(b) The due dates for the payment of corporation tax instalments by Hogg Ltd in respect of the ten months to 31 October 2007 are:

	£
14 July 2007	180,000
14 October 2007	180,000
14 January 2008	180,000
14 February 2008 (4th month of next accounting period) (balance)	60,000

Tutorial note: The amount of the instalments is $^3/_n \times CT = {^3/_{10}} \times £600,000 = £180,000$.

PART G

Practice activities

Practice activities are short activities directly related to the actual content of the corresponding chapter in this text.

chapter 1

Introduction to business taxation

Activity checklist

This checklist shows which performance criteria are covered by this activity. Full details of the performance criteria are shown on page (xiii) onwards. Tick off the activity when you complete it.

Activity		
1	☐	This is an introductory activity and no specific performance criteria are relevant to it

This activity covers Knowledge and Understanding points 2 and 4.

1 Income tax computation

John Smith has the following income and outgoings for the tax year 2005/06.

		£
(i)	Taxable trading profits	45,000
(ii)	Interest on a deposit account with the Scotia Bank	1,000
(iii)	Dividends on UK shares	1,000

Tasks

(a) Prepare a schedule of income for 2005/06, clearly showing the distinction between non-savings, savings and dividend income. John Smith's personal allowance should be deducted as appropriate.

(b) Calculate the income tax liability for 2005/06.

2090
32400
32401

chapter 2

Computing trading income

Activity checklist

This checklist shows which performance criteria are covered by each activity in this chapter. Full details of the performance criteria are shown on page (xiii) onwards. Tick off each activity as you complete it.

Activity		
2		Performance Criteria 18.2A
3		Performance Criteria 18.2A and 18.2B
4		Performance Criteria 18.1A and 18.2A

2 Idaho

Idaho has been in business as a sole trader for many years, making up accounts to 31 December. His profit and loss account for the year ended 31 December 2005 is as follows.

	£	£
Gross trading profit		275,000
Interest received on building society investment account		270
Rent received on office space let to tenants		5,700
		280,970
Expenses		
Wages	105,000	
Depreciation	10,000	
Repairs	6,500	
Overdraft interest on the business bank account	450	
Donation to a political party	700	
Legal charges	1,700	
Rent of premises	18,000	
Bad and doubtful debts	1,850	
		144,200
Net profit		136,770

Notes

(a) Wages include £12,000 paid to Idaho.

(b) Repairs include a £500 general provision for repairs to be undertaken in 2006, and £3,000 for the redecoration of office premises, one third of which are let to tenants.

(c) The overdraft interest paid in the year was £400. There was a closing accrual of £50.

(d) Legal charges comprised the following.

	£
Debt collection	500
Renewal of a lease of premises used wholly by the business for 40 years	300
Service contract for a senior employee	200
Conduct of a tax appeal which Idaho won	700
	1,700

(e) The rent paid includes £12,000 in respect of office premises, one third of which are let to tenants.

(f) The bad and doubtful debts account shows an opening general provision of £10,000 and a closing general provision of £8,800.

(g) During the year Idaho took goods for his own use. They had cost £1,500 and would normally have been sold for £2,600. Idaho credited the sales account and debited his drawings account with £1,500.

(h) No assets qualify for capital allowances.

Task

Compute Idaho's taxable trading profits based on these accounts.

Guidance notes

1. You are asked to compute the adjusted profit. You should therefore start by setting out a pro forma, starting with the accounts profit and leaving plenty of space for adding disallowable items, and rather less space for deducting any items not taxable as trading income. It does not matter if you end up not using all the space.
2. You should then work systematically through the detailed profit and loss account and the notes, taking any items for which an adjustment is needed to your pro forma as you go.
3. Finally, add up your adjusted profit computation.

3 George

George carries on a trade as a drapery wholesaler making up accounts to 31 January in each year.

His trading and profit and loss account for the year ended 31 January 2006 is as follows.

	£	£
Sales		825,630
Less: opening stock	105,966	
purchases	720,273	
	826,239	
less closing stock	(83,203)	
		(743,036)
Gross profit		82,594
Less: wages	22,504	
rent, rates, light and heat	26,492	
repairs	7,206	
professional charges	1,000	
sundry expenses	3,962	
travelling and entertaining	9,041	
bad debts	1,336	
depreciation	2,874	
		(74,415)
Profit for the year		8,179

Notes

		£
(a)	Professional charges	
	Debt collection	150
	Accountancy	760
	Advice regarding trading agreement	90
		1,000
(b)	Sundry expenses	
	Chamber of Commerce subscription	22
	Donations to local charities	18
	Sundry allowable expenses	3,922
		3,962

		£
(c)	Travelling and entertaining	
	General travelling including travellers' car expenses	7,527
	Expenses of George's car	640
	Entertaining	874
		9,041
(d)	Bad debts	
	Amounts written off trade debtors	541
	Further general provision	795
		1,336

The private use by George of his car is 25%.

Task

Compute the taxable trading profits for income tax purposes based on these accounts. Ignore capital allowances

4 Analyses of items

When submitting accounts to the Revenue, it may be necessary to provide an analysis of the following profit and loss items.

(a) Repairs
(b) Legal expenses
(c) Gifts and entertainment

Task

Summarise the rules which determine how the items appearing under each of the above headings will be dealt with in arriving at the taxable trading profit or loss.

chapter 3

Capital allowances

Activity checklist

This checklist shows which performance criteria, are covered by each activity in this chapter. Full details of the performance criteria are covered on page (xiii) onwards. Tick off each activity as you complete it.

Activity		
5	☐	Performance Criteria 18.1C
6	☐	Performance Criteria 18.1B
7	☐	Performance Criteria 18.1B
8	☐	Performance Criteria 18.1B
9	☐	Performance Criteria 18.1B
10	☐	Performance Criteria 18.1B
11	☐	Performance Criteria 18.1B

5 Saruman

Saruman is the sole proprietor of a small engineering business. He prepares accounts annually to 31 March.

General pool brought forward on 1 April 2005	£52,000
Tax written down value of motor car for Saruman's use on 1 April 2005.	£600

Private use of this car is 25%.

The following events occurred during the year ended 31 March 2006.

Disposals:	20 April 2005	–	Plant £12,000 (original cost £10,000)
	21 May 2005	–	Motor car for Saruman's own use £920 (original cost £1,896)
	20 June 2005	–	Plant £800 (original cost £3,000)
Additions:	1 May 2005	–	New plant £5,000
	21 May 2005	–	New car for Saruman's use £19,000
	1 October 2005	–	Estate car for use of sales representative £4,800

Saruman's business is a small enterprise for first year allowance purposes.

Tasks

Calculate capital allowances for the year ending 31 March 2006.

Guidance notes

1. When tackling a capital allowances computation, the first step is to set out the headings of the columns clearly, leaving plenty of space for items that need individual treatment (such as assets with private use).
2. Deal systematically with the additions and disposals, and calculate the total for each column before working out the capital allowances available.
3. Don't forget FYA where relevant.

6 Dexter Ltd

Dexter Ltd, makes accounts to 30 June. Despite substantial investment in new equipment, business has been indifferent and the company will cease trading on 31 December 2005. Its last accounts will be prepared for the six months to 31 December 2005.

The tax written down value of fixed assets at 1 July 2001 was as follows.

Pool	£
General	29,700

Fixed asset additions and disposals have been as follows.

		£
20.9.01	Digging machine cost	1,917
25.6.02	Computer cost	3,667
15.7.03	Car for managing director's use cost	13,400
14.7.04	Plant sold for	340
10.5.05	Computer sold for	2,000

An election to depool the computer was made when it was acquired in 2002. Private use of the managing director's car was 20% for all years.

At the end of 2005, the plant would be worth £24,000, the managing director's car £10,600.

Task

Calculate the capital allowances for the periods from 1 July 2001 to 31 December 2005. Dexter Ltd has always been a medium sized enterprise for First Year Allowance purposes.

7 Green Ltd

On 1 April 2005 the tax written down values of plant and machinery in Green Ltd's tax computations were as follows.

	£
Pool	106,000
Expensive car	7,000
Short life asset (spring end grinding machine)	17,500

The short-life asset was purchased on 7 August 2000 and was sold on 19 November 2005 for £5,000.

On 1 January 2006 the expensive car was traded in for £6,000 against a new car costing £14,000 (the full price before the trade-in allowance).

There were no other purchases or sales during the year. The company had always prepared accounts to 31 March.

Task

Calculate the maximum capital allowances available in the year ended 31 March 2006.

8 Chilterns Ltd

Chilterns Ltd is a small UK trading company with an accounting year-end of 31 March. The following transactions in plant took place in the year ending 31 March 2006:

Purchases		
15 May 2005	A second hand machine	£5,000
14 June 2005	A new machine	£9,000
17 August 2005	A new car	£10,000
Disposals		
12 June 2005	A machine (original cost £3,500)	£4,000

In addition to the above, a car which had cost £18,000 some years ago was traded in for a new car. The trade in value of the old car was £6,000 and additional cash of £9,000 was paid for the new car.

The tax written down values brought forward as at 1 April 2005 were:

Plant and machinery	£16,000
Expensive car	£8,500

Chilterns Ltd is a small enterprise for capital allowance purposes.

Task

Calculate the maximum capital allowances that can be claimed by Chilterns Ltd for its accounting period ending 31 March 2006.

9 Industrial Building

A plc bought a new small factory from a builder for a total cost of £40,000, including land £10,000 and office accommodation £3,000. The factory was purchased and brought into use on 10 September 2005. The company prepares accounts to 31 December each year.

Task

Show what industrial buildings allowances the company will be entitled to in its year to 31 December 2005.

Guidance notes

1 When dealing with industrial buildings allowances, two dates are critical: the date the building is brought into use and the final day of the period concerned. No WDAs are due before a building is brought into use and it is the use the building is put to on the final day of the period that determines whether an allowance is due for the period.

2 IBAs are never available on land. Are they available on the office accommodation?

10 Biswas Ltd

On 1 September 2005 Biswas Ltd purchased a second hand factory for £80,000. This had cost the original purchaser £100,000 on 1 September 1995 and had always been in industrial use. Biswas Ltd immediately used the factory as an industrial building.

Biswas Ltd had purchased its current factory (still in use) in August 2000 for a total cost of £190,000. This cost had been made up as follows:

Land	£55,000
Tunnelling	£10,000
Showroom	£35,000
Factory	£85,000

Task

Calculate the maximum IBAs that can be claimed by Biswas Ltd for its accounting period ended 31 March 2006.

11 Extensions Ltd

Extensions Ltd bought a factory in January 1998 for £40,000. The cost of administration offices included in the purchase price of £40,000 was £5,000. A second factory was built in 1999 and cost £70,000 of which £25,000 was for administration offices.

In June 2005 £22,500 was paid to erect a third factory on a nearby industrial estate. Extensions Ltd started to use the third factory in April 2006.

The first and second factories were both in use for industrial purposes at 31 March 2006.

Task

Calculate the maximum industrial buildings allowances available in the year end 31.3.06.

chapter 4

Basis of assessment for unincorporated businesses

Activity checklist

This checklist shows which performance criteria, are covered by each activity in this chapter. Full details of the performance criteria on page (xiii) onwards. Tick off each activity as you complete it.

Activity		
12	☐	Performance Criteria 18.2D
13	☐	Performance Criteria 18.2D
14	☐	Performance Criteria 18.2D.
15	☐	Performance Criteria 18.1C and 18.2D.

12 Rachel

Rachel commenced in business as a fashion designer on 1 July 2003, and made up her first accounts to 30 April 2005. Her profit for the period, adjusted for taxation, was £33,000.

Tasks

(a) Calculate the taxable profit for the first three tax years.
(b) Calculate the 'overlap profits'.

13 Jackie Smith

Jackie Smith started her picture framing business on 1 May 2001. Due to falling profits she ceased to trade on 28 February 2006.

Her profits for the whole period of trading were as follows.

	£
1 May 2001 – 31 July 2002	18,000
1 August 2002 – 31 July 2003	11,700
1 August 2003 – 31 July 2004	8,640
1 August 2004 – 31 July 2005	4,800
1 August 2005 – 28 February 2006	5,100

Task

Calculate the total assessable profits for each of the tax years concerned.

You are to assume that ALL possible claims are made.

14 Otto

Otto is a self-employed television engineer. He commenced in business on 1 June 2002 and makes up accounts to 30 November each year.

Otto's recent results have been:

	£
1.6.02 – 30.11.02	7,000
1.12.02 – 30.11.03	16,000
1.12.03 – 30.11.04	19,000
1.12.04– 30.11.05	25,000

Task

Calculate the amounts chargeable to income tax as taxable trading profits for the years 2002/03, 2003/04, 2004/05 and 2005/06. Show any amounts of overlap relief available to carry forward.

15 Miss Farrington

Miss Farrington started to trade as a baker on 1 January 2003 and made up her first accounts to 30 April 2004. Adjusted profits before capital allowances are as follows.

	£
Period to 30 April 2004	20,710
Year to 30 April 2005	15,125

Miss Farrington incurred the following expenditure on plant and machinery.

Date	Item	£
4.1.03	General plant	3,835
1.3.03	Secondhand oven acquired from Miss Farrington's father	1,200
25.3.03	Delivery van	1,800
15.4.03	Typewriter	425
15.5.03	Car for Miss Farrington	6,600
15.1.05	General plant	1,000
30.1.05	Computer	1,556

In addition Miss Farrington brought into the business on 1 January 2003 a desk and other office furniture. The agreed value was £940.

The agreed private use of the car is 35%. Miss Farrington's business is a small enterprise for capital allowance purposes.

Task

(a) Calculate Miss Farrington's capital allowances for her first two periods of account.

(b) Compute Miss Farrington's trading profits for her first two periods of account.

(c) Calculate the taxable trading profits for the first four tax years and the overlap profits carried forward.

chapter 5

Trading losses

Activity checklist

This checklist shows which performance criteria, are covered by each activity in this chapter. Full details of the performance criteria on page (xiii) onwards. Tick off each activity as you complete it.

Activity		
16		Performance Criteria 18.2A
17		Performance Criteria 18.2A and 18.2D

16 Mr N

The following information relates to Mr N who has run a shop for many years. Mr N's taxable trading profits and losses have been, or are expected to be, as follows:

		£
Year ended 30 June 2004	Profit	4,000
Year ended 30 June 2005	Loss	(11,000)
Year ended 30 June 2006	Profit (projected)	14,000

Mr N's other income (Rental income) is as follows.

	£
2004/05	0
2005/06	19,000
2006/07	12,000

Tasks

(a) State the ways in which Mr N may obtain relief for the loss of £11,000.

(b) Calculate Mr N's taxable income for 2005/06 to 2006/07 assuming that loss relief is claimed in the most efficient way.

Assume that the personal allowance and rates of tax applicable to 2005/06 apply to all the years involved.

Guidance notes

1 You must first work out the year in which the loss arose and Mr N's options for relieving this loss. These should be listed, briefly stating the income against which the loss would be relieved.

2 You must then choose the best form of loss relief. You should find that there is only one option which both gives relief quickly and does not set the loss against income which would otherwise be covered by the personal allowance.

3 Having made your choice, you should set out a working with a column for each year covered and a line for each source of income, a line for loss relief and a line for the personal allowance. Also allow space for sub-totals.

4 You can now insert the figures from the question into your working, and get the taxable income for each year.

17 Malcolm

Malcolm is a self-employed builder who has been trading for a number of years. His adjusted trading results for the past three accounting periods have been as follows:

		£
Year ended 31 December 2004	Profit	23,000
Year ended 31 December 2005	Loss	(14,000)
Year ended 31 December 2006	Profit	26,000

Malcolm's other income is as follows:

	£
2004/05	7,000
2005/06	8,000
2006/07	9,000

Tasks

(a) State Malcolm's options for obtaining relief for his loss.

(b) Calculate the effect of the two best options on his taxable income and comment on their implications.

Assume that the personal allowances and rates of tax for 2005/06 apply throughout.

Malcom can get releif for his loss by offsetting against income for

chapter 6

Partnerships

Activity checklist

This checklist shows which performance criteria are covered by each activity in this chapter. Full details of the performance criteria are shown on page (xiii) onwards. Tick off each activity as you complete it.

Activity		
18	☐	Performance Criteria 18.2C, 18.2D
19	☐	Performance Criteria 18.2C
20	☐	Performance Criteria 18.2C, 18.2D
21	☐	Performance Criteria 18.2C, 18.2D

18 Fred and Joe

Fred and Joe started a business on 1 January 2005, making up accounts for calendar years. It initially made profits of £3,000 a month before any remuneration for Fred and Joe. These profits rose to £4,000 a month from 1 January 2006.

Task

Compute the total income of Fred and Joe for 2004/05, 2005/06, 2006/07 and 2007/08 if Fred and Joe are equal partners. Show the overlap profits of each partner.

19 Bob, Annie and John

Bob, Annie and John started their partnership on 1 June 2000 and make accounts up to 31 May each year. The accounts have always shown taxable profits.

For the period up to 31 January 2005 each partner received a salary of £15,000 per annum and the remaining profits were shared 50% to Bob and 25% each to Annie and John. There was no interest on capital or drawings.

Bob left the partnership on 1 February 2005. The profit sharing ratio, after the same salaries, changed to 50% each to Annie and John.

Profits for the years ending 31 May 2005 and 31 May 2006 were £90,000 and £120,000 respectively.

Task

Calculate each partner's share of the profits for the periods to 31 May 2005 and 31 May 2006 respectively. (Allocation should be done on a monthly basis.)

20 Anne and Betty

Anne and Betty have been in partnership since 1 January 2000 sharing profits equally. On 30 June 2005 Betty resigned as a partner, and was replaced on 1 July 2005 by Chloe. Profits continued to be shared equally. The partnership's taxable trading profits are as follows:

	£
Year ended 31 December 2005	60,000
Year ended 31 December 2006	72,000

As at 6 April 2005 Anne and Betty each have unrelieved overlap profits of £3,000.

Task

Calculate the taxable trading profits for Anne, Betty and Chloe for 2005/06.

21 Partnerships

Clare and Justin commenced trading in partnership on 1 October 2002, initially sharing profits and losses as to Clare one third and Justin two thirds. They prepared their first set of accounts to 31 January 2003. Accounts were prepared to 31 January thereafter.

Malcolm joined the partnership on 1 May 2004. From this date the profit and losses were shared equally. Taxable trading profits were as follows:

	£
1.10.02 – 31.01.03	26,400
y/e 31.01.04	60,000
y/e 31.01.05	117,000
y/e 31.01.06	108,108

Task

(a) Calculate each partner's share of the above profits.

(b) Calculate the amount on which each partner will be assessed for 2002/03 to 2005/06 inclusive.

chapters 7 and 8

Chargeable gains

Activity checklist

This checklist shows which performance criteria are covered by each activity in this chapter. Full details of the performance criteria are shown on page (xiii) onwards. Tick off each activity as you complete it.

Activity		
22		Performance Criteria 18.3A, 18.3C and 18.3D
23		Performance Criteria 18.3A, 18.3C and 18.3D
24		Performance Criteria 18.3A and 18.3C
25		Performance Criteria 18.3A, 18.3C and 18.3D

22 John

John carried out the following disposals of assets during 2005/06.

(a) On 6 June 2005 he sold land used in his business for £23,000. John had purchased the land in December 2000 for £26,000.

(b) On 2 October 2005 he sold his 1956 motor car to a friend for £2,000. He had purchased the car in December 2004 for £300 and had spent many hours restoring it as a hobby.

(c) On 30 January 2006 he sold for £80,000 his business premises, which had been acquired in July 1985 for £20,000.

John had unused capital losses carried forward at 5 April 2003 of £2,500 and transactions in the following two years gave rise to gains and losses as follows.

	Gains	*Losses*
	£	£
2003/04	6,800	1,000
2004/05	11,500	2,000

Task

Compute John's taxable gains for 2005/06 after taking into account all available exemptions, reliefs and losses. Assume an annual exemption of £8,500 for all years.

Assume indexation factors:

July 1985 – April 1998 = 0.708

23 Mr Johnson

Mr Johnson ran a very successful antiques business. He sold the business and other assets to an unconnected third party on 1 March 2006 as follows.

	Proceeds
	£
Shop	180,000
Goodwill	61,410
Fixtures	38,000
Stock	80,000

The shop and goodwill were purchased on 1 May 1993 at a cost of £40,000 and £10,000 respectively. A fixture sold for £33,000 had cost £30,000 in August 1993 and one sold for £5,000 had cost £2,000 in May 1996. The stock had been purchased for £35,000 throughout 2005.

His taxable income (all earned income), after personal allowances, for income tax purposes during 2005/06 amounted to £24,000.

There were no other disposals during the year and no capital losses b/fwd.

Task

Calculate the capital gains tax payable by Mr Johnson for 2005/06.

Indexation factors

May 1993 – April 1998	0.152
August 1993 – April 1998	0.151
May 1996 – April 1998	0.063

24 Dove plc

Dove plc made the following disposals of assets during its 12 month accounting period ending 31 December 2005.

- 14 April 2005 – A factory for £230,000. This had originally been purchased April 1986 for £140,000.
- 18 July 2005 – A warehouse for £80,000. This had been purchased in May 1999 for £100,000.
- 17 September 2005 – Another factory for £280,000. This had been purchased in June 1991 for £85,000.
- 14 November 2005 – Two offices for £140,000. These had been part of a large office block from which Dove plc has traded. The whole block had cost £250,000 in August 1995 and in November 2005 the remaining offices had a market value of £320,000.

Tasks

(a) Calculate the chargeable gain arising on the disposal of the factory sold on 14.4.05.

(b) Calculate the allowable loss on disposal of the warehouse.

(c) Calculate the chargeable gain arising on disposal of the factory sold on 17.9.05.

(d) Calculate the chargeable gain arising on disposal of the offices.

(e) Calculate the net chargeable gains that Dove plc will include in its computation of PCTCT for the year ended 31 December 2005.

Indexation factors

April 1986 – April 2005	0.940
May 1999 – July 2005	0.148
June 1991 – September 2005	0.421
August 1995 – November 2005	0.268

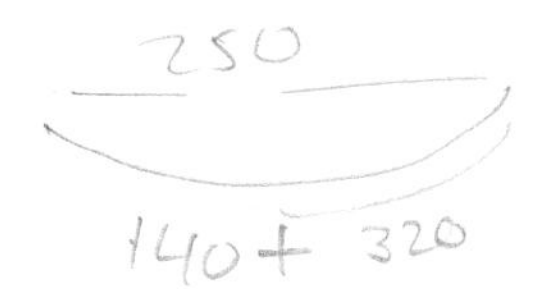

25 Hilary Spencer

Hilary Spencer disposed of the following capital items during the tax year 2005/06.

- A building which she had used for business purposes. The building was purchased for £28,000 in July 1991 and was sold for £106,000 in August 2005.
- A chattel, used for business purposes, was sold for £7,000 on 14 February 2006. It had originally cost £5,000 on 18 October 1999.
- A chattel, used for business purposes, was sold for £5,000 in 14 March 2006. This had cost £7,000 on 14 March 2002.

Task

Calculate Hilary's total amount chargeable to capital gains tax (CGT) for the year 2005/06.

Assume indexation

July 1991 to April 1998	0.215
July 1991 to August 2005	0.422

chapter 9

Shares and securities

Activity checklist

This checklist shows which performance criteria are covered by each activity in this chapter. Full details of the performance criteria are covered on page (xiii) onwards. Tick off each activity as you complete it.

Activity		
26	☐	Performance Criteria 18.3C
27	☐	Performance Criteria 18.3B

26 Brooklyn

Brooklyn sold 11,000 ordinary shares in Biggs Ltd a trading company on 17 May 2005 for £66,000. She had bought ordinary shares in the company, for which she worked full time, on the following dates.

	No of shares	*Cost*
		£
19 September 1982	2,000	1,700
17 January 1985	2,000	6,000
12 December 1985	2,000	5,500
29 June 2003	3,000	11,500
3 November 2004	2,000	12,800

Task

Calculate, after taper relief but before the annual exemption, the capital gain for 2005/06. The shares are a business asset for taper relief purposes.

Assume indexation factors

September 1982 – April 1985	0.158
January 1985 – April 1985	0.039
April 1985 –December 1985	0.013
December 1985 – April 1998	0.694

Guidance notes

1. Disposals should initially be matched with post 6.4.98 acquisitions. There will be no indexation allowance on these disposals but there may be taper relief.
2. Next build up the FA 1985 pool (including all the first three acquisitions). Indexation is first given up to April 1985, and then up to each later purchase or sale. Remember that the FA 1985 pool closes on 5 April 1998 so the final indexation allowance calculation will be to that date.
3. Gains and losses arising in a year must be set against each other even if this means wasting the annual exemption. Losses are set off in the most beneficial way before taper relief.

27 Box plc

Box plc makes up accounts to 31 March each year. In its 12-month period ending 31 March 2006 it has the following transactions in capital assets.

26 May 2005

22,000 shares in Crate Ltd sold for £136,400. These shares had been acquired as follows.

26 May 1992	Purchased	4,000 shares for	£24,000
30 June 1993	1 for 2 bonus issue		
24 October 2000	Purchased	5,000 shares for	£27,500
22 May 2005	Purchased	11,000 shares for	£67,800

Task

Calculate the total chargeable gain to be included in Box plc's profits chargeable to corporation tax (PCTCT) for the year ending 31 March 2006.

Assume indexation factors

May 1992 –October 2000	0.232
October 2000 – May 2005	0.105

chapter 10

Deferral reliefs

Activity checklist

This checklist shows which performance criteria are covered by each activity in this chapter. Full details of the performance criteria are shown on page (xiii) onwards. Tick off each activity as you complete it.

Activity		
28	☐	Performance Criteria 18.3C and 18.3D
29	☐	Performance Criteria 18.3C and 18.3D
30	☐	Performance Criteria 18.3C and 18.3D
31	☐	Performance Criteria 18.3C and 18.3D

28 Miss Bathsheba

Miss Bathsheba has traded for many years as a retail and wholesale dealer in children's toys. During 2005/06 the following disposals took place.

(a) A freehold shop was sold on 1 December 2005 for £120,000, net of all costs of disposal. The shop cost £44,000 on 31 March 1992 and was extended in December 2004 at a cost of £15,000.

(b) A yard attached to the storage depot was sold on 31 January 2006 for £80,000 less solicitors' fees of £1,200. The whole storage complex was acquired on 31 March 1992 for £110,000 and on 31 January 2005 the value of the remaining part of the complex was £230,000.

Miss Bathsheba hopes, within the next few years, to purchase a freehold shop in Manchester for approximately £300,000.

Tasks

(a) Calculate the capital gains arising from the above, assuming that no claims are made.
(b) Describe any claim that might be made in respect of the above events.

Assume indexation factors

March 1992 – April 1998	0.189

29 Walter and Darren

Walter purchased his business premises in October 1982 for £10,000. In May 1985 he gave them to his son Darren when the value was £50,000. The appropriate joint election for gift relief was made. On 14 April 2005 Darren sold the premises to an unconnected third party for £200,000. From the date of the gift Darren used the premises in his business.

Task

Calculate Darren's capital gain for 2005/06, after taper relief but before the annual exemption.

Assume indexation factors

October 1982 – May 1985	0.157
May 1985 – April 1998	0.708

30 E Ltd

On 31 March 1995 E Ltd acquired for £60,000 a workshop where it carried on its trade as a furniture maker. On 6 April 2005 it sold the workshop for £180,000 and moved on 10 April 2005 to larger premises which cost £184,000.

Tasks

(a) Calculate E Ltd's capital gain for its year ended 31 December 2005 before any claim to reduce its capital gain.

(b) State what relief is available to E Ltd to reduce its capital gain and explain the effect on a future disposal of the larger premises.

Assume indexation factors

March 1995 – April 1998	0.102
March 1995 – April 2005	0.285

31 K Ltd

During its accounting period of 12 months to 31 March 2006, K Ltd made the disposals which are detailed below.

(a) 30 November 2005

Sold a property that had been used in the trade for £174,500. This had been acquired on 31 May 1983 at a cost of £85,000. This cost had been funded using the full proceeds of the sale of an asset on the same day with rollover relief for the gain of £16,800 being claimed.

(b) 31 January 2006

Sold a painting, which had been hanging in the boardroom, for £5,800. This had cost £10 in January 1996.

(c) 3 March 2006

Sold a holding of shares in Z plc for £40,000. This holding had been acquired in March 2002 at a cost of £28,000.

(d) On 15 February 2006 £185,000 was invested in a new freehold warehouse. It is the company's policy to defer gains where possible.

Task

Compute the amount to be included in the corporation tax computation of K Ltd in respect of capital gains for the year ended 31 March 2006.

Use the following RPI factors.

May 1983 – November 2005	1.246	March 2002 – March 2006	0.099
January 1996 – January 2006	0.274		

chapter 11

An outline of corporation tax

Activity checklist

This checklist shows which performance criteria are covered by each activity in this chapter. Full details of the performance criteria are shown on page (xiii) onwards. Tick off each activity as you complete it.

Activity		
32		Performance Criteria 18.4A and 18.4C
33		Performance Criteria 18.4A and 18.4C
34		Performance Criteria 18.4A and 18.4C
35		Performance Criteria 18.4C
36		Performance Criteria 18.4A and 18.4C

32 Corporation tax computation

Abel Ltd, a UK trading company, produced the following results for the year ended 31 March 2006.

	£
Income	
Taxable trading profits	245,000
Rental income	15,000
Bank deposit interest	4,000
Capital gains: 25 September 2005	35,000
28 March 2006	7,000
(There were capital losses of £8,000 brought forward at 1 April 2005.)	
Dividends from UK companies (including tax credits)	15,000
Charges paid	
Gift aid donation	7,000

Task

Compute the corporation tax payable by Abel Ltd for the above accounting period.

Guidance notes

1 In working out a company's profits chargeable to corporation tax (PCTCT), we must bring together all taxable profits, including gains. You must therefore start by drawing up a working, and picking out from the question all relevant profit figures.

2 Once you have found the PCTCT, you can consider the rate of tax. You should find that small companies marginal relief applies. If you do not, look carefully to see whether you have missed anything.

33 A Company plc

A Company plc has one associated company. It accounts for the year to 31 December 2005 showed the following.

	£	£
Gross trading profit		400,000
Investment income		14,000
Profit on sale of investments		19,320
		433,320
Less: depreciation	65,000	
directors' emoluments	80,000	
audit and accountancy fees	16,320	
legal costs	21,000	
salaries	86,000	
miscellaneous expenses	47,000	
		(315,320)
Net profit for year		118,000

Notes

1 Legal costs comprised the following.

	£
Costs re directors' service agreements	5,000
Costs re issue of debentures	6,000
Costs re issue of shares	10,000

2 Miscellaneous expenses comprised the following.

	£
Installation costs for a new machine	12,000
Painting offices	1,500
Staff party	2,500
Entertaining suppliers	31,000

3 Investment income comprised the following.

	£
Dividends from non-associated UK companies (including tax credit) on 1.8.05	8,000
Bank interest (received August 2005)	6,000

4 The profit on the sale of investments resulted from the sale of one of the company's holdings of quoted ordinary shares on 30 November 2005. £18,000 is the chargeable gain.

5 Capital allowances have been agreed at £31,000.

Tasks

(a) Calculate the taxable trading profits for the year to 31 December 2005.

(b) Calculate the corporation tax payable in respect of the above accounting period.

34 Polar (UK) Ltd

Polar UK Ltd is a UK trading company making up accounts each year to 31 March. The results of its most recent 12-month accounting period ending on 31 March 2006 showed the following amounts of income and expenditure:

	£
Income:	
Adjusted trading profit after capital allowances	20,000
Chargeable gain	4,000
Bank interest received (amount credited to account) – 1 May	14,500
Dividends from UK companies (cash amount)	6,300
Expenditure:	
Gift aid donation (gross amount) – 29 June	4,500
Dividend paid	10,000

Notes

1 There were no accruals of bank interest at the beginning or end of the year.

2 All of Polar (UK) Ltd's shareholders are individual shareholders.

Task

Calculate the corporation tax payable by Polar UK Ltd for the period ending 31 March 2006.

35 Dealers plc and Springer Ltd

(a) Dealers plc had profits chargeable to corporation tax of £420,000 for its year ended 31 December 2005.

Task

Compute Dealers plc's corporation tax liability for the year.

(b) Springer Ltd had profits chargeable to corporation tax of £6,200 in the year to 31 December 2005.

Springer Ltd distributed £1,000 of its PCTCT as a dividend in the year to non-corporate shareholders.

Task

Calculate Springer Ltd's corporation tax liability for the year.

36 Traders Ltd

Traders Ltd's profit and loss account for the year to 31 March 2006 was as follows.

	£		£
General expenses	73,611	Gross trading profit	246,250
Repairs and renewals	15,000	Bad debts recovered	
Legal and accountancy charges	1,200	(previously written off)	373
Subscriptions and donations	7,000	Commissions	800
Bad debts written off	500	Profit on sale of investment	5,265
Directors' remuneration	20,000	Building society interest (gross)	1,100
Salaries and wages	18,000		
Depreciation	15,000		
Rent and rates	1,500		
Net profit	101,977		
	253,788		253,788

Notes

1 General expenses include the following.

	£
Travelling expenses of staff, including directors	1,000
Entertaining suppliers	600

2 Repairs and renewals include the following.

	£
Redecorating existing premises	300
Renovations to new premises to remedy wear and tear of previous owner (the premises were usable before these renovations)	500

3 Legal and accountancy charges are made up as follows.

	£
Debt collection service	200
Staff service agreements	50
Tax consultant's fees for special advice	30
45 year lease on new premises	100
Audit and accountancy	820
	1,200

4 Subscriptions and donations include the following.

	£
Donations under the gift aid scheme	5,200
Donation to a political party	500
Sports facilities for staff	500
Contribution to a local enterprise agency	200

5 The commissions received were not incidental to the trade.

6 The chargeable gain arising on the sale of investments was £770.

7 The amounts received were the same as the amounts accrued in the year.

8 The company paid dividends of £10,000 in the year. 60% of these dividends were to non-corporate shareholders.

Tasks

(a) Compute Traders Ltd's taxable trading profits for the year to 31 March 2006.
(b) Compute Traders Ltd's profits chargeable to corporation tax for the year to 31 March 2006.
(c) Compute Traders Ltd's corporation tax liability for the year to 31 March 2006.

chapter 12

Corporation tax losses

Activity checklist

This checklist shows which performance criteria are covered by each activity in this chapter. Full details of the performance criteria are shown on page (xiii) onwards. Tick off each activity as you complete it

Activity		
37	☐	Performance Criteria 18.4B
38	☐	Performance Criteria 18.4B
39	☐	Performance Criteria 18.4B

37 P Ltd

P Ltd is a UK resident company, it has no associated companies.

The following details relate to the 12 month accounting period ending 31 March 2006.

	£
Income	
Taxable trading profit	360,000
Rental income	18,000
Bank deposit interest	6,000
Capital gain	14,000
Dividend (cash amount received)	10,800
Payments	
Gift aid payment (gross amount)	6,000

A capital loss of £15,000 and a trading loss of £10,000 were brought forward as at 1 April 2005.

Task

Calculate the corporation tax payable for the year ending 31 March 2006.

38 Galbraith Ltd

Galbraith Ltd started to trade on 1 April 2003. The company's results for the first three years are as follows.

	Year ended 31 March		
	2004	*2005*	*2006*
	£	£	£
Trading profit/(loss) (as adjusted for taxation)	125,000	(465,000)	50,000
Bank interest accrued	263,000	10,000	24,000
Chargeable gains/(allowable loss)	60,360	(7,000)	3,000
Dividends received from UK companies (net) (January)	6,750	3,000	3,750
Gift aid donation	40,000	47,000	30,000
Dividends paid	–	–	12,000

All of Galbraith Ltd's shareholders are corporate shareholders.

Tasks

(a) Calculate the corporation tax liabilities for the three years after claiming maximum loss relief at the earliest possible times. Comment on the effectiveness of the reliefs. Assume FY 2005 rates and allowances apply throughout.

(b) State any amounts that remain to carry forward at 1 April 2006.

Guidance notes

1 First, set out the figures for trading profits and leave space for losses carried forward under s 393(1) ICTA 1988.

2 Set out the remainder of the profits subject to tax and then deduct losses from the total. Questions usually require loss relief to be claimed as quickly as possible. Remember that s 393A(1) ICTA 1988 requires losses to be set off first against total profits of the loss-making accounting period. Only after these have been extinguished can losses be carried back. Any remaining losses are carried forward, but may only be set against trading profits (not total profits).

3 Remember that the corporation tax charge may need to be adjusted if distributions are made to non-corporate shareholders. Is this the case here?

39 Ferraro Ltd

Ferraro Ltd has the following results.

	y/e 31.12.03	*9m to 30.9.04*	*y/e 30.9.05*
	£	£	£
Trading profit (loss)	6,200	4,320	(100,000)
Bank deposit interest accrued	80	240	260
Rents receivable	1,420	1,440	1,600
Capital gain		12,680	
Allowable capital loss	5,000		9,423
Gift Aid donation paid (gross)	0	1,000	1,500

Tasks

(a) Compute all profits chargeable to corporation tax, claiming loss reliefs as early as possible.

(b) State any amounts carried forward as at 30 September 2005.

chapter 13

National insurance

Activity checklist

This checklist shows which performance criteria are covered by each activity in this chapter. Full details of the performance criteria are shown on page (xiii) onwards. Tick off each activity as you complete it.

Activity		
40	☐	Performance Criteria 18.4E
41	☐	Performance Criteria 18.2F
42	☐	Performance Criteria 18.2C, 18.2F

40 Josephine

Josephine receives a weekly salary of £402. In one week she receives a book token for £100 from her employer as a bonus. She also receives vouchers of £10 per week for meals on her employer's premises. Josephine is provided with a company car by her employer. The taxable benefit arising in respect of this car was £6,850 in 2005/06.

Task

Calculate the national insurance contributions payable by Josephine's employer for the year 2005/06.

41 Zoë

Zoë is a self employed author. In the year to 31 December 2005 she had taxable trading profits of £80,000.

Tasks

(a) Calculate the NICs payable by Zoë for 2005/06.
(b) State the date by which a self employed person must notify that he or she is liable to Class 2 NICs.

42 Paula

Wendy and Jayne have been in partnership as interior designers for many years, trading as Dramatic Decors.

On 1 January 2006, Wendy and Jayne admitted Paula to the partnership. From that date, partnership profits were shared 40% to each of Wendy and Jayne and 20% to Paula. The partnership continued to make up its accounts to 31 December and the trading profit for the year to 31 December 2006 was £100,000.

Paula had not worked for many years prior to becoming a partner in Dramatic Decors.

Tasks

(a) Compute the share of profits taxable on Paula for 2005/06 and 2006/07 and identify the overlap profits to carry forward.

(b) Calculate the Class 4 National Insurance Contributions payable by Paula for 2005/06.

chapter 14

Administration of income tax and CGT

Activity checklist

This checklist shows which performance criteria are covered by each activity in this chapter. Full details of the performance criteria are shown on page (xiii) onwards. Tick off each activity as you complete it.

Activity		
43	☐	Performance Criteria 18.2E
44	☐	Performance Criteria 18.2E
45	☐	Performance Criteria 18.2A, 18.2B, 18.2F and 18.2G

43 Self assessment for individuals

Tasks

(a) State the latest date by which an individual taxpayer should submit the tax return if:

(i) he wishes the Revenue to calculate his income tax liability; and
(ii) he wishes to calculate his own liability.

(b) State:

(i) the normal dates of payment of income tax for a sole trader in respect of the fiscal year 2005/06; and
(ii) how the amounts of these payments are arrived at.

(c) State the circumstances in which a payment on account is not required to be made by a taxpayer.

(d) State:

(i) the fixed penalties for late submission of tax returns and when they apply;

(ii) the circumstances under which the penalties will be reduced; and

(iii) the further penalties which may be imposed where the Revenue believe that the fixed penalties will not result in the submission of the return.

44 Enquiries

The Revenue have to give written notice before the commencement of an enquiry into the completeness and accuracy of a self-assessment tax return.

Tasks

(a) State the date by which this written notice must normally be issued;

(b) State the circumstances under which the Revenue can extend the deadline in (a) within which an enquiry may be commenced together with the relevant time limits;

(c) State the three main reasons for the commencement of an enquiry;

(d) State what action the taxpayer may take where the Revenue have amended the self assessment to show an additional liability as a result of an enquiry.

45 Martin

Martin has been trading as a greengrocer for many years, under the name of Martin's The Greengrocer. He makes up accounts to 31 March each year.

In the year to 31 March 2006, Martin had the following results:

	£	£
Turnover	100,000	
Less: cost of sales	(40,000)	
Gross profit		60,000
Less: wages (N1)	35,000	
rent and rates	7,000	
administration expenses	1,000	
depreciation	3,000	
motor expenses (N2)	2,500	
entertaining (N3)	1,000	
bank interest	500	
legal costs (N4)	1,250	
other allowable expenses	3,750	
		(55,000)
Net profit		5,000

Notes

1 The figure for wages includes Martin's wages of £15,000.

2 20% of motor expenses relate to Martin's private use.

3 Entertaining suppliers £750; entertaining staff £250.

4 Legal expenses include £450 for the costs for the grant of a lease for 20 years.

5 There are capital allowances of £1,600 for the year to 31 March 2006. These arose on various shop fittings purchased for the business.

Tasks

(a) Compute Martin's taxable trading profits for 2005/06.
(b) Calculate the National Insurance contributions payable by Martin as a self-employed individual for 2005/06.
(c) Complete the attached self-employment pages for Martin for 2005/06.

Tutorial note

The examiner has stated that the two attached self employment pages are the only two self employment pages that you will be expected to complete in your examination.

SELF EMPLOYMENT PAGES

Income for the year ended 5 April 2006

SELF-EMPLOYMENT

Fill in these boxes first

Name

Tax reference

If you want help, look up the box numbers in the Notes

Business details

Name of business **3.1**

Description of business **3.2**

Address of business **3.3**

Postcode

Accounting period - *read the Notes, page SEN3 before filling in these boxes*

Start **3.4** / /

End **3.5** / /

- Tick box 3.6 if details in boxes 3.1 or 3.3 have changed since your last Tax Return **3.6**
- Date of commencement if after 5 April 2002 **3.7** / /
- Date of cessation if before 6 April 2006 **3.8** / /
- Tick box 3.9 if the special arrangements for particular trades apply - *read the Notes, pages SEN11 and SEN12* **3.9**
- Tick box 3.10 if you entered details for all relevant accounting periods on last year's Tax Return and boxes 3.14 to 3.73 and 3.99 to 3.115 will be blank *(read Step 3 on page SEN2)* **3.10**
- Tick box 3.11 if your accounts do not cover the period from the last accounting date (explain why in the 'Additional information' box, box 3.116) **3.11**
- Tick box 3.12 if your accounting date has changed (only if this is a permanent change and you want it to count for tax) **3.12**
- Tick box 3.13 if this is the second or further change (explain in box 3.116 on Page SE4 why you have not used the same date as last year) **3.13**

Capital allowances - summary

	Capital allowances	Balancing charges
• Cars costing more than £12,000 (excluding cars with low CO_2 emissions) (A separate calculation must be made for each car.)	**3.14** £	**3.15** £
• Other business plant and machinery (including cars with low CO_2 emissions and cars costing less than £12,000) *read the Notes, page SEN4*	**3.16** £	**3.17** £
• Agricultural or Industrial Buildings Allowance (A separate calculation must be made for each block of expenditure.)	**3.18** £	**3.19** £
• Other capital allowances claimed (Separate calculations must be made.)	**3.20** £	**3.21** £
Total capital allowances/balancing charges	total of column above **3.22** £	total of column above **3.23** £

- Tick box 3.22A if box 3.22 includes enhanced capital allowances for environmentally friendly expenditure **3.22A**

Income and expenses - annual turnover below £15,000

If your annual turnover is £15,000 or more, ***ignore*** *boxes 3.24 to 3.26. Instead fill in Page SE2*

If your annual turnover is below £15,000, ***fill in boxes 3.24 to 3.26 instead of Page SE2****. Read the Notes, page SEN6.*

- Turnover including other business receipts and goods etc. taken for personal use (and balancing charges from box 3.23) **3.24** £
- Expenses allowable for tax (including capital allowances from box 3.22) **3.25** £

Net profit (put figure in brackets if a loss) box 3.24 *minus* box 3.25 **3.26** £

You must now fill in Page SE3

SA103

BS 12/04net

TAX RETURN ■ SELF-EMPLOYMENT: PAGE SE1

Income and expenses - annual turnover £15,000 or more

You must fill in this Page if your annual turnover is £15,000 or more - read the Notes, pages SEN2, SEN6 to SEN7

If you were registered for VAT, do the figures in boxes 3.29 to 3.64, include VAT? **3.27** [ ] or exclude VAT? **3.28** [ ]

Sales/business income (turnover) **3.29** £

	Disallowable expenses included in boxes 3.46 to 3.63	Total expenses	
• Cost of sales	3.30 £	3.46 £	
• Construction industry subcontractor costs	3.31 £	3.47 £	
• Other direct costs	3.32 £	3.48 £	box 3.29 *minus* (boxes 3.46 + 3.47 + 3.48)
		Gross profit/(loss)	3.49 £
		Other income/profits	3.50 £
• Employee costs	3.33 £	3.51 £	
• Premises costs	3.34 £	3.52 £	
• Repairs	3.35 £	3.53 £	
• General administrative expenses	3.36 £	3.54 £	
• Motor expenses	3.37 £	3.55 £	
• Travel and subsistence	3.38 £	3.56 £	
• Advertising, promotion and entertainment	3.39 £	3.57 £	
• Legal and professional costs	3.40 £	3.58 £	
• Bad debts	3.41 £	3.59 £	
• Interest	3.42 £	3.60 £	
• Other finance charges	3.43 £	3.61 £	
• Depreciation and loss/(profit) on sale	3.44 £	3.62 £	
• Other expenses	3.45 £	3.63 £	total of boxes 3.51 to 3.63
	Put the total of boxes 3.30 to 3.45 in box 3.66 below	Total expenses	3.64 £
			boxes 3.49 + 3.50 *minus* 3.64
		Net profit/(loss)	3.65 £

Tax adjustments to net profit or loss

	boxes 3.30 to 3.45	
• Disallowable expenses	3.66 £	
• Adjustments (apart from disallowable expenses) that increase profits. Examples are goods taken for personal use and amounts brought forward from an earlier year because of a claim under ESC B11 about compulsory slaughter of farm animals	3.67 £	
• Balancing charges (from box 3.23)	3.68 £	boxes 3.66 + 3.67 + 3.68
Total additions to net profit (deduct from net loss)		3.69 £
• Capital allowances (from box 3.22)	3.70 £	boxes 3.70 + 3.71
• Deductions from net profit (add to net loss)	3.71 £	3.72 £
		boxes 3.65 + 3.69 *minus* 3.72
Net business profit for tax purposes (put figure in brackets if a loss)		3.73 £

BS 12/04net Tax Return ■ Self-employment: page SE2 *Now fill in Page SE3*

chapter 15

Payment of tax by companies

Activity checklist

This checklist shows which performance criteria are covered by each activity in this chapter. Full details of the performance criteria are shown on page (xiii) onwards. Tick off each activity as you complete it.

Activity		
46	☐	Performance Criteria 18.4F and 18.4G
47	☐	Performance Criteria 18.1B, 18.4A, 18.4C, 18.4D, 18.4F and 18.4G

46 Alphabetic Ltd

(a) Alphabetic Ltd makes up annual accounts to 30 September. It paid four quarterly instalments of corporation tax of £156,000 each in respect of the accounting period to 30 September 2005. These were paid on 14 April 2005, 14 July 2005, 14 October 2005 and 14 January 2006. It subsequently transpired that the actual liability for the period was £800,000 and the balance of £176,000 was subsequently paid on 1 July 2006.

Alphabetic Ltd has always paid corporation tax at the full rate.

Task

State the amounts on which interest will be charged in respect of the above accounting period and the dates from which it will run.

(b) **Task**

State what action a company should take if it does not receive a corporation tax return and the penalty for not taking such action.

(c) **Task**

State:

(i) the fixed rate penalties for failing to submit a corporation tax return on time; and
(ii) the tax-geared penalties for failing to submit a corporation tax return on time.

Your answers to (c)(i) and (c)(ii) should indicate under what circumstances these penalties are triggered.

(d) Large companies must normally pay their corporation tax liability by instalments.

Task

State the circumstances in which such a company does not need to make instalment payments.

47 Cranmore Ltd

Cranmore Ltd is a trading company manufacturing specialist engineering tools. It makes up its accounts to 31 March each year. It is a small enterprise for capital allowance purposes with no associated companies.

For the year to 31 March 2006, the company had the following results:

	£
Turnover	525,000
Trading profit before capital allowances	405,000
Interest received from building society deposit	3,000
Rental income from letting out part of factory	10,000
Gross patent royalty received (non-trade) from Mr Wilkes	6,000
	424,000

The tax written down value of the general pool at 1 April 2005 was £12,000. The company made the following purchases during the year:

	£
Car for salesman	10,000
Car for managing director	25,000
Computer for office	6,250
	40,000

Tasks

(a) Compute the capital allowances for Cranmore Ltd for the year to 31 March 2006.

(b) Compute the corporation tax payable for the year to 31 March 2006.

(c) Complete the attached pages of Form CT 600.

Tutorial note: The examiner has said that you will only see the short version of the CT 600 return form in your examination.

CT600 RETURN FORM

Page 2

Company Tax Calculation

Turnover

1 Total turnover from trade or profession		1 £

Income

3 Trading and professional profits	3 £	
4 Trading losses brought forward claimed against profits	4 £	
5 Net trading and professional profits		box 3 minus box 4 5 £
6 Bank, building society or other interest, and profits and gains from non-trading loan relationships		6 £
11 Income from UK land and buildings		11 £
14 Annual profits and gains not falling under any other heading		14 £

Chargeable gains

16 Gross chargeable gains	16 £	
17 Allowable losses including losses brought forward	17 £	
18 Net chargeable gains		box 16 minus box 17 18 £

21 Profits before other deductions and reliefs		sum of boxes 5, 6, 11, 14 & 18 21 £

Deductions and Reliefs

24 Management expenses under S75 ICTA 1988	24 £	
30 Trading losses of this or a later accounting period under S393A ICTA 1988	30 £	
31 *Put an 'X' in box 31 if amounts carried back from later accounting periods are included in box 30*	31	
32 Non-trade capital allowances	32 £	
35 Charges paid	35 £	

37 Profits chargeable to corporation tax		box 21 minus boxes 24, 30, 32 and 35 37 £

Tax calculation

38 Franked investment income	38 £	
39 Number of associated companies in this period or	39	
40 Associated companies in the first financial year	40	
41 Associated companies in the second financial year	41	
42 *Put an 'X' in box 42 if the company claims to be charged at the starting rate or the small companies' rate on any part of its profits, or is claiming marginal rate relief*		42

Enter how much profit has to be charged and at what rate of tax

Financial year *(yyyy)*	Amount of profit	Rate of tax	Tax
43	44 £	45	46 £ p
53	54 £	55	56 £ p

63 Corporation tax		total of boxes 46 and 56 63 £ p
64 Marginal rate relief	64 £ p	
65 Corporation tax net of marginal rate relief	65 £ p	
66 Underlying rate of corporation tax	66 • %	
67 Profits matched with non-corporate distributions	67	
68 Tax at non-corporate distributions rate	68 £ p	
69 Tax at underlying rate on remaining profits	69 £ p	
70 Corporation tax chargeable		enter value of box 63 or 65 or the total of boxes 68 and 69 if greater 70 £ p

CT600 (Short) (2004) Version 2

79 Tax payable under S419 ICTA 1988		79 £ p
80 *Put an 'X' in box 80 if you completed box A11 in the Supplementary Pages CT600A*	80	
84 Income tax deducted from gross income included in profits		84 £ p
85 Income tax repayable to the company		85 £ p
86 **Tax payable - this is your self-assessment of tax payable**		total of boxes 70 and 79 minus box 84 86 £ p

Tax reconciliation

91 Tax already paid (and not already repaid)	91 £ p
92 Tax outstanding	box 86 minus box 91 92 £ p
93 Tax overpaid	box 91 minus box 86 93 £ p

Information about capital allowances and balancing charges

Charges and allowances included in calculation of trading profits or losses

	Capital allowances	Balancing charges
105 - 106 Machinery and plant - long-life assets	105 £	106 £
107 - 108 Machinery and plant - other (general pool)	107 £	108 £
109 - 110 Cars outside general pool	109 £	110 £
111 - 112 Industrial buildings and structures	111 £	112 £
113 - 114 Other charges and allowances	113 £	114 £

Charges and allowances not included in calculation of trading profits or losses

	Capital allowances	Balancing charges
115 - 116	115 £	116 £
117 *Put an 'X' in box 117 if box 115 includes flat conversion allowances*	117	

Expenditure

118	Expenditure on machinery and plant on which first year allowance is claimed	118 £
119	*Put an 'X' in box 119 if claim includes enhanced capital allowances for energy-saving investments* 119	
120	Qualifying expenditure on machinery and plant on long-life assets	120 £
121	Qualifying expenditure on machinery and plant on other assets	121 £

Losses, deficits and excess amounts

122 Trading losses Case I	calculated under S393 ICTA 1988 122 £	124 Trading losses Case V	calculated under S393 ICTA 1988 124 £
125 Non-trade deficits on loan relationships and derivative contracts	calculated under S82 FA 1996 125 £	127 Schedule A losses	calculated under S392A ICTA 1988 127 £
129 Overseas property business losses Case V	calculated under S392B ICTA 1988 129 £	130 Losses Case VI	calculated under S396 ICTA 1988 130 £
131 Capital losses	calculated under S16 TCGA 1992 131 £	136 Excess management expenses	calculated under S75(3) ICTA 1988 136 £

CT600 (Short) (2004) **Version 2**

Answers to practice activities

Chapter 1 Introduction to business taxation

1 Income tax computation

(a) INCOME TAX COMPUTATION

	Non-savings	*Savings (excl dividend)*	*Dividend*	*Total*
	£	£	£	£
Taxable trading profits	45,000			
Dividend			1,000	
Bank deposit interest		1,000		
	45,000	1,000	1,000	47,000
Less personal allowance	(4,895)			
Taxable income	40,105	1,000	1,000	42,105

(b)

	£
Tax on non – savings income	
£2,090 × 10%	209
£30,310 × 22%	6,668
£7,705 × 40%	3,082
Tax on savings (excl dividend) income £1,000 × 40%	400
Tax on dividend income £1,000 × 32.5%	325
Tax liability	10,684

Chapter 2 Computing trading income

2 Idaho

		£	£
Net profit per accounts			136,770
Add:	wages paid to proprietor	12,000	
	depreciation	10,000	
	repairs £(500 + (3,000 × 1/3))	1,500	
	donation to a political party	700	
	legal charges re tax appeal	700	
	rent £12,000 × 1/3	4,000	
	profit on goods taken £(2,600 – 1,500)	1,100	
			30,000
			166,770
Less:	interest received	270	
	rent received	5,700	
	fall in general provision for bad debts £(10,000 – 8,800)	1,200	
			(7,170)
Taxable trading profit			159,600

Tutorial notes

1 The wages paid to Idaho are an appropriation of profit which must be added back in computing the taxable trading profits.

2 The interest received must be excluded from taxable trading profits. It is taxed as savings (excluding dividend) income. The rent received is taxed as rental income.

3 Increases in general provisions are never deductible for tax purposes. Similarly, decreases are never taxable and, therefore, the decrease must be deducted from the accounts profit.

4 The expenditure relating to the office space let to tenants qualifies as a rental expenses. As it is not a trading deduction it must be added in the computation of taxable trading profits.

3 George

		£	£
Net profit per accounts			8,179
Add:	car expenses (25% × £640)	160	
	entertaining	874	
	increase in general provision	795	
	depreciation	2,874	
			4,703
Taxable trading profit			12,882

4 Analyses of items

(a) *Repairs*

Expenditure on repairs is in general deductible, so that no adjustment to the accounts profit is required. However, charges to create a provision for future repairs are not deductible and must be added back. Similarly, **expenditure may be capital in nature and must then be added back**. The following guidelines may be derived from case law.

(i) The cost of restoration of an asset by, for instance, replacing a subsidiary part of the asset will be treated as revenue expenditure. It was held that expenditure on a new factory chimney replacement was allowable since the chimney was a subsidiary part of the factory *(Samuel Jones & Co (Devondale) Ltd v CIR 1951)*. However, in another case a football club demolished a spectators' stand and replaced it with a modern equivalent. This was held not to be repair, since repair is the restoration by renewal or replacement of subsidiary parts of a larger entity, and the stand formed a distinct and separate part of the club *(Brown v Burnley Football and Athletic Co Ltd 1980)*.

(ii) The cost of initial repairs to improve an asset recently acquired to make it fit to earn profits will be treated as disallowable capital expenditure. In *Law Shipping Co Ltd v CIR 1923* the taxpayer failed to obtain relief for expenditure on making a newly bought ship seaworthy prior to using it.

(iii) The cost of initial repairs to remedy normal wear and tear of recently acquired assets will be treated as allowable. *Odeon Associated Theatres Ltd v Jones 1971* can be contrasted with the *Law Shipping* judgement. Odeon were allowed to charge expenditure incurred on improving the state of recently acquired cinemas.

(b) *Legal expenses*

Legal expenses relating to capital or non-trading items are not deductible. These include expenses incurred in acquiring new capital assets or legal rights or in issuing shares. Legal expenses incurred on tax appeals are not deductible, because appealing against assessments is not wholly and exclusively for the purposes of the trade.

Expenses incurred are deductible when they relate directly to trading. Deductible items include:

(i) legal expenses incurred defending the taxpayer's title to fixed assets
(ii) expenses connected with an action for breach of contract
(iii) expenses of the *renewal* (not the grant) of a lease for less than 50 years
(iv) expenses of trade debt collection

(c) *Gifts and entertainment*

The costs of entertainment of and gifts to employees are normally deductible although where gifts are made, or the entertainment is excessive, a charge to tax may arise on the employee under the benefits in kind legislation. **Gifts to customers not costing more than £50 per donee per year are allowed if they carry a conspicuous advertisement for the business and are not food, drink, tobacco or vouchers exchangeable for goods.** All other expenditure on entertaining and gifts is non-deductible (except for certain gifts to charities and educational institutions).

Tutorial note. For each type of expenditure, you should have given a balanced treatment, indicating what is deductible as well as what is not deductible.

Chapter 3 Capital allowances

5 Saruman

		Pool	*Saruman's car (75%)*	*Allowances/ (charges)*
	£	£	£	£
WDV b/f		52,000	600	
Additions (no FYAs)		4,800		
Disposals		(10,800)	(920)	
		46,000		
Balancing charge			(320)×75%	(240)
Private use car			19,000	
WDA restricted			(3,000)×75%	2,250
WDA 25%		(11,500)		11,500
Addition FYA	5,000			
FYA 40%	(2,000)			2,000
		3,000		
WDV c/f		37,500	16,000	15,510

Tutorial notes.

1. Where disposal proceeds exceed original cost the deduction for capital allowances purposes is limited to the cost. This means that only £10,000 is deducted for the disposal on 20 April 2005.
2. Don't forget the first year allowance for the addition of plant in May 2005 (not available for motor cars).
3. The maximum WDA on the car is £3,000.

6 Dexter Ltd

	FYA	*Pool*	*Expensive car*	*Short life assets*	*Allowances*
	£	£	£	£	£
Year ended 30.6.02					
WDV b/f		29,700			
WDA @ 25%		(7,425)			7,425
Additions	1,917			3,667	
FYA @ 40%	(767)			(1,467)	2,234
		1,150			9,659
		23,425		2,200	
Year ended 30.6.03					
WDA @ 25%		(5,856)		(550)	£6,406
		17,569		1,650	

	FYA	Pool	Expensive car	Short life assets	Allowances
	£	£	£	£	£
Year ended 30.6.04					
Acquisitions			13,400		
WDA @ 25%		(4,392)	(3,000)	(413)	£7,805
		13,177	10,400	1,237	
Year ended 30.6.05					
Disposals		(340)		(2,000)	
		12,837		(763)	
Balancing charge				763	(763)
WDA @ 25%		(3,209)	(2,600)		5,809
		9,628	7,800		5,046
Period ended 31.12.05					
Disposals		(24,000)	(10,600)		
Balancing charge		(14,372)	(2,800)		£(17,172)

Tutorial notes

1 There is never any private use restriction when calculating capital allowances for companies.

2 Since Dexter Ltd is a medium sized enterprise, 100% FYA for computers is not available (only small enterprises qualify). However, a 40% FYA is available.

7 Green Ltd

	Pool	Expensive car	Short life assets	Allowances
	£	£	£	£
WDV b/f	106,000	7,000	17,500	
Transfer	17,500		(17,500)	
	123,500		0	
Disposals	(5,000)	(6,000)		
Balancing allowance		1,000		1,000
	118,500			
Addition		14,000		
WDA	(29,625)	(3,000)		32,625
WDV c/f	88,875	11,000		33,625

Tutorial note. If a short life asset has not been disposed of within four years of the end of the accounting period in which it was acquired, it must be transferred to the general pool.

8 Chilterns Ltd

Chilterns Ltd – Capital Allowances y/e 31 March 2006

Plant and machinery

	FYA	*Pool*	*Car (1)*	*Car (2)*	*CAs*
	£	£	£	£	£
WDV b/f		16,000	8,500		
Additions					
not with FYAs		10,000		15,000	
		26,000			
Disposals **(restricted to cost)**		(3,500)	(6,000)		
		22,500			
BA			2,500		2,500
WDA @25%		(5,625)		(3,000) max	8,625
		16,875			
Additions	14,000				
FYA @ 40%	(5,600)	8,400			5,600
WDV c/f		25,275		12,000	
CAs					16,725

Tutorial Note. Disposal proceeds in a capital allowances computation cannot exceed the original cost of an asset.

9 Industrial Building

	£
Cost excluding land	30,000
WDA 4%	(1,200)
WDV c/f	28,800

IBA = £1,200

Tutorial note. IBAs are not available on the cost of land but they are available on the cost of office accommodation as the office accommodation cost less than 25% of £30,000.

10 Biswas Ltd

New factory

As Biswas Ltd is the second owner, it will write off the lower of the original cost (£100,000) or its own cost (£80,000) ie £80,000.

The tax life of the building is 25 years from 1 September 1995. 15 years of the tax life remain.

The allowance for y/e 31 March 2006 is therefore:

$$\frac{£80{,}000}{15} = \underline{£5{,}333}$$

Original factory

Qualifying expenditure was:

	£
Tunnelling	10,000
Factory	85,000
	95,000

The cost of the land is not qualifying. The showroom is a non-qualifying part exceeding more than 25% of the expenditure so must be excluded.

The allowance for y/e 31 March 2006 is:

£95,000 × 4% = £3,800

Total allowances are therefore:

£(5,333 + 3,800) = £9,133

11 Extensions Ltd

Industrial buildings allowances: year ended 31.3.06

	£
Factory bought in 1998 £40,000 × 4%	1,600
Factory built in 1999 £(70,000 – 25,000) × 4% (£25,000 is more than 25% of £70,000)	1,800
Third factory (the factory was not in use at the end of the period)	0
	3,400

Tutorial note. Industrial buildings allowances are not available if a factory is not in industrial use at the end of a period.

Chapter 4 Basis of assessment for unincorporated businesses

12 Rachel

(a) *Taxable profits*

Tax year	*Basis period*	*Taxable profits*
		£
2003/04	(1.7.03 – 5.4.04) $\frac{9}{22} \times$ £33,000 =	13,500
2004/05	(6.4.04 – 5.4.05) $\frac{12}{22} \times$ £33,000 =	18,000
2005/06	(1.5.04 – 30.4.05) $\frac{12}{22} \times$ £33,000 =	18,000

(b) *Overlap profits*

The profits taxed twice are those for the period 1.5.04 to 5.4.05:

$\frac{11}{22} \times$ £33,000 = £16,500

Tutorial note. Overlap profits are the profits taxed twice in the early years.

13 Jackie Smith

	£	£
2001/02		
1st year – 1.5.01 to 5.4.02		
11/15 × £18,000		13,200
2002/03		
2nd year 12 months to 31.7.02 (1.8.01 – 31.7.02)		
12/15 × £18,000		14,400
2003/04		
3rd year y/e 31.7.03		11,700
2004/05		
y/e 31.7.04		8,640
2005/06		
y/e 31.7.05	4,800	
p/e 28.2.06	5,100	
	9,900	
Less: Overlap profits (W)	(9,600)	300

Working

Overlap profits

Overlap period is 1 August 2001 to 5 April 2002, ie 8/15 × £18,000 = £9,600

14 Otto

		£
2002/03	(1.6.02 – 5.4.03)	
	£7,000 + 4/12 × £16,000	12,333
2003/04	(1.12.02 – 30.11.03)	16,000
2004/05	(1.12.03 – 30.11.04)	19,000
2005/06	(1.12.04 – 30.11.05)	25,000

Overlap profits on commencement were £16,000 × 4/12 = £5,333. The overlap period was 4 months long.

15 Miss Farrington

(a)

	FYA @ 50%	*FYA@ 40%*	*Pool*	*Car (65%)*	*Allowances*
	£	£	£	£	£
1.1.03 – 30.4.04					
Car				6,600	
WDA @ 25% × 16/12				(2,200) × 65%	1,430
Desk and office furniture		940			
General plant		3,835			
Secondhand oven		1,200			
Delivery van		1,800			
Typewriter		425			
		8,200			
FYA @ 40%		(3,280)			3,280
			4,920	4,400	4,710
Year ended 30.4.05					
WDA @ 25%			(1,230)	(1,100) × 65%	1,945
			3,690	3,300	
General plant	1,000				
FYA @ 50%	(500)				500
			500		
Computer	1,556				
FYA @ 50%	(778)		778		778
WDV c/f			4,968	3,300	3,223

(b) Profits are as follows.

Period	*Profit*	*Capital allowances*	*Trading profits*
	£	£	£
1.1.03 – 30.4.04	20,710	4,710	16,000
1.5.04 – 30.4.05	15,125	3,223	11,902

(c) The taxable profits are as follows.

Year	*Basis period*	*Working*	*Taxable trading profits*
			£
2002/03	1.1.03 – 5.4.03	£16,000 × 3/16	3,000
2003/04	6.4.03 – 5.4.04	£16,000 × 12/16	12,000
2004/05	1.5.03 – 30.4.04	£16,000 × 12/16	12,000
2005/06	1.5.04 – 30.4.05		11,902

The overlap profits are the profits from 1 May 2003 to 5 April 2004: £16,000 × 11/16 = £11,000.

Tutorial notes

1 Writing down allowances are time apportioned in a long period of account but first year allowances are not.

2 As Miss Farrington's business is a small enterprise she is entitled to 50% FYAs on the plant purchased on 15.1.05. and 50% FYA on the computer. When different rates of FYA are available, as here, we suggest that your computation deals with the different rates of FYA in different columns as we have done here. The key to getting a capital allowance question correct is to set up a proforma with the various columns that we have shown here.

3 Don't forget that the private use of an asset restricts the allowances available to a sole trader.

Chapter 5 Trading losses

16 Mr N

(a) The loss of £11,000 is a loss for 2005/06.

Possible loss relief claims are:

(i) against total income for 2004/05
(ii) against total income for 2005/06
(iii) under (i) and then the remaining loss under (ii)
(iv) against the taxable trading profits of £14,000 in 2006/07

(b) (i) (and therefore (iii)) should be avoided, as loss relief in 2004/05 would cover income which would in any case be covered by the personal allowance. Both (ii) and (iv) save tax at 22%. However, as (ii) saves tax more quickly it is more beneficial from a cashflow point of view.

	2004/05	*2005/06*	*2006/07*
	£	£	£
Taxable trading profits	4,000	0	14,000
Rental income	0	19,000	12,000
	4,000	19,000	26,000
Less s 380 loss relief	0	(11,000)	0
	4,000	8,000	26,000
Less personal allowance	(4,895)	(4,895)	(4,895)
Taxable income	0	3,105	21,105

Tutorial note. If you set out the alternative loss relief claims clearly, the computation should have been straightforward. It is important to practise giving finished answers to questions which require you to list alternative claims; do not assume that a scrappy note will do and that neatness and clarity will come naturally in the real examination.

17 Malcolm

(a) The tax year of the loss is 2005/06

The options for offsetting the £14,000 trading loss are:

(i) Carry the loss forward and set against the taxable trading profits of 2006/07.
(ii) Set the trading loss against the other income of 2005/06.
(iii) Set the loss against the other income of 2004/05.
(iv) Set the loss against the other income of 2005/06 and 2004/05.

(b) The two best options are:

(i)

	2004/05	*2005/06*	*2006/07*
	£	£	£
Taxable trading profits	23,000	0	26,000
Less: loss relief s385			(14,000)
			12,000
Other income	7,000	8,000	9,000
	30,000	8,000	21,000
Less: personal allowance	(4,895)	(4,895)	(4,895)
Taxable income	25,105	3,105	16,105

This option makes full use of personal allowances but there will be a delay in obtaining the tax benefit.

(i)

	2004/05	*2005/06*	*2006/07*
	£	£	£
Taxable trading profits	23,000	0	26,000
Other income	7,000	8,000	9,000
	30,000	8,000	35,000
Less: loss relief s380	(14,000)	0	0
	16,000	8,000	35,000
Less: personal allowance	(4,895)	(4,895)	(4,895)
Taxable income	11,105	3,105	30,105

This option makes full use of personal allowances and obtains the benefit of the loss relief at the earliest opportunity.

Chapter 6 Partnerships

18 Fred and Joe

The profits for each period of account are:

	£
y/e 31.12.05 (£3,000 × 12)	36,000
y/e 31.12.06 (£4,000 × 12)	48,000
y/e 31.12.07 (£4,000 × 12)	48,000

Fred and Joe are equal partners from the beginning so the above profits must be divided equally.

Year	*Basis period*	*Working*	*Profits Per partner* £
2004/05	1.1.05 – 5.4.05	(£36,000 × 50%) × 3/12	4,500
2005/06	1.1.05 – 31.12.05	£36,000 × 50%	18,000
2006/07	1.1.06 – 31.12.06	£48,000 × 50%	24,000
2007/08	1.1.07 – 31.12.07	£48,000 × 50%	24,000
			70,500
Overlap profits of each partner are from 1.1.05 – 5.4.05: £4,500			£4,500

Tutorial note. Apply the opening year rules to each partner's share of the partnership profits.

19 Bob, Annie and John

Y/e 31.5.05

	Total	*Bob*	*Annie*	*John*
	£	£	£	£
1.6.04 – 31.1.05				
Salaries £15,000 × 8/12	30,000	10,000	10,000	10,000
Balance				
£(90,000 × 8/12 – 30,000) = £30,000	30,000	15,000	7,500	7,500
1.2.05 – 31.5.05				
Salaries £15,000 × 4/12	10,000	n/a	5,000	5,000
Balance				
£(90,000 × 4/12 – 10,000) = £20,000	20,000	n/a	10,000	10,000
Totals	90,000	25,000	32,500	32,500

Y/e 31.5.06

	Total	*Annie*	*John*
	£	£	£
Salaries	30,000	15,000	15,000
Balance			
£(120,000 – 30,000) = £90,000 × 50%	90,000	45,000	45,000
Totals	120,000	60,000	60,000

20 Anne and Betty

	Total	*Anne*	*Betty*	*Chloe*
	£	£	£	£
1.1.05 – 31.12.05				
January to June	30,000	15,000	15,000	–
July to December	30,000	15,000	–	15,000
Totals	60,000	30,000	15,000	15,000
1.1.06 – 31.12.06	72,000	36,000	–	36,000

Taxable trading profits 2005/06

	Anne	*Betty*	*Chloe*
	£	£	£
Profits y/e 31.12.05	30,000		
Profits 1.1.05 – 30.6.05		15,000	
Profits 1.7.05 – 31.12.05			15,000
Profits 1.1.06 – 5.4.06			
3/12 × £36,000			9,000
	30,000	15,000	24,000
Less: overlap relief for Betty on cessation		(3,000)	
Profits assessable 2005/06	30,000	12,000	24,000

Betty leaves the partnership so the cessation rules apply to her in 2005/06.

Chloe joins the partnership so the opening year rules apply to Chloe in 2005/06.

21 Partnerships

(a) Each partner's share of the profits is

		Total	Clare	Justin	Malcolm
		£	£	£	£
1.10.02 – 31.1.03		26,400	8,800	17,600	0
Y/e 31.1.04		60,000	20,000	40,000	0
Y/e 31.1.05					
1.2.04 – 30.4.04					
(3/12 × £117,000)	29,250		9,750	19,500	0
1.5.04 – 31.1.05					
(9/12 × £117,000)	87,750		29,250	29,250	29,250
		117,000	39,000	48,750	29,250
Y/e 31.1.06		108,108	36,036	36,036	36,036

(b) The partners will be taxed on the above profits in the following tax years.

	Clare	Justin	Malcolm
2002/03 (1.10.02 – 5.4.03)	£	£	
1.10.02 – 31.1.03	8,800	17,600	
1.2.03 – 5.4.03 (2/12 × (£20,000/£40,000)	3,333	6,667	
	12,133	24,267	
2003/04 (Y/e 31.1.04)	£20,000	£40,000	
2004/05			
(Y/e 31.1.05)	£39,000	£48,750	
			£
(1.5.04 – 5.4.05)			29,250
1.5.04 – 31.1.05			6,006
1.2.05 – 5.4.05 (2/12 × £36,036)			35,256
2005/06			
(y/e 31.1.06)	£36,036	£36,036	£36,036

The commencement rules apply to Malcolm in 2004/05 as he joined the partnership in that year.

Chapters 7 and 8 Chargeable gains

22 John

	£
Motor car: exempt asset	0
Gain on business premises (W1)	45,840
Less allowable loss on land (W2)	(3,000)
	42,840
Less loss brought forward (W3)	(1,500)
Gain before taper relief	41,340
Gain after taper relief (25%) (see note)	10,335
Less annual exemption	(8,500)
Taxable gains	1,835

Tutorial notes.

1 Taper relief reduces the gain on the business asset sale to 25% of the chargeable gain as there are seven complete years of ownership post 5.4.1998.

2 Losses are deducted from gains before taper relief is applied.

Workings

1 *The disposal of the business premises*

	£
Proceeds	80,000
Less cost	(20,000)
	60,000
Less indexation allowance to April 1998 0.708 × £20,000	(14,160)
	45,840

2 *The disposal of the business land*

	£
Proceeds	23,000
Less cost	(26,000)
Allowable loss	(3,000)

3 *Losses brought forward*

	£
Loss brought forward at 6 April 2003 and at 6.4.2004	2,500
Loss set-off in 2004/05 (£11,500 – £2,000 – £8,500)	(1,000)
Loss carried forward to 2005/06	1,500

The brought forward loss is not used in 2003/04 as the gain in that year does not exceed the annual exemption.

23 Mr Johnson

CAPITAL GAINS TAX COMPUTATION

		£	£
1	Shop		
	Proceeds	180,000	
	Less cost	(40,000)	
		140,000	
	Less indexation allowance 0.152 × £40,000	(6,080)	
		133,920	
	Taper relief applies: 25% × £133,920		33,480
2	Goodwill		
	Proceeds	61,410	
	Less cost	(10,000)	
		51,410	
	Less indexation allowance 0.152 × £10,000	(1,520)	
		49,890	
	Taper relief applies: 25% × £49,890		12,473
3	Fixtures: value > £6,000		
	Proceeds	33,000	
	Less cost	(30,000)	
		3,000	
	Less indexation allowance 0.151 × £30,000 (restricted)	(3,000)	
		Nil	Nil
4	Fixtures: value < £6,000 exempt		Nil
5	Stock: not subject to CGT		Nil
	Total business gains		45,953

	£
Total business gains	45,953
Less annual exemption	(8,500)
Chargeable gains	37,453

CGT payable:

	£
(£32,400 – £24,000) = £8,400 × 20%	1,680
£(37,453 – 8,400) = £29,053 × 40%	11,621
	13,301

Tutorial note. Chattels costing/worth less than £6,000 are exempt from CGT, as is trading stock.

24 Dove plc

Capital gains/losses

(a) *Factory – 14.4.05*

	£
Proceeds	230,000
Less: cost	(140,000)
Unindexed gains	90,000
Less: 0.940 × £140,000 (restricted)	(90,000)
	nil

(b) *Warehouse – 18.7.05*

	£
Proceeds	80,000
Less: cost	(100,000)
Loss	(20,000)
Indexation allowance cannot increase loss	

(c) *Factory – 17.9.05*

	£
Proceeds	280,000
Less: cost	(85,000)
Unindexed gains	195,000
Less: IA	
0.421 × £85,000	(35,785)
Indexed gains	159,215

(d) *Offices – 14.11.04*

	£
Proceeds	140,000
Less: Cost	
$£250{,}000 \times \dfrac{140{,}000}{320{,}000 + 140{,}000}$	(76,087)
Unindexed gain	63,913
Less: IA	
0.268 × £76,087	(20,391)
Indexed gain	43,522

(e) Summary

	£
(i)	nil
(ii)	(20,000)
(iii)	159,215
(iv)	43,522
Net gains for accounting period	182,737

25 Hilary Spencer

Hilary Spencer – CGT 2005/06

Summary

	Business
	£
Building (W1) – 7 years taper (25%)	71,980
Plant (W2) – 6 years taper (25%)	1,667
	73,647
Less: loss	(1,000)
Net gains before taper relief	72,647
Gains after taper relief	
25% × £72,647	18,162
Total gains	18,162
Less: annual exemption	(8,500)
Gains chargeable to CGT 2005/06	9,662

Tutorial notes

1. As both assets are subject to the same amount of taper relief it does not matter how the loss is offset.
2. You are given an indexation factor in the question which is a 'red herring'. The examiner has said she will give you 'red herrings' in the exam so you must ensure you know which indexation factor to use.

Workings

1 Building

	£
Proceeds	106,000
Less: cost	(28,000)
Unindexed gain	78,000
Less: indexation allowance to 4.98 0.215 × £28,000	(6,020)
Gain before taper relief	71,980
Taper relief ownership period – 6.4.98 – 5.4.05 = 7 years	

2 Chattel

	£
Proceeds	7,000
Less: cost	(5,000)
Gain before taper relief	2,000
Restricted to 5/3 × £(7,000 – 6,000)	1,667
Taper relief ownership period – 18.10.99 – 17.10.05 = 6 years	

3 Chattel

	£
Proceeds [presumed]	6,000
Less: cost	(7,000)
Loss	(1,000)

Chapter 9 Shares and securities

26 Brooklyn

Post 6.4.98 acquisitions are treated as disposed of on a LIFO basis:

(a) 3.11.04 acquisition

	£
Proceeds (2,000/11,000) × £66,000)	12,000
Less: Cost	(12,800)
Allowable loss	(800)

(b) 29.6.03 acquisition

	£
Proceeds (3,000/11,000 × £66,000)	18,000
Less: Cost	(11,500)
Gain before taper relief	6,500

The shares are a business asset. They have been held for one complete year so taper relief is available, but see below.

(c) The FA 1985 pool

	Shares	*Cost*	*Indexed cost*
		£	£
Acquisition 19.9.82	2,000	1,700	1,700
Indexation to April 1985			
0.158 × £1,700			269
Acquisition 17.1.85	2,000	6,000	6,000
Indexation to April 1985			
0.039 × £6,000			234
	4,000	7,700	8,203
Indexed rise to December 1985			
£8,203 × 0.013			107
Acquisition 12.12.85	2,000	5,500	5,500
	6,000	13,200	13,810
Indexed rise to April 1998			
£13,810 × 0.694			9,584
Value when pool closes (5.4.98)	6,000	13,200	23,394
Disposal 17.5.05	(6,000)	(13,200)	(23,394)
	0	0	0

	£
Proceeds $\frac{6,000}{11,000} \times$ £66,000	36,000
Less cost	(13,200)
	22,800
Less indexation allowance £(23,394 – 13,200)	(10,194)
Chargeable gain	12,606

There are seven complete years of post 5 April 1998 so the chargeable gain must be reduced by taper relief.

Losses may be set against gains in the most beneficial way before taper relief is applied:

	£	£
Gain on sale of 29.6.03 acquisition	6,500	
Less: loss on 3.11.04 acquisition	(800)	
Gain before taper relief	5,700	
Gain after taper relief (50%)		2,850
Gain on FA 1985 pool shares after taper relief (25%)		3,152
Gain after taper relief		6,002

Tutorial note. You should always set losses against gains with the lowest amount of taper relief attached.

27 Box plc

Box plc: Chargeable gains y/e 31.3.2006

Summary of gains and losses

	£
Shares: last nine days (W1)	400
FA 1985 pool (W2)	5,140
	5,540

Workings

1 *Crate Ltd shares – acquisition in last nine days*

	£
Proceeds 11,000/22,000 × £136,400	68,200
Less: cost	(67,800)
Gain	400

2 *Crate Ltd shares – FA 1985 pool*

	No.	*Cost*	*Indexed cost*
		£	£
26.5.92			
Acquisition	4,000	24,000	24,000
30.6.93 Bonus issue	2,000		
24.10.00			
IA			
0.232 × £24,000			5,568
			29,568
Acquisition	5,000	27,500	27,500
c/f	11,000	51,500	57,068
22.5.05			
IA 0.105 × £57,068			5,992
			63,060
Disposal	(11,000)	(51,500)	(63,060)
c/f	nil	nil	nil

Gain

	£
Proceeds 11,000/22,000 × £136,400	68,200
Less: cost	(51,500)
Unindexed gain	16,700
Less indexation allowance	
£(63,060 – 51,500)	(11,560)
Indexed gain	5,140

Tutorial notes

1 For companies, indexation is available to the date of disposal of an asset.

2 A bonus issue merely effects the number of shares in issue. As bonus shares have no cost there is no need to index the Finance Act 1985 pool to the date of the bonus issue.

Chapter 10 Deferral reliefs

28 Miss Bathsheba

(a) CAPITAL GAINS

	£	£
The shop		
Proceeds		120,000
Cost	44,000	
Extension	15,000	
		(59,000)
		61,000
Less indexation allowance to April 1998		
On original cost only:		
0.189 × £44,000		(8,316)
		52,684

The chargeable gain before taper relief is £52,684.

	£
The yard	
Proceeds	80,000
Less costs of disposal	(1,200)
	78,800
Less: Cost	
$£110,000 \times \frac{80,000}{80,000 + 230,000}$	(28,387)
	50,413
Less: Indexation allowance to April 1998	
0.189 × £28,387	(5,365)
	45,048

The chargeable gain before taper relief is £45,048.

Total chargeable gains before taper relief are £(52,684 + 45,048) = £97,732.

Taper relief is available on the disposal of both business assets leaving 25% of the original gains as taxable = £24,433. (Seven complete years of ownership.) Note that there is no restriction on the taper relief in respect of the extension made in December 2004.

(b) If the new shop is acquired within 36 months after the above disposals, a claim may be made to roll over the gains before taper relief against the cost of the new shop. Any tax already paid on the gains will be repaid, and the cost of the new shop for capital gains tax purposes will be reduced by the gains rolled over. Miss Bathsheba can make a provisional rollover claim, to avoid paying the tax and then getting it back.

If all of the above proceeds are invested in a new shop, the full amount of the gains may be rolled over. However, the gains will remain chargeable to the extent that any of the proceeds are not reinvested.

Tutorial note. Costs must be allocated on a part disposal using the formula $\frac{A}{A+B}$ where A = gross disposal proceeds and B = value of the remainder.

29 Walter and Darren

The gain covered by gift relief is as follows.

	£
Market value at gift	50,000
Less cost	(10,000)
	40,000
Less indexation allowance	
0.157 × £10,000	(1,570)
Gain relieved	38,430

The gain in 2005/06 is as follows.

	£	£
Proceeds		200,000
Less cost	50,000	
Less gift relief	(38,430)	
		(11,570)
		188,430
Less indexation allowance to April 1998		
0.708 × £11,570		(8,192)
Chargeable gain		180,238

Taper relief will reduce the chargeable gain on this business asset to £45,060 (25%) due to the seven complete years of ownership post 5 April 1998.

Tutorial note. The gain deferred by gift relief is deducted from the base cost of the asset given away.

30 E Ltd

(a) **The workshop**

	£
Proceeds	180,000
Less cost	(60,000)
Unindexed gain	120,000
Less indexation allowance	
0.285 × £60,000	(17,100)
	102,900

(b) Since E Ltd has reinvested the proceeds of sale of the workshop into the larger premises, it can rollover the gain of £102,900. This means there will be no chargeable gain in the year ended 31 December 2005.

The base cost of the large premises will be £(184,000 – 102,900) = £81,100. Therefore, the unindexed gain arising on the disposal of these premises will be increased by £102,900.

Tutorial notes.

1. Companies are not eligible for taper relief but they do get indexation to the date of disposal.

2. One of the indexation factors given to you in this question was a "red herring". In the examination you may well be given indexation factors which are 'red herrings' so you must make sure that you know which indexation factor to use.

31 K Ltd

(a) **The property**

	£
Proceeds	174,500
Less cost (£85,000 – £16,800)	(68,200)
	106,300
Less indexation allowance to November 2005 – 1.246 × £68,200	(84,977)
Chargeable gain	21,323

(b) **The painting**

There will be no chargeable gain, because the painting is a chattel sold for not more than £6,000.

(c) **The shares in Z plc**

	£
Proceeds	40,000
Less cost	(28,000)
Unindexed gain	12,000
Less: indexation allowance to March 2006	
0.099 × £28,000	(2,772)
Gain	9,228

(d) Rollover relief can be claimed to defer the gain on the property as the proceeds were reinvested in the freehold warehouse.

(e) **Summary**

	£
The property (rolled over)	0
The painting	0
The shares in Z plc	9,228
Gains for year ended 31 March 2006	9,228

Tutorial notes

1 It is not possible to rollover the gain arising on the sale of the shares, as shares are not a qualifying asset for rollover relief purposes.

2 As the amount invested in the new warehouse exceeded the sale proceeds on the sale of property in November 2005, the full amount of the gain can be rolled over. If the amount invested in the warehouse had been less than the sale proceeds, an amount of the gain equal to the sale proceeds not reinvested would have remained chargeable.

Chapter 11 An outline of corporation tax

32 Corporation tax computation

CORPORATION TAX COMPUTATION FOR THE ACCOUNTING PERIOD ENDED 31 MARCH 2006

	£	£
Taxable trading profits		245,000
Rental income		15,000
Interest		4,000
Capital gains £(35,000 + 7,000)	42,000	
Less losses brought forward	(8,000)	
		34,000
		298,000
Less charges		(7,000)
PCTCT		291,000
Dividends plus tax credits		15,000
Profits for small companies rate purposes		306,000

	£
Corporation tax £291,000 × 30%	87,300
Less small companies marginal relief	
$£(1{,}500{,}000 - 306{,}000) \times \frac{291{,}000}{306{,}000} \times 11/400$	(31,225)
	56,075

33 A Company plc

(a) *The adjustment of profits*

		£	£
Net profit per accounts			118,000
Add:	depreciation	65,000	
	legal costs: re issue of shares	10,000	
	entertaining suppliers	31,000	
	installation of machinery	12,000	
			118,000
			236,000
Less:	investment income	14,000	
	profit on sale of investments	19,320	
	capital allowances	31,000	
			(64,320)
			171,680

(b) **CORPORATION TAX COMPUTATION**

	£
Taxable trading profits (Part (a) above)	171,680
Interest	6,000
Chargeable gains	18,000
PCTCT	195,680
Dividends received plus tax credits	8,000
'Profits' for small companies rate purposes	203,680

The associated company halves the lower and upper limits for small companies' rate purposes.

Upper limit for small companies rate purposes	750,000
Lower limit for small companies rate purposes	150,000

Corporation tax	£
£195,680 × 30%	58,704
Less small companies marginal relief	
$£(750,000 - 203,680) \times \frac{195,680}{203,680} \times 11/400$	(14,434)
Corporation tax	44,270

34 Polar (UK) Ltd

Polar UK Ltd Corporation Tax Payable y/e 31.3.06

	£	£
Taxable trading profits		20,000
Interest:		
bank interest received	14,500	
		14,500
Chargeable gain		4,000
Total profits		38,500
Less: charges on income		
gift aid		(4,500)
PCTCT		34,000
Add: dividend received (gross up)		
£6,300 × 100/90		7,000
'Profits'		41,000

Tax liability

	£
Starting rate upper limit	£50,000
Starting rate lower limit	£10,000
Starting rate marginal relief applies	

	£
£34,000 × 19%	6,460
Less: starting rate marginal relief	
$(£50,000 - £41,000) \times \frac{34,000}{41,000} \times \frac{19}{400}$	(355)
Corporation tax	6,105

Underlying tax rate $\frac{6,105}{34,000} = 17.956\%$

This underlying rate must be increased to 19% for dividends paid to non-corporate shareholders:

	£
£10,000 × 19%	1,900
£24,000 × 17.956%	4,309
Corporation tax due	6,209

35 Dealers plc and Springer Ltd

(a) Dealers plc's profits for small companies rate purposes are £420,000 so tax is payable at the marginal rate in both FY04 and FY05.

	FY 2004 and FY 2005
	£
Profits chargeable to corporation tax	420,000
'Profits'	420,000
Upper limit	1,500,000
Lower limit	300,000

Corporation tax

	£
FY 2004 and FY 2005	
£420,000 × 30%	126,000
Less small companies marginal relief	
£(1,500,000 – 420,000) × 11/400	(29,700)
	96,300

(b) Springer Ltd's 'profits' are £6,200. This means they qualify for the starting rate in both FY 2005 and FY 2004:

	£
FY 2004 and FY 2005	
£6,200 × 0%	NIL
	NIL

Springer Ltd's underlying tax rate is 0%. The tax rate must be increased to 19% in respect of dividends paid to non-corporate shareholders.

	£
£1,000 × 19%	190
£5,200 × 0%	0
Corporation tax due	190

36 Traders Ltd

(a) **Taxable trading profits**

		£	£
Net profit per accounts			101,977
Add:	entertaining	600	
	tax consultancy	30	
	lease on new premises	100	
	gift aid donation	5,200	
	political donation	500	
	depreciation	15,000	
			21,430
			123,407
Less:	commissions (chargeable as other income)	800	
	profit on sale of investment	5,265	
	building society interest	1,100	
			(7,165)
Taxable trading profits			116,242

(b)

Taxable trading profits	116,242
Interest	1,100
Other income	800
Chargeable gain	770
	118,912
Less charges paid	(5,200)
Profits chargeable to corporation tax	113,712

(c) The profits for small companies rate purposes are below the lower limit, so the small companies rate applies.

The corporation tax liability is £113,712 × 19% — £21,605

Tutorial notes

1 You are extremely likely to be required to adjust accounts profit for tax purposes in the examination. The best way to familiarise yourself with the adjustments required is to practice plenty of questions like this.

2 As the company pays tax at 19%, there is no additional tax to pay in respect of the distributions to non-corporate shareholders.

Chapter 12 Corporation tax losses

37 P Ltd

Corporation tax y/e 31.3.06

	£	£
Taxable trading profits	360,000	
Less: loss b/f	(10,000)	
		350,000
Interest – bank interest		6,000
Rental income		18,000
Capital gain	14,000	
Loss b/f	(14,000)	nil
Loss c/f £(15,000 – 14,000) = £1,000		
Total profits		374,000
Less: gift aid payment (charge)		(6,000)
PCTCT		368,000

	£
PCTCT	368,000
Dividends (10,800 × 100/90)	12,000
'Profits'	380,000

'Profits' are above £300,000 but below £1,500,000 so SCR marginal relief applies.

Tax payable

	£
Corporation tax on PCTCT	
£368,000 × 30%	110,400
Less: small companies' marginal relief	
$£(1{,}500{,}000 - 380{,}000) \times \frac{368{,}000}{380{,}000} \times \frac{11}{400}$	(29,827)
Tax payable	80,573

Tutorial notes

1 The capital loss can only be set against the capital gain. The unrelieved loss must be carried forward.

2 Bought forward trading losses can only be set against taxable profits.

38 Galbraith Ltd

(a)

	Year ended 31 March		
	2004	*2005*	*2006*
	£	£	£
Taxable trading profits	125,000	0	50,000
Less s 393(1) loss relief	0	0	(6,640)
	125,000	0	43,360
Interest	263,000	10,000	24,000
Chargeable gains (loss c/f)	60,360	0	0
	448,360	10,000	67,360
Less s 393A(1) current loss relief	0	(10,000)	0
	448,360	0	67,360
Less: s 393A carry back	(448,360)	0	0
Less: gift aid donation	0	0	(30,000)
Profits chargeable to corporation tax	0	0	37,360
Unrelieved gift aid donation	40,000	47,000	0

The loss available for carry back is £465,000 – £10,000 = £455,000. The loss remaining to carry forward is £455,000 – £448,360 = £6,640.

There is no corporation tax liability for either of the first two years.

For the third year, the position is as follows.

Profits chargeable to corporation tax = £37,360

'Profits' = £37,360 + (£3,750 × 100/90) = £41,527. As 'profits' are between the starting rate upper and lower limits of £50,000 and £10,000 respectively, starting rate marginal relief applies.

	£
Corporation tax	
£37,360 × 19%	7,098
Less: starting rate marginal relief	
$^{19}/_{400}$ (£50,000 – £41,527) × $\frac{37,360}{41,527}$	(363)
	6,735

As all dividends are paid to corporate shareholders, there is no need to adjust the amount of tax payable.

The current year set off is in some ways not worth taking in this question as the company's profits **would otherwise be covered by the gift aid donation.** However, if a current year set off is not made a s 393A carryback claim cannot be made. In this case carrying the loss back saves tax at 32.75%, 19% and 23.75%. The claim must be for the whole of the loss under s 393A. If s 393A claims were not made the loss would have to be carried forward and based on current year profits relief would be at 23.75%, 19% and 0% in future years. Full relief would not be available for several years.

Tutorial note. It was necessary to spot that starting rate marginal relief would apply in the year to 31 March 2006.

(b) A capital loss of £4,000 is carried forward at 1 April 2006.

Tutorial note. Capital losses can only be carried forward to set against current and future capital gains. They can not be carried back.

39 Ferraro Ltd

(a)

	Accounting periods		
	12m to 31.12.03	*9m to 30.9.04*	*12m to 30.9.05*
	£	£	£
Taxable trading profits	6,200	4,320	0
Interest	80	240	260
Rental income	1,420	1,440	1,600
Chargeable gain (£12,680 – £5,000 b/f)	0	7,680	0
	7,700	13,680	1,860
Less: s 393A – current	0	0	(1,860)
	7,700	13,680	0
Less: s 393A – c/b	(1,925)	(13,680)	(0)
Less: charges	(0)	(0)	(0)
PCTCT	5,775	0	0

(b) The loss carried forward against future profits of the same trade is £100,000 – £(1,925 + 13,680 + 1,860) = £82,535.

The allowable capital loss of £9,423 during the year ended 30 September 2005 is carried forward against future chargeable gains.

The gift aid donation made in the 9 months to 30.9.04 remains unrelieved. Similarly the unrelieved gift aid donation in the year 30.9.05 remains unrelieved. Unrelieved gift aid donations cannot be carried forward.

Tutorial notes

1 The loss is carried back to set against profits arising the previous 12 months. This means that the set off in the y/e 31.12.03 is restricted to 3/12 × £7,700 = £1,925.

2 The pro-forma for loss relief is important. If you learn the proforma you should find that the figures just slot into place. Note that the result of a losses claim may be that, as here, gift aid donations become unrelieved.

Chapter 13 National Insurance

40 Josephine

Earnings for NICs

Salary per week for 51 weeks	£402
Salary per week for 1 week plus book token	£502

Meal vouchers for meals on employer premises are not earnings for NIC purposes.

Class 1 secondary contributions – payable by employer

	£
12.8% × £(402 – 94) = £39.42 × 51	2,010.42
12.8% × £(502 – 94)	52.22
	2,062.64

Class 1A contributions – payable by employer

£6,850 × 12.8%	£876.80

41 Zoë

(a) Class 2 = £2.10 × 52 = £109.20

		£
Class 4	£(32,760 – 4,895) × 8% (main)	2,229.20
	£(80,000 – 32,760) × 1% (additional)	472.40
		2,701.60

(b) A self employed person must notify the Revenue that he or she is liable to Class 2 NICs within three months of the end of the month in which he or she becomes self employed.

42 Paula

(a) Share of profits for y/e 31.12.06 is £100,000 × 20% = £20,000

2005/06

1.1.05 to 5.4.05

3/12 × £20,000 = £5,000

2006/07

1.1.06 to 31.12.06 = £20,000

Overlap period is 1.1.06 to 5.4.06 so overlap profits are £5,000.

(b) *Class 4 NICs for 2005/06*

£(5,000 – 4,895) = £105 × 8% = £8.40

Chapter 14 Administration of income tax and CGT

43 Self assessment for individuals

Tutorial note. It was important to confine your answer to the points asked for in the question.

(a) (i) In general, the later of 30 September following the tax year to which the return relates and 2 months after the notice to file the return was issued. However, if an individual is issued with a short tax return, the Revenue will calculate the tax provided that the return is submitted by the 31 January following the end of the tax year.

(ii) The later of 31 January following the tax year to which the return relates and 3 months after notice to file the return was issued.

(b) (i) The normal payment dates for income tax are:

- 31 January in the tax year for the first payment on account, ie 31.1.05
- 31 July following the tax year for the second payment on account, ie 31.7.05
- 31 January following the tax year for the final payment, ie 31.1.06

(ii) **Each of the payments on account is normally equal to half of the income tax liability for the preceding year, (in this case 2004/05).**

The **final payment is the balancing payment**. It is the difference between the tax which is finally due for 2005/06 and the payments on account which have already been made in respect of the year.

(c) Payments on account are not required if the relevant amount falls below £500.

Also, payments on account are not required from taxpayers who paid 80% or more of their tax liability for the previous year under PAYE or other deduction at source arrangements.

(d) (i) The **fixed penalty** for not making a tax return by the filing date (31 January following the tax year) when required to do so is initially **£100**. If the **delay is more than six months** from the filing date, and the Revenue did not apply for a daily penalty within those six months, there is a **further £100 fixed penalty**.

(ii) The total of the £100 fixed penalties is reduced to the amount of the final payment of tax, if that is less than that total. The commissioners can set aside the fixed £100 penalties if they find that the taxpayer had a reasonable excuse for his conduct.

(iii) Where the Revenue are of the opinion that the fixed penalties imposed will not result in the return being submitted they may ask the Commissioners to apply further penalties of up to £60 a day until the return is submitted.

44 Enquiries

(a) The Revenue must normally give notice of an enquiry by the first anniversary of the due filing date (not the actual filing date).

(b) If a return is filed late, the deadline by which the Revenue must give notice of an enquiry is extended to 12 months after the 31 January, 30 April, 31 July or 31 October next following the actual date of delivery of the return or amendment.

(c) The three main reasons why the Revenue commence enquiries into a return are:

(i) **random selection** of the return

(ii) **the return appears unusual**; there appears to be either an underdeclaration or income or allowances appear to have been incorrectly claimed

(iii) **the Revenue suspect or have been informed of irregularities** in the return

(d) If the taxpayer does not accept the Revenue's amendments he may **appeal to the commissioners within 30 days of the end of an enquiry**.

45 Martin

(a) *Taxable trading profits 2005/06*

	£	£
Net profit per accounts		5,000
Add: wages of proprietor	15,000	
private motor 20% × £2,500	500	
depreciation	3,000	
entertaining suppliers	750	
legal costs re grant of lease	450	
		19,700
		24,700
Less: capital allowances		(1,600)
Taxable trading profit		23,100

(b) *Class 2 NICs 2005/06*

£2.10 × 52 = £109.20

Class 4 NICs 2005/06

£(23,100 – 4,895) = £18,205 × 8% = £1,456.40

(c)

Box 3.1	Martin's The Greengrocer		
Box 3.2	Retail greengrocer		
Box 3.4	01/04/05		
Box 3.5	31/03/06		
Box 3.16	£1,600		
Box 3.22	£1,600		
Box 3.29	£100,000		
Box 3.46	£40,000		
Box 3.49	£60,000		
Box 3.33	£15,000	Box 3.51	£35,000
		Box 3.52	£7,000
		Box 3.54	£1,000
Box 3.37	£500	Box 3.55	£2,500
Box 3.39	£750	Box 3.57	£1,000
Box 3.40	£450	Box 3.58	£1,250
		Box 3.60	£500
Box 3.44	£3,000	Box 3.62	£3,000
		Box 3.63	£3,750
Box 3.64	£55,000		
Box 3.65	£5,000		
Box 3.66	£19,700		
Box 3.69	£19,700		
Box 3.70	£1,600		
Box 3.72	£1,600		
Box 3.73	£23,100		

Chapter 15 Payment of tax by companies

46 Alphabetic Ltd

(a) Alphabetic Ltd is a 'large' company and as such should have paid its corporation tax liability for the year to 30 September 2005 in four quarterly instalments. The underpayments were:

Due date	*Amount Due*	*Underpaid*
	£	£
14.4.05	200,000	44,000
14.7.05	200,000	44,000
14.10.05	200,000	44,000
14.1.06	200,000	44,000

Interest will run on each of the amounts of £44,000 underpaid from the due date until the date of payment, 1 July 2006.

(b) If a company has not received a return it must notify the Revenue of its liability to corporation tax with 12 months of the end of its accounting period.

The maximum penalty for not taking such action is 100% of the corporation tax unpaid twelve months after the end of the accounting period.

(c) (i) Fixed rate penalties

(1) Where the return is up to 3 months late – £100

(2) Where the return is more than 3 months late – £200

(3) Where the return is the third consecutive one to be filed late the above penalties are increased to £500 and £1,000 respectively.

(ii) A tax geared penalty is triggered in addition to the fixed penalties if a return is more than six months late. The penalty is 10% of any tax unpaid six months after the return was due if the total delay is up to 12 months, but 20% of that tax if the return is over 12 months late.

(d) Companies that become large during an accounting period will not have to pay their corporation tax for that period by instalments if:

(i) their taxable profits for the period do not exceed £10 million (reduced if there are associated companies); and

(ii) they were not a large company in the previous period

A 'large company' is one that pays corporation tax at the full rate.

Also, there is a de minimis limit in that any company whose liability does not exceed £10,000 need not pay by instalments.

47 Cranmore Ltd

(a)

	FYA	Pool	Exp. car		Allowances
	£	£	£		£
TWDV b/f		12,000			
Additions		10,000	25,000		
		22,000	25,000		
WDA @ 25%		(5,500)	(3,000)	(max)	8,500
		16,500	22,000		
Addition	6,250				
FYA @ 40%	(2,500)	3,750			2,500
TWDV c/f		20,250	22,000		
Allowances					11,000

(b) *Corporation tax computation y/e 31.3.06*

	£
Taxable trading profits (£405,000 – £11,000)	394,000
Interest	3,000
Rental income	10,000
Other income	6,000
PCTCT	413,000

	£
£413,000 x 30%	123,900.00
Less: Small companies' marginal relief £(1,500,000 – 413,000) x 11/400	(29,892.50)
	94,007.50
Less: income tax deducted at source £6,000 x 22%	(1,320.00)
Corporation tax due	92,687.50

(c) You should have made the following entries on the form CT 600.

Taxable trading profits (box 3): £394,000
Net trading profits (box 5): £394,000
Interest (box 6): £3,000
Rental income (box 12): £10,000
Other income (box 14): £6,000
Profits (box 21): £413,000
Profits chargeable to corporation tax (box 37): £413,000
Franked investment income (box 38): £0
Associated companies (box 39): 0
Marginal relief (box 42): X
Financial year (box 43): 2005
Amount of profit (box 44): £413,000
Rate of tax (box 45): 30.00
Tax (box 46): £123,900.00
Corporation tax (box 63): £123,900.00
Marginal rate relief (box 64): £29,892.50

Corporation tax net of marginal rate relief (box 65): £94,007.50
Corporation tax chargeable (box 70): £94,007.50
Income tax deducted (box 84): £1,320.00
Tax payable (box 86): £92,687.50
Corporation tax outstanding (box 92): £92,687.50

Capital allowances
Machinery and plant (box 107): £8,000
Cars (box 109): £3,000
FYA expenditure (box 118): £6,250
Other expenditure on plant and machinery (box 121): £35,000

PART H

Full exam based assessments

PRACTICE EXAM PAPER 1

(December 2004 paper)

TECHNICIAN STAGE – NVQ4

Unit 18

Preparing business tax computations (BTC)

DO NOT OPEN THIS PAPER UNTIL YOU ARE READY TO START UNDER EXAM CONDITIONS

INSTRUCTIONS

This examination paper is in TWO SECTIONS.

You have to show competence in BOTH sections.

You should therefore attempt and aim to compete EVERY task in EACH section.

You should spend about 80 minutes on Section 1 and 100 minutes on Section 2.

COVERAGE OF PERFORMANCE CRITERIA

The following performance criteria are covered in this exam.

Element	PC Coverage
18.1	**Prepare capital allowances computations**
A	Classify expenditure on capital assets in accordance with the statutory distinction between capital and revenue expenditure
C	Made adjustments for private use by business owners
D	Ensure that computations and submissions are made in accordance with current tax law and take account of current Revenue practice
G	Maintain client confidentiality at all times
18.2	**Compute assessable business income**
A	Adjust trading profits and losses for tax purposes
C	Divide profits and losses of partnerships amongst partners
D	Apply the basis of assessment for unincorporated businesses in the opening and closing years
E	Identify the due dates of payment of Income Tax by unincorporated businesses, including payments on account
F	Identify the National Insurance Contributions payable by self-employed individuals
G	Complete correctly the self-employed and partnership supplementary pages to the Tax Return for individuals, together with relevant claims and elections, and submit them within statutory time limits
I	Give timely and constructive advice to clients on the maintenance of accounts and the recording of information relevant to tax returns
18.3	**Prepare capital gains computations**
A	Identify and value correctly any chargeable assets that have been disposed of
B	Identify shares disposed of by companies
C	Calculate chargeable gains and allowable losses
D	Apply reliefs, deferrals and exemptions correctly.
E	Ensure that computations and submissions are made in accordance with current tax law and take account of current Revenue practice
18.4	**Prepare corporation tax computations**
A	Enter adjusted trading profits and losses, capital allowances, investment income and capital gains in the Corporation Tax computation
B	Set-off and deduct loss reliefs and charges correctly
C	Calculate Corporation Tax due, taking account of marginal relief
F	Identify the amount of Corporation Tax payable and the due dates of payment, including payments on account

TAXATION TABLES FOR BUSINESS TAX

Capital allowances:

	%
Writing down allowance	
Plant and machinery	25
First year allowance	
Plant and machinery, after 2 July 1998 – all businesses	40
Year commending 6 April 2004 – small businesses	50

National insurance contributions:

Class 2	
Weekly contribution	£2.10
Small earnings exemption limit	£4,345
Class 4	
Lower profits limited	£4,895
Upper profits limit	£32,760
Rate on profits between upper and lower limits	8%
Rate on profits over upper limit	1%

Capital gains indexation factors:

July 1995 to April 1998	0.091
November 2001 to March 2006	0.110

Tapering relief for business assets:

No of years held after 5 April 1998	*% of gain chargeable*
0	100
1	50
2 or more	25

Corporation tax:

	FY 2005	FY 2004
Starting rate	0%	0%
Lower limit	£10,000	£10,000
Upper limit	£50,000	£50,000
Marginal relief fraction	19/400	19/400
Small companies rate	19%	19%
Lower limit	£300,000	£300,000
Upper limit	£1,500,000	£1,500,000
Marginal relief fraction	11/400	11/400
Full rate	30%	30%

SECTION 1

(Suggested time allowance: 80 minutes)

DATA

You work in the tax department of a small firm of Chartered Accountants. One of the firm's clients, Angela Graham, has just given you the information you need to complete her 2005/06 tax return.

Trading profits

Angela ceased trading on 30 September 2005. Her summarised profit and loss account for the nine-month period showed:

	£
Sales	257,200
Cost of sales	79,400
Gross profit	177,800
Expenses	124,800
Net profit	53,000

All expenses were allowable for taxation purposes.

On 31 December 2004, the balances for capital allowances purposes were:

	£
General pool	7,330
Car, private usage 30%	9,570

The plant and machinery in the general pool was sold on 30 September 2005 for £8,200. Angela decided to keep the car after the business ceased trading. The market value of the car on 30 September 2005 was £6,000. It had originally cost £15,570. The overlap profit brought forward from commencement of trade was £21,050.

Capital Transactions

On 31 January 2006, Angela disposed of an asset that has been classified as a business asset for capital gains tax purposes. The proceeds were £225,000. She bought the asset in July 1995 for £82,500. She spent £17,000 on improving the asset in February 2003.

Payments on account

Angela paid £5,000 on both 31 January 2006 and 31 July 2006 as income tax payments on account for 2005/06.

Task 1.1

Calculate the capital allowances to the date of cessation.

Task 1.2

Calculate the net taxable trading profit for the final tax year of the business.

Task 1.3

Calculate the net gain chargeable to capital gains tax, before the annual exemption.

DATA

In the paper work received from Angela was a note saying that she wants to start another business with her sister. She wants to know:

- if the way in which a partnership is taxed is different to how she was taxed as a sole trader
- how tax payable by each partner is determined
- which National Insurance Contributions she and her sister will need to pay
- the records that should be kept to maintain the accounts to an acceptable level.

Task 1.4

Using the memo below, answer Angela's queries.

MEMO	
To: Angela Graham	**Subject: Various queries**
From: Accounting Technician	**Date: 30 November 2006**

Task 1.5

Assuming that Angela's final total tax liability for 2005/06 exceeds the £10,000 payments on account that she has already paid, explain how and when the remaining tax will be paid to the HMRC.

Task 1.6

As far as is possible given the available information, complete the attached tax return.

Income for the year ended 5 April 2006

SELF-EMPLOYMENT

Fill in these boxes first

Name

Tax reference

If you want help, look up the box numbers in the Notes

Business details

Name of business

3.1 Angela Graham

Description of business

3.2

Address of business

3.3

Postcode

Accounting period - *read the Notes, page SEN3 before filling in these boxes*

Start 3.4 / /

End 3.5 / /

- Tick box 3.6 if details in boxes 3.1 or 3.3 have changed since your last Tax Return 3.6
- Date of commencement if after 5 April 2002 3.7 / /
- Date of cessation if before 6 April 2006 3.8 / /
- Tick box 3.9 if the special arrangements for particular trades apply - *read the Notes, pages SEN11 and SEN12* 3.9
- Tick box 3.10 if you entered details for all relevant accounting periods on last year's Tax Return and boxes 3.14 to 3.73 and 3.99 to 3.115 will be blank *(read Step 3 on page SEN2)* 3.10
- Tick box 3.11 if your accounts do not cover the period from the last accounting date (explain why in the 'Additional information' box, box 3.116) 3.11
- Tick box 3.12 if your accounting date has changed (only if this is a permanent change and you want it to count for tax) 3.12
- Tick box 3.13 if this is the second or further change (explain in box 3.116 on Page SE4 why you have not used the same date as last year) 3.13

Capital allowances - summary

	Capital allowances	Balancing charges
• Cars costing more than £12,000 (excluding cars with low CO_2 emissions) (A separate calculation must be made for each car.)	3.14 £	3.15 £
• Other business plant and machinery (including cars with low CO_2 emissions and cars costing less than £12,000) *read the Notes, page SEN4*	3.16 £	3.17 £
• Agricultural or Industrial Buildings Allowance (A separate calculation must be made for each block of expenditure.)	3.18 £	3.19 £
• Other capital allowances claimed (Separate calculations must be made.)	3.20 £	3.21 £
Total capital allowances/balancing charges	total of column above 3.22 £	total of column above 3.23 £

- Tick box 3.22A if box 3.22 includes enhanced capital allowances for environmentally friendly expenditure 3.22A

Income and expenses - annual turnover below £15,000

*If your annual turnover is £15,000 or more, **ignore** boxes 3.24 to 3.26. Instead fill in Page SE2*

*If your annual turnover is below £15,000, **fill in boxes 3.24 to 3.26 instead of Page SE2**. Read the Notes, page SEN6.*

- Turnover including other business receipts and goods etc. taken for personal use (and balancing charges from box 3.23) 3.24 £
- Expenses allowable for tax (including capital allowances from box 3.22) 3.25 £

Net profit (put figure in brackets if a loss) — box 3.24 *minus* box 3.25 — 3.26 £

You must now fill in Page SE3

SA103

BS 12/04net

TAX RETURN ■ SELF-EMPLOYMENT: PAGE SE1

Income and expenses - annual turnover £15,000 or more

You must fill in this Page if your annual turnover is £15,000 or more - read the Notes, pages SEN2, SEN6 to SEN7

If you were registered for VAT, do the figures in boxes 3.29 to 3.64, include VAT? **3.27** [ ] or exclude VAT? **3.28** [ ]

Sales/business income (turnover) **3.29** £

	Disallowable expenses included in boxes 3.46 to 3.63	Total expenses	
• Cost of sales	3.30 £	3.46 £	
• Construction industry subcontractor costs	3.31 £	3.47 £	
• Other direct costs	3.32 £	3.48 £	box 3.29 *minus* (boxes 3.46 + 3.47 + 3.48)
		Gross profit/(loss)	3.49 £
		Other income/profits	3.50 £
• Employee costs	3.33 £	3.51 £	
• Premises costs	3.34 £	3.52 £	
• Repairs	3.35 £	3.53 £	
• General administrative expenses	3.36 £	3.54 £	
• Motor expenses	3.37 £	3.55 £	
• Travel and subsistence	3.38 £	3.56 £	
• Advertising, promotion and entertainment	3.39 £	3.57 £	
• Legal and professional costs	3.40 £	3.58 £	
• Bad debts	3.41 £	3.59 £	
• Interest	3.42 £	3.60 £	
• Other finance charges	3.43 £	3.61 £	
• Depreciation and loss/(profit) on sale	3.44 £	3.62 £	
• Other expenses	3.45 £	3.63 £	total of boxes 3.51 to 3.63
	Put the total of boxes 3.30 to 3.45 in box 3.66 below	Total expenses	3.64 £
			boxes 3.49 + 3.50 *minus* 3.64
		Net profit/(loss)	3.65 £

Tax adjustments to net profit or loss

• Disallowable expenses	boxes 3.30 to 3.45 3.66 £	
• Adjustments (apart from disallowable expenses) that increase profits. Examples are goods taken for personal use and amounts brought forward from an earlier year because of a claim under ESC B11 about compulsory slaughter of farm animals	3.67 £	
• Balancing charges (from box 3.23)	3.68 £	boxes 3.66 + 3.67 + 3.68
Total additions to net profit (deduct from net loss)		3.69 £
• Capital allowances (from box 3.22)	3.70 £	boxes 3.70 + 3.71
• Deductions from net profit (add to net loss)	3.71 £	3.72 £
		boxes 3.65 + 3.69 *minus* 3.72
Net business profit for tax purposes (put figure in brackets if a loss)		3.73 £

BS 12/04net TAX RETURN ■ SELF-EMPLOYMENT: PAGE SE2

Now fill in Page SE3

SECTION 2

(Suggested time allowance: 100 minutes)

DATA

You are employed by Horatio Ltd, and work in the accounts department. The Company Accountant has asked you to prepare the tax information before it is entered in the CT600 tax form.

The accounts department has supplied you with the accounts for the 15-month period ended 31 March 2006.

The profit and loss account shows:

	£	£
Gross profit		487,500
Profit on sale of shares (Note 1)		12,850
UK dividends received (Note 2)		4,500
Rental income (Note 3)		7,500
		512,350
General expenses (Note 4)	240,780	
Wages and salaries	120,650	
Administrative expenses	87,230	
Depreciation	14,600	463,260
Net profit		49,090

Notes

(1) Profit on sale of shares: Horatio Ltd sold all its shares in Yellow Ltd for £24,500 in March 2006. 2,000 shares had been bought in November 2001 for £11,650. In January 2003, Horatio Ltd received a bonus issue of 1 for 2 shares.

(2) UK dividends received: The dividends were received on 15 October 2005. The company that paid the dividends is not associated with Horatio Ltd.

(3) Rental income: Horatio Ltd received £500 per month in rental income.

(4) General expenses: These include:

	£
Gift aid donation (paid July 2005)	3,500
Entertaining customers	8,450

ADDITIONAL DATA

1. The capital allowances for the year ended 31 December 2005 are £8,750, and £2,600 for the period ended 31 March 2006.

2. Horatio Ltd has property income losses of £1,000 brought forward from the year ended 31 December 2004.

Task 2.1

Calculate the chargeable gain, or allowable loss, arising from the sale of the shares in Yellow Ltd.

Task 2.2

Calculate the adjusted trading profit, before capital allowances, for the 15-month period ended 31 March 2006.

Task 2.3

Calculate the PCTCT (profit chargeable to corporation tax) for the:

(a) 12 months ended 31 December 2005
(b) period ended 31 March 2006

Task 2.4

Calculate the corporation tax payable for the:

(a) 12 months ended 31 December 2005
(b) period ended 31 March 2006

DATA

You have received the following e-mail from the Managing Director of Horatio Ltd.

From: MD@horatio.co.uk
To: AAT@horatio.co.uk
Sent: 26 November 2006 13.25
Subject: Tax return

I know that you have recently joined the company, but we have a problem that I would like you to sort out.

For the year ended 31 December 2004, we calculated our corporation tax liability at £15,000. We paid this bill on time on 1 October 2005. We received the tax return in January 2005, but the Company Accountant didn't submit it until 30 September 2006.

We have recently had a demand from the HMRC stating that the corporation tax liability for the year was finally assessed at £19,600.

We have never done anything like this before, so hopefully the HMRC will be sympathetic to us, but we are really worried now that we will incur heavy penalties.

Please let us know what we need to do, and what penalties and interest the HMRC will impose.

Many thanks.

Managing Director

Task 2.5

Reply to the Managing Director's e-mail.

PRACTICE EXAM PAPER 2

(June 2004 paper)

TECHNICIAN STAGE – NVQ4

Unit 18

Preparing business tax computations (BTC)

DO NOT OPEN THIS PAPER UNTIL YOU ARE READY TO START UNDER EXAM CONDITIONS

COVERAGE OF PERFORMANCE CRITERIA

The following performance criteria are covered in this exam.

Element	PC Coverage
18.1	**Prepare capital allowances computations**
A	Classify expenditure on capital assets in accordance with the statutory distinction between capital and revenue expenditure
C	Make adjustments for private use by business owners
D	Ensure that computations and submissions are made in accordance with current tax law and take account of current Revenue practice
18.2	**Compute assessable business income**
A	Adjust trading profits and losses for tax purposes
B	Make adjustments for private use by business owners
C	Divide profits and losses of partnerships amongst partners
D	Apply the basis of assessment for unincorporated businesses in the opening and closing years
E	Identify the due dates of payment of Income Tax by unincorporated businesses, including payments on account
F	Identify the National Insurance contributions payable by self-employed individuals
18.3	**Prepare capital gains computations**
A	Identify and value correctly any chargeable assets that have been disposed of
B	Identify shares disposed of by companies
C	Calculate chargeable gains and allowable losses
D	Apply reliefs, deferrals and exemptions correctly
E	Ensure that computations and submissions are made in accordance with current tax law and take account of current Revenue practice
18.4	**Prepare corporation tax computations**
A	Enter adjusted trading profits and losses, capital allowances, investment income and capital gains in the Corporation Tax computation
B	Set-off and deduct loss reliefs and charges correctly
C	Calculate Corporation Tax due, taking account of marginal relief
D	Identify and set off income tax deductions and credits
F	Identify the amount of Corporation Tax payable and the due dates of payments, including payments on account
G	Complete Corporation Tax returns correctly and submit them, together with relevant claims and elections, within statutory time limits
I	Give timely and constructive advice on the maintenance of accounts and the recording of information relevant to tax returns
J	Maintain client confidentiality at all times

INSTRUCTIONS

This exam is in TWO sections.

You must show competence in BOTH sections. You should therefore attempt and aim to complete EVERY task in EACH section.

You are advised to spend approximately 100 minutes on Section 1 and 80 minutes on Section 2.

All essential workings should be included within your answers, where appropriate.

SECTION 1

(Suggested time allowance: 100 minutes)

DATA

You work for George and Carol Checkers, a partnership that makes and sells pottery. You prepare the tax information before completing the tax returns for the partners.

The profit and loss account for the year ended 31 January 2006 shows:

	£	£
Gross profit		256,550
General expenses (note 1)	85,480	
Bad and doubtful debts (note 2)	585	
Motor expenses (note 3)	7,880	
Wages and salaries	54,455	
Depreciation	21,080	
		169,480
Net profit		87,070

Notes

1 General expenses include:

	£
Gifts to customers – Christmas cakes costing £4.50 each	1,350
Cost of installing new machinery bought in August 2005	2,200

2 Bad and doubtful debts are made up of:

	£
Trade debts written off	350
Increase in general provision	400
Trade debts recovered	(165)
	585

3 Motor expenses

	Private usage %	*Annual expenses* £
George	25	4,680
Carol	15	3,200

ADDITIONAL INFORMATION

1 For capital allowances purposes, the balances brought forward from the year ended 31 January 2005 showed:

	Pool £	*George's car* £	*Carol's car* £
Balance	18,444	15,630	8,780

2 New machinery was bought in August 2005 for £24,200

3 On 1 August 2005, the business bought a new industrial building for £88,000. The building was in industrial use throughout the period.

4 The partnership agreement states that George and Carol share profits equally.

Task 1.1

Calculate the adjusted trading profit, before capital allowances, for the year ended 31 January 2006.

Task 1.2

(a) Calculate the capital allowances on the plant and machinery and motor vehicles for the year ended 31 January 2006.

(b) Calculate the industrial buildings allowance for the year ended 31 January 2006.

Task 1.3

Calculate the net trading profit for the year ended 31 January 2006.

Task 1.4

State the due dates of payment of the tax liability arising from the above profit, including any payments on account.

Task 1.5

Calculate the total National Insurance Contributions payable by Carol for the tax year 2005/06.

DATA

In March 2006 you receive a telephone call from George saying that he is thinking of giving his half of the business to his son, Elliot. He has heard of something called 'gift relief' but doesn't know anything about it. He asks for information on gift relief.

Task 1.6

State what information you would give to George.

DATA

You have received the following e-mail from George.

From: george007@boxmail.net
To: AATstudent@boxmail.net
Sent: 27 May 2006 16:22
Subject: Important news

I asked you a while ago about the implications of giving away my half of the business to my son.

However, Carol and I have now decided that we want to sell the business completely. We will therefore cease to trade on 31 May 2006.

As it is only four months since the last year end, I was wondering how the business income will be assessed in the closing years. We hope that we will make a profit in the four months from 1 February 2006 to 31 May 2006.

Thank you for your advice.

George

Task 1.7

Reply to George's email, explaining which profit periods will be assessed for the past two tax years. Your answer must include the impact of overlap relief.

Note Assume all tax rules are the same in 2005/06 as for 2006/07.

From: AATstudent@boxmail.net
To: george007@boxmail.net
Sent: 15 June 2006
Subject: Re: Important news

SECTION 2

(Suggested time allowance: 80 minutes)

DATA

You work in the tax department of a firm of Chartered Accountants. Abbey Ltd is a client of the firm, and has one associated company. You have been asked to do the tax work for the company for the year ended 31 March 2006.

Abbey Ltd has the following information for the year ended 31 March 2006.

1 The adjusted trading profit, after deducting capital allowances, was £623,024

2 In May 2005, Abbey Ltd sold 4,000 of the shares it held in Blue Ltd for £120,000. These shares had been acquired as follows:

	No of shares	£
April 1986	2,000	25,000
June 1991	2,000	35,000
July 1994 – bonus issue	1 for 10	
September 1999 – rights issue	1 for 5	£10 per share

3 In November 2005, Abbey Ltd sold its factory for £260,000. It bought the factory in December 1999 for £150,000. In March 2006, it bought a replacement factory for £230,000. The industrial buildings allowances adjustment has already been made in calculating taxable trading profits.

Task 2.1

Calculate the capital gain arising from the disposal of the shares in Blue Ltd.

Task 2.2

Calculate the capital gain arising from the disposal of the factory, and show the amount of rollover relief to be carried forward.

Task 2.3

Calculate the corporation tax payable for the year ended 31 March 2006, stating the due date for payment.

Task 2.4

Complete the following extract from the tax return for Abbey Ltd for the year ended 31 March 2006, using all the relevant information from above.

Page 1

Company - short tax return form

CT600 (Short) (2004) Version 2

for accounting periods ending on or after 1 July 1999

Your company tax return

If we send the company a *Notice* to deliver a company tax return (form *CT603*) it has to complete and send us a company tax return, at the latest by the filing date, or the company may face a penalty. A company tax return includes a company tax return form, any Supplementary Pages, accounts, computations and any relevant information.

Is this the right form for the company? Read the advice on pages 3 to 6 of the Company tax return guide (2004) (the *Guide*) before you start.

The forms in the CT600 series set out the information we need and provide a standard format for calculations. Use the Guide to help you complete the return form. It contains general information you may need and box by box advice.

Company information

Company name

Company registration number | **Tax Reference as shown on the CT603** | **Type of Company**

Registered office address

Postcode

About this return

This is the above company's return for the period

from (dd/mm/yyyy) to (dd/mm/yyyy)

Put an 'X' in the appropriate box(es) below

A repayment is due for this return period ☐

A repayment is due for an earlier period ☐

Making more than one return for this company now ☐

This return contains estimated figures ☐

Disclosure of tax avoidance schemes

Notice of disclosable avoidance schemes ☐

Transfer pricing

Compensating adjustment claimed ☐

Company qualifies for SME exemption ☐

Accounts

I attach accounts and computations for the period to which this return relates ☐

for a different period ☐

If you are not attaching accounts and computations, say why not

Supplementary Pages

If you are enclosing any Supplementary Pages put an 'X' in the appropriate box(es)

Loans to participators by close companies, form *CT600A* ☐

Charities and Community Amateur Sports Clubs (CASCs), form *CT600E* ☐

Disclosure of tax avoidance schemes, form *CT600J* ☐

BS11/04 CT600 (Short) (2004) Version 2

Page 2

Company Tax Calculation

Turnover

1 Total turnover from trade or profession		1 £

Income

3 Trading and professional profits	3 £	
4 Trading losses brought forward claimed against profits	4 £	
5 Net trading and professional profits		box 3 minus box 4 5 £
6 Bank, building society or other interest, and profits and gains from non-trading loan relationships		6 £
11 Income from UK land and buildings		11 £
14 Annual profits and gains not falling under any other heading		14 £

Chargeable gains

16 Gross chargeable gains	16 £	
17 Allowable losses including losses brought forward	17 £	
18 Net chargeable gains		box 16 minus box 17 18 £

21 Profits before other deductions and reliefs	sum of boxes 5, 6, 11, 14 & 18 21 £

Deductions and Reliefs

24 Management expenses under S75 ICTA 1988	24 £
30 Trading losses of this or a later accounting period under S393A ICTA 1988	30 £
31 *Put an 'X' in box 31 if amounts carried back from later accounting periods are included in box 30*	31
32 Non-trade capital allowances	32 £
35 Charges paid	35 £

37 Profits chargeable to corporation tax	box 21 minus boxes 24, 30, 32 and 35 37 £

Tax calculation

38 Franked investment income	38 £	
39 Number of associated companies in this period or	39	
40 Associated companies in the first financial year	40	
41 Associated companies in the second financial year	41	
42 *Put an 'X' in box 42 if the company claims to be charged at the starting rate or the small companies' rate on any part of its profits, or is claiming marginal rate relief*		42

Enter how much profit has to be charged and at what rate of tax

Financial year *(yyyy)*	Amount of profit	Rate of tax	Tax
43	44 £	45	46 £ p
53	54 £	55	56 £ p

63 Corporation tax		total of boxes 46 and 56 63 £ p
64 Marginal rate relief	64 £ p	
65 Corporation tax net of marginal rate relief	65 £ p	
66 Underlying rate of corporation tax	66 • %	
67 Profits matched with non-corporate distributions	67	
68 Tax at non-corporate distributions rate	68 £ p	
69 Tax at underlying rate on remaining profits	69 £ p	
70 Corporation tax chargeable		enter value of box 63 or 65 or the total of boxes 68 and 69 if greater 70 £ p

CT600 (Short) (2004) Version 2

Page 3

79 Tax payable under S419 ICTA 1988		79 £ p
80 *Put an 'X' in box 80 if you completed box A11 in the Supplementary Pages CT600A*	80	
84 Income tax deducted from gross income included in profits		84 £ p
85 Income tax repayable to the company		85 £ p
86 **Tax payable - this is your self-assessment of tax payable**		total of boxes 70 and 79 minus box 84 86 £ p

Tax reconciliation

91 Tax already paid (and not already repaid)	91 £ p
92 Tax outstanding	box 86 minus box 91 92 £ p
93 Tax overpaid	box 91 minus box 86 93 £ p

Information about capital allowances and balancing charges

Charges and allowances included in calculation of trading profits or losses

	Capital allowances	Balancing charges
105 - 106 Machinery and plant - long-life assets	105 £	106 £
107 - 108 Machinery and plant - other (general pool)	107 £	108 £
109 - 110 Cars outside general pool	109 £	110 £
111 - 112 Industrial buildings and structures	111 £	112 £
113 - 114 Other charges and allowances	113 £	114 £

Charges and allowances not included in calculation of trading profits or losses

	Capital allowances	Balancing charges
115 - 116	115 £	116 £
117 *Put an 'X' in box 117 if box 115 includes flat conversion allowances*	117	

Expenditure

118 Expenditure on machinery and plant on which first year allowance is claimed		118 £
119 *Put an 'X' in box 119 if claim includes enhanced capital allowances for energy-saving investments*	119	
120 Qualifying expenditure on machinery and plant on long-life assets		120 £
121 Qualifying expenditure on machinery and plant on other assets		121 £

Losses, deficits and excess amounts

122 Trading losses Case I	calculated under S393 ICTA 1988 122 £	124 Trading losses Case V	calculated under S393 ICTA 1988 124 £
125 Non-trade deficits on loan relationships and derivative contracts	calculated under S82 FA 1996 125 £	127 Schedule A losses	calculated under S392A ICTA 1988 127 £
129 Overseas property business losses Case V	calculated under S392B ICTA 1988 129 £	130 Losses Case VI	calculated under S396 ICTA 1988 130 £
131 Capital losses	calculated under S16 TCGA 1992 131 £	136 Excess management expenses	calculated under S75(3) ICTA 1988 136 £

CT600 (Short) (2004) **Version 2**

DATA

One of your friends works for Abbey Ltd. He knows that you have prepared the accounts for the company for the year ended 31 March 2006 and he has contacted you to find out if the company is making a profit.

Task 2.5

State how you should respond to this query from your friend.

TAX TABLES

Capital allowances

	%
Writing down allowance	
Plant and machinery	25
Industrial buildings	4
First year allowance	
Plant and machinery, after 02 July 1998 – all businesses	40
Year commencing 6 April 2004 – small enterprises	50

National Insurance contributions

Class 2	
Weekly contribution	£2.10
Small earnings exemption limit	£4,345
Class 4	
Lower profits limit	£4,895
Upper profits limit	£32,760
Rate on profits between upper and lower limits	8%
Rate on profits over upper limit	1%

Capital gains indexation factors

April 1986 to June 1991	0.373
June 1991 to July 1994	0.074
June 1991 to September 1999	0.239
July 1994 to September 1999	0.154
September 1999 to May 2005	0.141
December 1999 to November 2005	0.136

Corporation tax

	Full rate	*Small Co rate*	*Taper relief fraction*	*Upper limit*	*Lower limit*
FY 2005	*30%*	*19%*	*11/400*	*1,500,000*	*300,000*

Formula: Fraction × (M – P) × 1/P

PRACTICE EXAM PAPER 3

(December 2003 paper)

TECHNICIAN STAGE – NVQ4

Unit 18

Preparing business tax computations (BTC)

DO NOT OPEN THIS PAPER UNTIL YOU ARE READY TO START UNDER EXAM CONDITIONS

INSTRUCTIONS

This examination paper is in TWO SECTIONS.

You have to show competence in BOTH sections.

You should therefore attempt and aim to compete EVERY task in EACH section.

You should spend about 100 minutes on Section 1 and 80 minutes on Section 2.

COVERAGE OF PERFORMANCE CRITERIA

The following performance criteria are covered in this exam.

Element	PC Coverage
18.1	**Prepare capital allowances computations**
A	Classify expenditure on capital assets in accordance with the statutory distinction between capital and revenue expenditure
B	Ensure that entries and calculations relating to the computation of capital allowances for a company are correct.
C	Make adjustments for private use by business owners
D	Ensure that computations and submissions are made in accordance with current tax law and take account of current Revenue practice
18.2	**Compute assessable business income**
A	Adjust trading profits and losses for tax purposes
B	Make adjustments for private use by business owners
C	Divide profits and losses of partnerships amongst partners
D	Apply the basis of assessment for unincorporated businesses in the opening and closing years
F	Identify the National Insurance Contributions payable by self-employed individuals
18.3	**Prepare capital gains computations**
A	Identify and value correctly any chargeable assets that have been disposed of
B	Identify shares disposed of by companies
C	Calculate chargeable gains and allowable losses
D	Apply reliefs, deferrals and exemptions correctly.
E	Ensure that computations and submissions are made in accordance with current tax law and take account of current Revenue practice
18.4	**Prepare corporation tax computations**
A	Enter adjusted trading profits and losses, capital allowances, investment income and capital gains in the Corporation Tax computation
B	Set-off and deduct loss reliefs and charges correctly
C	Calculate Corporation Tax due, taking account of marginal relief
F	Identify the amount of Corporation Tax payable and the due dates of payment, including payments on account

TAXATION TABLES

Capital allowances:

	%
Writing down allowance	
Plant and machinery	25
Industrial buildings	4
First year allowance	
Plant and machinery, after 02/07/98 – all businesses	40
Plant and machinery (6.4.04-5.4.05) – small enterprises	50

National Insurance contributions:

Class 2	
Weekly contribution	£2.10
Small earnings exemption limit	£4,345
Class 4	
Rate	8%
Lower profits limit	£4,895
Upper profits limit	£32,760

Capital gains indexation factors:

February 1994 to November 1997	0.123
November 1997 to May 1999	0.038
May 1999 to August 2005	0.149

Corporation tax:

	Full rate	*Small Co rate*	*Taper relief fraction*	*Upper limit*	*Lower limit*
FY 2004	30%	19%	11/400	1,500,000	300,000
FY 2005	30%	19%	11/400	1,500,000	300,000

Formula: Fraction x (M – P) x $\frac{I}{P}$

SECTION 1

(Suggested time allowance: 100 minutes)

DATA

You work in the tax department of a firm of Chartered Accountants.

James Reed and Linda Cann are new clients who commenced trading as JL Traders on 1 January 2004. You have been asked to do the tax work for the business from the date of commencement to the tax year of 2005/06.

The accounting department supplies you with the following information.

1. Adjusted trading profits, before deducting capital allowances:

	£
Period ended 30 September 2004	14,363
Year ended 30 September 2005	38,114

2. Fixed asset additions and disposals:

Additions		£
March 2004	Car, 25% private use	13,800
May 2004	Plant and machinery	10,200
December 2004	Plant and machinery	16,902
August 2005	Car, no private use	10,000
Disposals		
January 2005	Plant and machinery	2,500
	Original cost	£4,890

Neither of the cars bought has low emissions.

3. In April 2004, a new industrial building was bought for the business, costing £95,000. The building was in industrial use throughout the period of ownership.

4. The partnership agreement states that the profit share ratio is 2/3 for James and 1/3 for Linda.

5. The business is a small enterprise for capital allowance purposes.

Task 1.1

(a) Calculate the capital allowances on the plant and machinery for each accounting period.

Task 1.1 (continued)

(b) Calculate the Industrial Buildings Allowance for each accounting period.

Task 1.2

Calculate the net taxable trading profit for each accounting period.

Task 1.3

Calculate the taxable profits for each partner for all tax years, from commencement of trade to 2005/06, clearly showing all relevant dates and the amount of overlap profit.

Task 1.4

Explain which National Insurance Contributions James and Linda are required to pay, and calculate the NIC payable by each for 2005/06.

Task 1.5

James Reed informs you that nine months after buying the car in March 2004, £300 was paid for new tyres. He wants to know how this expenditure will be treated for taxation purposes.

Explain how such expenditure would be treated in a taxation computation, providing reasons for the treatment.

DATA

You received the following e-mail from James Reed.

From:	Jreed@boxmail.net
To:	AATStudent@boxmail.net
Sent:	27 November 2006 11:37
Subject:	Buildings

During September 2006, we sold the industrial building that we bought in April 2004. We immediately replaced it with another new industrial building. However, we are concerned that the sale will give rise to a Capital Gains Tax liability.

We would be grateful if you could explain to us the Capital Gains Tax implications of these transactions.

Many thanks.

James Reed

Task 1.6

Reply to James's e-mail, explaining to him how rollover relief for Capital Gains Tax purposes works.

Note: Assume that the rules governing rollover relief are the same in 2006/07 as they were in 2005/06.

From:	AATStudent@boxmail.net
To:	Jreed@boxmail.net
Sent:	5 December 2006 15:45
Subject:	Buildings

This page is for the continuation of the email. You may not need all of it.

SECTION 2

(Suggested time allowance: 80 minutes)

DATA

You work for a company, Quinten Ltd, preparing its tax information prior to being entered in the CT600 tax form.

The Chief Accountant for Quinten Ltd has supplied you with the accounts for the twelve month period ended 31 December 2005.

The profit and loss account shows:

	£	£
Gross profit		935,750
Profit on the sale of shares (Note 1)		32,800
General expenses (Note 2)	386,740	
Bad debts and doubtful debts (Note 3)	4,890	
Administrative expenses	65,900	
Salaries and wages	250,660	
Depreciation	98,320	
		(806,510)
Net profit		162,040

Notes

1. *Profit on the sale of shares:*

   In August 2005, Quinten Ltd sold all of its shares in Hart Ltd for £72,300. These shares had been acquired as follows:

	No of Shares	£
February 1994	5,000	16,900
November 1997 – rights issue	1 for 10	£2 per share
May 1999	5,000	21,600

2. *General expenses includes:*

	£
Entertaining customers	1,640
Gifts to customers (1,000 calendars with Quinten Ltd clearly visible)	2,000
Staff Christmas party (45 people)	750

3. *Bad debts are made up of:*

	£
Debts written off – trade	6,830
Decrease in general provision	(1,500)
Bad debts recovered – trade	(440)
	4,890

Additional information:

1. The capital allowances for the year ended 31 December 2005 are £23,700
2. Quinten Ltd has capital losses brought forward from 2004 of £3,962.
3. Quinten Ltd has no associated companies.

Task 2.1

Calculate the capital gain arising from the disposal of the shares in Hart Ltd.

Task 2.2

Calculate the adjusted trading profit, after capital allowances, for the year ended 31 December 2005.

Task 2.3

Show the PCTCT (profit chargeable to corporation tax) for the year ended 31 December 2005.

Task 2.4

Calculate the Corporation Tax payable for the year ended 31 December 2005, stating the due date for payment.

DATA

The Chief Accountant for Quinten Ltd informs you that the company is considering acquiring an associated company during 2006. He asks for your advice regarding the taxation implications of such a purchase.

Task 2.5

Using the headed paper below, write a memo to the Chief Accountant explaining how the purchase of an associated company will affect the taxation computation of Quinten Ltd.

MEMO	
To: Chief Accountant	**Subject: Associated Companies**
From: Accounting Technician	**Date: December 2005**

PRACTICE EXAM PAPER 4

(AAT Specimen Exam Paper – 2003 Standards)

NVQ/SVQ IN ACCOUNTING, LEVEL 4

UNIT 18

Preparing Business Tax Computations

This examination paper is in TWO sections.

You have to show competence in BOTH sections.

You should therefore attempt and aim to complete EVERY task in EACH section.

You should spend about 90 minutes on Section 1 and 90 minutes on Section 2.

COVERAGE OF PERFORMANCE CRITERIA

The following performance criteria are covered in this exam.

Element	PC Coverage
18.1	**Prepare capital allowances computations**
A	Classify expenditure on capital assets in accordance with the statutory distinction between capital and revenue expenditure
B	Ensure that entries relating to the capital allowance computations of a company are correct.
C	Make adjustments for private use by business owners
D	Ensure that computations and submissions are made in accordance with current tax law and take account of current Revenue practice
18.2	**Compute assessable business income**
A	Adjust trading profits and losses for tax purposes
B	Make adjustments for private use by business owners
D	Apply the basis of assessment for unincorporated businesses in the opening and closing years
E	Identify the due dates of payment of Income Tax by unincorporated businesses, including payments on account
F	Identify the National Insurance Contributions payable by self-employed individuals
18.3	**Prepare capital gains computations**
A	Identify and value correctly any chargeable assets that have been disposed of
B	Identify shares disposed of by companies
C	Calculate chargeable gains and allowable losses
E	Ensure that computations and submissions are made in accordance with current tax law and take account of current Revenue practice
18.4	**Prepare corporation tax computations**
A	Enter adjusted trading profits and losses, capital allowances, investment income and capital gains in the Corporation Tax computation
B	Set-off and deduct loss reliefs and charges correctly
C	Calculate Corporation Tax due, taking account of marginal relief

SECTION 1

(Suggested time allowance: 90 minutes)

DATA

You work in the tax department of a firm of chartered accountants. One of your colleagues, Samantha, who works in the Small Business Accounts department, has contacted you about a new client, Joe Dunn. He commenced trading on 1 January 2003, but has not prepared any accounts. Samantha has completed the accounts for the period ended 30 June 2003, and the two years ended 30 June 2004 and 2005. She asks you to carry out tax work for Joe Dunn for all tax years, up to and including 2005/06.

Samantha supplies you with the following information.

1 Adjusted trading profits, before deducting capital allowances:

	£
Period ended 30 June 2003	27,055
Year ended 30 June 2004	31,496
Year ended 30 June 2005	30,047

2 Fixed asset additions and disposals:

		£
Additions		
January 2003	Plant and machinery	26,400
February 2003	Motor car, no private usage	11,600
February 2003	Motor car, 30% private usage	10,000
June 2003	Plant and machinery	17,050
November 2003	Computer	3,200
May 2004	Motor car, no private usage	13,000
Disposals		
December 2003	Plant and machinery	4,600

3 Joe Dunn's business is a small enterprise for capital allowance purposes

4 Joe Dunn has paid no National Insurance Contributions since he started trading.

5 Joe Dunn wants to take his brother into partnership to help him run the business, from January 2006.

Task 1.1

Calculate the capital allowances for all relevant years.

Task 1.2

Calculate the net trading profits taxable profit for each accounting period.

27055 - 19705 7350
31496 - 15636 15860
30047 - 9577 20470

Task 1.3

Calculate the taxable profits for all tax years, from commencement of trade to 2005/06, clearly showing the dates and amount of overlap profits.

1/1/03 - 5.4.3 3/6 x 7350 7350
1.1.3 - 31/12/3 12/12 x 7350
30/6/3 6/12 x 15860

54

Task 1.4

Calculate the total amount of NIC Class 4 payable by Joe Dunn for 2005/06.

2.10 x 52 = 109.20
20470 - 4895 ~~18~~ 8% 1246
1355.20

Task 1.5

Explain the implications for Joe Dunn of his failure to:

- Notify the Revenue of his chargeability to taxation
- Complete and submit his tax returns by the due dates, stating what the due dates were

Task 1.6

Outline the key points that you would like to make to Joe Dunn regarding the taxation implications of a business being operated as a partnership.

SECTION 2

(Suggested time allowance: 90 minutes)

Data

You work for a company, Delta Ltd, preparing its tax information prior to being entered in the CT600 tax form. The company has traded for many years, using a year end of 31 December. However it has now changed its year end to 31 March.

The Chief Accountant for Delta Ltd has supplied you with the account for the fifteen month period ended 31 March 2006.

The profit and loss accounts shows:

	£	£
Gross profit		1,131,950
Profit on the sale of shares (Note 3)		23,800
General expenses (Note 1)	425,380	
Bad debts (Note 2)	5,850	
Salaries and wages	280,645	
Depreciation	125,630	
		(837,505)
Net profit		318,245

Notes

1 General expenses includes:

	£
Entertaining customers	2,300
Parking fines paid for employees	650
Gifts to customers (100 bottles of wine)	1,000
Staff Christmas party (30 people)	600

2 Bad debts are made up of:

		£
Debts written off	trade	3,800
	employee loan	800
Increase in general provision		1,600
Bad debts recovered – trade		(350)
		5,850

3 Profit on the sale of shares

In January 2006, Delta Ltd sold 30,000 shares in Alpha Ltd for £58,500. These shares had been acquired as follows.

	No. of shares	£
June 1995	20,000	12,000
November 1999	10,000	16,000

In May 1996, Alpha Ltd made a bonus issue of 1 for 10.

Additional information

1. You have already calculated the capital allowances for the plant and machinery at £35,060 for the year ended 31 December 2005, and £9,409 for the period ended 31 March 2006.
2. In September 1990, Delta Ltd had acquired a new industrial building for £250,000. The building had been in industrial use throughout the period of ownership.
3. Delta Ltd has no associated companies.

Task 2.1

Calculate the capital gain arising from the disposal of the shares in Alpha Ltd.

Task 2.2

Calculate the adjusted trading profit, before capital allowances, for the fifteen month period ended 31 March 2006.

Task 2.3

Show the PCTCT (profit chargeable to corporation tax) for the year ended 31 December 2005, and the period ended 31 March 2006.

Task 2.4

Calculate the corporation tax payable for the twelve month period ended 31 December 2005.

Task 2.5

Calculate the Corporation Tax payable for the three month period ended 31 March 2006.

Task 2.6

DATA

The Chief Accountant tells you that he anticipates that Delta Ltd will make a loss in the year ended 31 March 2006. He has asked if you could advise him about the tax implications of such a loss.

Using the headed paper provided write a memo to the Chief Accountant, setting out the options available to Delta Ltd for the set-off of the potential loss.

MEMO

To:	Chief Accountant	Date:	1 February 2007
From:	Accounting Technician	Ref:	Corporation tax losses

Taxation tables

Capital allowances

	%
Writing down allowance	
Plant and machinery	25
Industrial buildings	4
First year allowance – small enterprise	
Plant and machinery 02.07.98 to 05.04.04 and after 05.04.05	40
Plant and machinery between 06.04.04 and 05.04.05	50
ICT acquired 01.04.00 to 31.03.04	100

National insurance contributions

Class 2	
Weekly contribution	£2.10
Small earnings exemption limit	£4,345
Class 4	
Rate	8%
Lower profits limit	£4,895
Upper profits limit	£32,760

Capital gains indexation factors

June 1995 to November 1999	0.113
November 1999 to January 2006	0.148

Corporation tax

	Full rate	*Small company rate*	*Taper relief fraction*	*Upper limit*	*Lower limit*
FY 2004	30%	19%	11/400	1,500,000	300,000
FY 2005	30%	19%	11/400	1,500,000	300,000

Part I

Lecturers' resource pack activities

Note to Students

The answers to these activities and assessments are provided to your lecturers, who will distribute them in class.

If you are not on a classroom based course, a copy of the answers can be obtained from Customer Services on 020 8740 2211 or e-mail publishing @bpp.com.

Note to Lecturers

The answers to these activities and assessments are included in the Lecturers' Resource Pack, provided free to colleges.

If your college has not received the Lecturers' Resource Pack, please contact Customer Services on 020 8740 2211 or e-mail publishing @bpp.com.

Lecturers' Practice Activities

1 Harry

Harry has the following income for 2005/06:

- Taxable trading profits £30,150
- building society interest £2,250
- dividends £5,000

Task

Calculate his tax liability.

2 Peter

The profit and loss account of Peter, who runs a carpentry business, for the year ended 31 March 2006 showed a loss of £42,000 after accounting for the under-noted items.

Expenditure	£	£	*Income*	£
Depreciation		11,500	Discount received	3,200
Patent fees (not royalties)		4,000	Insurance recovery re flood	
Loss on sale of lorry		6,000	damage to stock	6,500
Bad debts:			Rents received	10,000
Amounts written off	4,000		Gain on sale of plant	9,040
Increase special provision	2,000			
	6,000			
Less: Reduction general provision	(1,000)			
		5,000		
Entertainment expenses (N1)		2,600		
Legal fees:				
Re recovery of loan to former employee		4,400		
Re employees' service contracts		600		
General expenses (N2)		4,000		
Repairs and renewals (N3)		6,400		

Capital allowances for the period of account were agreed at £7,160.

Notes

1 Entertainment consists of expenditure on:

	£
Entertaining customers	1,200
Staff dance (40 people)	800
Gifts to customers of food hampers	600
	2,600

2 General expenses comprise:

	£
Penalty for late VAT return	2,500
Fees for employees attending courses	1,500
	4,000

3 Included in this figure for repairs is an amount of £5,000 incurred in installing new windows in a recently-acquired second-hand warehouse. This building had suffered fire damage resulting in all of its windows being blown out shortly before being acquired by Peter. Other repairs were of a routine nature.

Task

Compute the taxable trading profit or loss for the above period.

Explain your reasons for your treatment of each of the above items including those items not included in your computation.

3 DB Ltd

DB Ltd commenced trading as a tool manufacturer on 1 October 2001, and made up accounts each year to 30 June. The company ceased trading on 30 April 2005.

The company's adjusted profits before the deduction of capital allowances for each period of trading were:

	£
Period to 30 June 2002	180,000
Year ended 30 June 2003	120,000
Year ended 30 June 2004	84,000
Period to 30 April 2005	146,000

The following purchases and sales of capital items took place:

		£
Purchases:		
September 2001	General plant and equipment	60,000
May 2002	Motor car for employee (no private use)	10,000
August 2002	General plant and equipment	10,000
September 2002	Motor car (40% private use by director)	18,000
August 2003	Computer	4,000
Sales:		
April 2005	Plant sold for	25,000
	Employee's car	10,000
	Director's car sold for	8,000
	Computer sold for	2,500

DB Ltd is a small enterprise.

Tasks

(a) Compute the maximum capital allowances for each accounting period.
(b) Compute the taxable trading profits for each accounting period.

4 Porcupine Ltd

Porcupine Ltd, a UK-resident company, makes up accounts each year to 31 October. It occupies a factory which it bought on 1 November 2002, the cost comprising:

	£
Land	20,000
Preparing site	10,000
Factory	110,000
Office unit	30,000
	170,000

On 1 November 2004 the company bought two additional factories:

(1) A secondhand factory which cost it £80,000.

This had cost the original owner £100,000 on 1 November 1998.

(2) A newly constructed factory.

This cost £100,000 (including £26,000 for office accommodation).

Task

Compute the maximum industrial buildings allowance (IBA) which may be claimed by Porcupine Ltd for its accounting period of 12 months to 31 October 2005.

5 Mr T

Mr T, who is 30 years of age, commences trading on 1 July 2002 and makes up accounts each year at 31 December.

The profits, before capital allowances, for the first four periods of trading are as follows.

	£
Six months to 31 December 2002	12,000
Year to 31 December 2003	20,000
Year to 31 December 2004	36,000
Year to 31 December 2005	60,000

The only acquisitions of assets during the above periods on which capital allowances may be claimed are as follows.

		£
1 July 2002	Car for employee (no private use)	10,000
10 May 2003	Grinding machines	3,750
30 May 2004	Private motor car (private use 60%)	14,000

Mr T's business is a small enterprise for first year allowance purposes.

Task

(a) Compute the capital allowances for the first four periods of trading.

(b) Compute the taxable trading profits for the first four periods of account.

(c) Compute the taxable trading profits for 2002/03 to 2005/06 and state the overlap profits carried forward.

6 Godard, Karina and Anna

Godard, Karina and Anna have been trading in partnership for the last ten years.

Their agreed profit and loss sharing ratio and salaries have always been follows.

Godard: salary £2,000 and 40% of remaining profits or losses.
Karina: salary £1,000 and 35% of remaining profits or losses.
Anna: salary £3,000 and 25% of remaining profits or losses.

The tax-adjusted trading results of the partnership for the last two years have been as follows.

	£
12 months to 30 November 2004	10,000 profit
12 months to 30 November 2005	24,000 profit

Task

Show each partner's share of the profits for income tax purposes for each of the above two accounting years.

7 Ming

In 2005/06, Ming made the following disposals.

Asset	*Gain/(loss) before taper relief* £
Motor car	(3,000)
Factory used in his business	15,100
Gilt-edged securities	45,000
Unquoted shares (business asset)	24,000

All assets were sold for their market values. The factory had been purchased in June 2004 and was sold in December 2005. The unquoted shares were bought in June 1995.

Ming is single. His taxable income for 2005/06 (after deduction of the personal allowance) was £27,815.

Task

Compute Ming's capital gains tax liability for 2005/06.

8 Patricia

On 1 May 2005 Patricia sold a freehold shop used in her business as a greengrocer, for £225,000. She bought the shop on 10 January 1996, paying £114,000. Patricia had an allowable capital loss of £10,000 brought forward on 6 April 2005.

Task

Calculate the chargeable gain arising on the sale after taper relief but before the annual exemption.

Assume an indexation factor January 1996 to April 1998 is 0.083.

9 Harriet

Harriet acquired 2,500 shares, a 25% holding, in Black Ltd on 6 October 1992 for £4,000. She sold the shares on 6 June 2005 for £41,780. The shares are a business asset for taper relief purposes.

Harriet's only source of income for 2005/06 was taxable trading profits of £32,890, and she sold no other assets.

Task

Calculate the capital gains tax payable by Harriet and state when the tax is payable.

Assume an indexation factor October 1992 to April 1998 of 0.163.

10 B Ltd

During B Ltd's twelve-month accounting period ended 31 March 2006, it made the following disposals:

(1) *April 2005*

A warehouse was sold for £120,000. This has been purchased in June 1996 for £80,000 as an investment property. It was immediately rented to a major supplier and was never used for the purpose of B Ltd's trade.

(2) *May 2005*

Two offices were sold for £40,000. These offices were part of a group of six offices purchased by the company for £50,000 in June 1993. All of the offices had been used for the purpose of B Ltd's trade up to May 2005. At the time of sale, the agreed value of the four offices retained by the company was £60,000.

(3) *June 2005*

Sold 10,000 £1 ordinary shares in T Ltd for £10 each. These shares were part of a holding of 14,000 shares acquired as follows:

May 1983	10,000 shares were purchased at £1.90 each.
June 1985	A bonus issue of one share for every five held was made.
August 1999	2,000 shares were purchased at £7 each.

Tasks

(a) Compute the chargeable gains arising as a result of each of the above disposals.

(b) Prepare a report to the directors of B Ltd setting out the opportunities of deferring the corporation tax payable on each of the above gains.

Indexation Factors which should be used in answering this question

May 1983 – April 1985	0.121
April 1985 – August 1999	0.746
June 1993 – May 2005	0.345
June 1996 – April 2005	0.239
August 1999 – June 2005	0.141

11 Maxwell

Maxwell bought a workshop used in his trade on 31 March 1992 for £75,000. He gave it to his son on 1 January 2006 when its market value was £210,000.

Task

Calculate the chargeable gain on disposal of the workshop and the new base cost of the asset if:

(a) no gift relief claim is made;
(b) such a claim is made.

Assume indexation March 1992 to April 1998 = 0.189

12 Newdeal Ltd

Newdeal Ltd has no associated companies and makes up its accounts to 31 March each year. The company's profit and loss account for the year ended 31 March 2006 was as follows.

		£	£
Gross trading profit			361,400
Add:	profit on sale of house (note (iv))	7,000	
	bank interest accrued (received in May)	1,000	
	dividends received from UK companies in June (net)	1,752	
			9,752
			371,152
Less:	wages and salaries	25,102	
	directors' fees	11,000	
	donations (note 1)	1,700	
	depreciation	2,650	
	professional charges (note 2)	3,200	
	miscellaneous (note 3)	3,600	
			(47,252)
Net profit			323,900

Notes

1 Donations comprised the following.

	£
Local political party	200
Local charities for trading purposes	150
Works sport and social club (employees only)	1,350
	1,700

The charitable donations were not made under the gift aid scheme

2 Professional charges comprised the following.

	£
Accountancy fee re annual audit	2,400
Legal fees re collection of trade debt	800
	3,200

3 Miscellaneous expenses comprised the following.

	£
Entertaining suppliers	1,000
Round sum expenses allowances to company salesmen	2,600
	3,600

4 During the year the company sold a house, the asset disposal account showing the following.

ASSET DISPOSAL ACCOUNT

	£		£
Original cost (1.4.99)	6,000	Accumulated depreciation	2,524
Profit and loss a/c	7,000	Sale proceeds (10.12.05)	10,476
	13,000		13,000

5 The written down values of capital assets at 1 April 2005 were as follows.

	£
Plant and machinery pool	12,800
Industrial building	36,800

The industrial building was purchased unused on 1 December 2002 for £40,000 and was brought into use immediately. There were no disposals or additions during the year.

Task

Compute the corporation tax for the accounting period to 31 March 2006.

Assume the following indexation factor

April 1999 – December 2005 0.157

13 J Ltd

J Ltd has been trading for a number of years. The company has always made modest profits. However, due to a market downturn in trade it suffered a substantial trading loss in respect of the accounting period of nine months to 31 December 2005.

The following information is provided.

	12 months to 31.3.04	*12 months to 31.3.05*	*9 months ended 31.12.05*
	£	£	£
Taxable trading profits(loss)	24,000	6,000	(88,000)
Rental income	12,000	6,000	3,000
Capital gains			28,000
Capital losses		20,000	
Gift aid donations paid	1,000	1,000	1,000

Tasks

Assuming the company claims loss relief as early as possible, show, for each of the above accounting periods:

(a) the amount of profits chargeable to corporation tax;

(b) the treatment of charges and the amount remaining to carry forward to future periods.

14 Tony and James

Tony is a self employed electrician. Tony's taxable trading profits for the year ended 31 March 2006 were £47,000. Tony has one employee, James. James is paid a salary of £2,800 a month.

Task

Calculate the NICs that Tony must pay for 2005/06.

15 Mr Brown

Mr Brown's income tax liability for 2004/05 was £16,000. He had suffered tax by deduction at source of £4,000 and paid two payments on account of £6,000 each on the due dates. He submitted his 2004/05 return on 31 January 2006. Mr Brown made a claim to reduce his payments on account for 2005/06 on the basis that this total liability for 2005/06 would be £14,000 with tax suffered of £5,000. He made the payments on account of £4,500 on 28 February and 14 August 2006. Finally, on 13 March 2007 he submitted his return for 2005/06 which showed total tax due of £17,000 and tax deducted at source of £4,000. He therefore paid a further £4,000 on the same date.

Required

(a) Outline the time limits for submission of returns and payments of tax under self assessment and detail the provisions for failure to comply.

(b) Calculate the interest on overdue tax chargeable in respect of Mr Brown's tax payments for 2005/06. You are not required to compute any surcharges payable.

Note. Assume interest is charged at 6.5% per annum.

16 Rosie Ltd

Rosie Ltd's corporation tax liability for the year to 31 December 2005 is £800,000. A notice requiring a corporation tax return to be filed for this year was issued on 1 January 2006.

Rosie Ltd has always paid corporation tax at the full rate. Until now Rosie Ltd's accountant has always ensured that its corporation tax return is filed on time.

Tasks

(a) State the date(s) by which Rosie Ltd should have paid its corporation tax for the year to 31 December 2005.

(b) State the date by which Rosie Ltd will be required to file its corporation tax return for the year ended 31 December 2005 and the penalties that will arise if the return is filed late.

BPP
PROFESSIONAL EDUCATION

Lecturers' Practice Exam

LECTURERS' PRACTICE EXAM

TECHNICIAN STAGE – NVQ4

UNIT 18

Preparing Business Taxation Computations (FA 2005)

Time allowed – 3 hours plus 15 minutes' reading time.

DO NOT OPEN THIS PAPER UNTIL YOU ARE READY TO START UNDER TIMED CONDITIONS

INSTRUCTIONS

This examination paper is in TWO sections.

You have to show competence in BOTH sections.

You should therefore attempt and aim to complete EVERY task in EACH section.

You should spend about 60 minutes on Section 1 and 120 minutes on Section 2.

COVERAGE OF THE PERFORMANCE CRITERIA

The following performance criteria are covered in this practice exam.

Element	PC Coverage
18.1	**Prepare capital allowances computations**
A	Classify expenditure on capital assets in accordance with the statutory distinction between capital and revenue expenditure
B	Ensure that entries and calculations relating to the computation of capital allowances for a company are correct.
D	Ensure that computations and submissions are made in accordance with current tax law and take account of current Revenue practice
E	Consult with Revenue staff in an open and constructive manner
F	Give timely and constructive advice to clients on the maintenance of accounts and the recording of information relevant to tax returns
G	Maintain client confidentiality at all times
18.2	**Compute assessable business income**
A	Adjust trading profits and losses for tax purposes
D	Apply the basis of assessment for unincorporated businesses in the opening and closing years
F	Identify the National Insurance Contributions payable by self-employed individuals
18.3	**Prepare capital gains computations**
A	Identify and value correctly any chargeable assets that have been disposed of
C	Calculate chargeable gains and allowable losses
18.4	**Prepare corporation tax computations**
A	Enter adjusted trading profits and losses, capital allowances, investment income and capital gains in the Corporation Tax computation
E	Identify the National Insurance Contributions payable by employers
F	Identify the amount of Corporation Tax payable and the due dates of payment, including payments on account
G	Complete corporation tax returns correctly and submit them, together with relevant claims and elections within the statutory time limits.
I	Give timely and constructive advice to clients on the maintenance of accounts and the recording of information relevant to tax returns

SECTION 1

Data

You are a qualified accounting technician, working in the tax department of firm of accountants, Badger and Co. You report to the tax department manager, Edwina Smith. One of your clients is Cordelia Travers, trading as Cordelia's Shoe Shop.

Cordelia started to trade selling shoes from a local shop, on 1 December 2004. Edwina Smith has prepared the following computation of taxable trading profits:

Cordelia's Shoe Shop

Computation of taxable trading profits for the period 1 December 2004 to 30 June 2005

		£	£
Net profit per the accounts			6,789
Add:	Depreciation	2,739	
	Work clothes	115	
	Private telephone (£291 × 70%)	204	
	Private car expenses (£495 + £275) × 40%	308	
	Non trade magazine subscription	25	
			3,391
Less:	Capital allowances		(3,180)
			7,000

Cordelia estimates her trading profit for the year ended 30 June 2006 will be £18,000.

Task 1.1

Calculate the taxable trading profits taxable on Cordelia for 2004/05, 2005/06 and 2006/07 based on the information available.

Task 1.2

Calculate the overlap profits and explain how they will be relieved.

Task 1.3

Compute the national insurance contributions payable by Cordelia as a self employed individual for 2004/05, 2005/06 and 2006/07. Assume FA 2005 tax rates apply throughout.

Task 1.4

Cordelia has one employee, Jane. Throughout 2005/06 Jane was paid £387 a week. She was also given £100 worth of Marks and Spencer's gift vouchers on Christmas Eve. Calculate the national insurance contributions that Cordelia will have to pay in respect of Jane.

SECTION 2

Data

You are given the following information regarding Unicorn Trading Ltd for the year ended 31 December 2005:

Profit and loss account for the year ended 31 December 2005

		£
Turnover		43,446
Less:	Administration expenses	(30,498)
	Operating charges	(1,220)
		11,828
Add:	Interest receivable and similar income	124,900
Profit before tax		136,728

Notes

Administration expenses include the following items:

1 Entertaining

	£
Staff Christmas party	250
Entertaining customers	2,312
	2,562

2 Professional fees

	£
Legal fees for updating employee service contracts	125
Accounting fees: Dealing with routine computations and completion of corporation tax returns	450
Dealing with an appeal against a decision by the Inspector of Taxes	224
	799

3 Bad debts

	£
General provision (2% of debtors at 1 January 2005)	(220)
Specific trade debt written off	500
Loan to former employee written off	250
General provision (2% of debtors at 31 December 2005)	180
Charge to profit and loss account	710

4 Depreciation = £9,133

Interest receivable and similar income is made up as follows:

	£
Bank investment account interest receivable	20,000
Profit on the sale of fixed assets	104,900
	124,900

The tax written down values of assets brought forward at 1 January 2005 is as follows:

	£
General pool	17,750
Expensive car (Land Rover)	23,600

You are given the following analysis of fixed asset additions and disposals:

Additions

1	*Plant and machinery*	Total £10,000	
	Cardboard box making machine	£10,000	Date of purchase: 10 March 2005
2	*Motor vehicles*	Total £6,000	
	Nissan Micra car	£6,000	Date of purchase: 1 March 2005

Disposals

1	Land and buildings	Sale of plot of land(N)	Date of sale: 10 December 2004
	Sale proceeds	£200,000	
	Original cost (1 January 1996)	£100,000	
	Note:* (Company had hoped to build new premises on this land, but planning permission was refused.)		
2	Plant machinery: Sale of various machines		Date of sale: 1 May 2005
	Sale proceeds	£13,000	
	Original cost	£15,000	
	Note: All items sold for less than original cost		
3	Motor vehicles: Sale of Ford Fiesta car		Date of sale: 28 February 2005
	Sale proceeds	£4,500	
	Original cost	£5,000	

Unicorn Ltd is a small enterprise for capital allowances purposes.

Task 2.1

Prepare a computation of the company's capital allowances for the year ended 31 December 2005.

Task 2.2

Prepare a calculation of taxable trading profits for Unicorn Trading Ltd for the year ended 31 December 2005.

Task 2.3

Prepare a computation of the chargeable gain on the disposal of the land sold by Unicorn Trading Limited during the year ended 31 December 2005.

Task 2.4

Prepare the corporation tax computation of the company for the year ended 31 December 2005.

Task 2.5

Complete the enclosed pages taken from the corporation tax return, Form CT600, for the company for the year ended 31 December 2005.

Task 2.6

Write a covering letter, on my behalf, to John Jones, the Finance Director of Unicorn Trading Limited, enclosing the corporation tax computation and return, and advising him of the amount of corporation tax to be paid and of the due date by which payment should be made.

TAX TABLES

National insurance (not contracted out rates) 2005/06

Class 1 contributions

Employer

Earnings threshold	£4,895 (£94 pw)
Employer contributions	12.8% on earnings above earnings threshold

Class 1A contributions

Rate 12.8%

Class 2 contributions

Rate	£2.10 pw
Small earnings exception	£4,345 pa

Class 4 contributions

Main rate between LEL and UEL	8%
Additional rate above UEL	1%
Lower earnings limit	£4,895
Upper earnings limit	£32,760

Capital gains

Indexation factor

January 1996 – December 2005 0.272

Corporation tax

1 *Rates*

Financial year	*Full rate*	*Small companies rate*	*Starting rate*	*Starting rate marginal relief fraction*	*Lower limit for starting rate*	*Upper limit for starting rate*	*Small companies' rate marginal relief*	*Upper limit for SCR*	*Lower Limit for SCR*
	%	%			£	£		£	£
2004	30	19	0	19/400	10,000	50,000	11/400	1,500,000	300,000
2005	30	19	0	19/400	10,000	50,000	11/400	1,500,000	300,000

2 *Marginal relief*

(M – P) × I/P × Marginal relief fraction

CT600 RETURN FORM

Page 1

Company - short tax return form

CT600 (Short) (2004) Version 2

for accounting periods ending on or after 1 July 1999

Your company tax return

If we send the company a *Notice* to deliver a company tax return (form *CT603*) it has to complete and send us a company tax return, at the latest by the filing date, or the company may face a penalty. A company tax return includes a company tax return form, any Supplementary Pages, accounts, computations and any relevant information.
Is this the right form for the company? Read the advice on pages 3 to 6 of the Company tax return guide (2004) (the *Guide*) before you start.
The forms in the CT600 series set out the information we need and provide a standard format for calculations. Use the Guide to help you complete the return form. It contains general information you may need and box by box advice.

Company information

Company name

Company registration number | **Tax Reference as shown on the CT603** | **Type of Company**

Registered office address

Postcode

About this return

This is the above company's return for the period
from (dd/mm/yyyy) to (dd/mm/yyyy)

Put an 'X' in the appropriate box(es) below

A repayment is due for this return period

A repayment is due for an earlier period

Making more than one return for this company now

This return contains estimated figures

Disclosure of tax avoidance schemes

Notice of disclosable avoidance schemes

Transfer pricing

Compensating adjustment claimed

Company qualifies for SME exemption

Accounts

I attach accounts and computations for the period to which this return relates

for a different period

If you are not attaching accounts and computations, say why not

Supplementary Pages

If you are enclosing any Supplementary Pages put an 'X' in the appropriate box(es)

Loans to participators by close companies, form *CT600A*

Charities and Community Amateur Sports Clubs (CASCs), form *CT600E*

Disclosure of tax avoidance schemes, form *CT600J*

BS11/04

CT600 (Short) (2004) Version 2

Page 2

Company Tax Calculation

Turnover

1 Total turnover from trade or profession		1 £

Income

3 Trading and professional profits	3 £	
4 Trading losses brought forward claimed against profits	4 £	
5 Net trading and professional profits		box 3 minus box 4 5 £
6 Bank, building society or other interest, and profits and gains from non-trading loan relationships		6 £
11 Income from UK land and buildings		11 £
14 Annual profits and gains not falling under any other heading		14 £

Chargeable gains

16 Gross chargeable gains	16 £	
17 Allowable losses including losses brought forward	17 £	
18 Net chargeable gains		box 16 minus box 17 18 £

21 Profits before other deductions and reliefs	sum of boxes 5, 6, 11, 14 & 18 21 £

Deductions and Reliefs

24 Management expenses under S75 ICTA 1988	24 £
30 Trading losses of this or a later accounting period under S393A ICTA 1988	30 £
31 *Put an 'X' in box 31 if amounts carried back from later accounting periods are included in box 30*	31
32 Non-trade capital allowances	32 £
35 Charges paid	35 £

37 Profits chargeable to corporation tax	box 21 minus boxes 24, 30, 32 and 35 37 £

Tax calculation

38 Franked investment income	38 £	
39 Number of associated companies in this period or	39	
40 Associated companies in the first financial year	40	
41 Associated companies in the second financial year	41	
42 *Put an 'X' in box 42 if the company claims to be charged at the starting rate or the small companies' rate on any part of its profits, or is claiming marginal rate relief*		42

Enter how much profit has to be charged and at what rate of tax

Financial year *(yyyy)*	Amount of profit	Rate of tax	Tax
43	44 £	45	46 £ p
53	54 £	55	56 £ p

63 Corporation tax		total of boxes 46 and 56 63 £ p
64 Marginal rate relief	64 £ p	
65 Corporation tax net of marginal rate relief	65 £ p	
66 Underlying rate of corporation tax	66 • %	
67 Profits matched with non-corporate distributions	67	
68 Tax at non-corporate distributions rate	68 £ p	
69 Tax at underlying rate on remaining profits	69 £ p	
70 Corporation tax chargeable		enter value of box 63 or 65 or the total of boxes 68 and 69 if greater 70 £ p

CT600 (Short) (2004) Version 2

Page 3

79 Tax payable under S419 ICTA 1988		79 £ p
80 *Put an 'X' in box 80 if you completed box A11 in the Supplementary Pages CT600A*	80	
84 Income tax deducted from gross income included in profits		84 £ p
85 Income tax repayable to the company		85 £ p
86 **Tax payable - this is your self-assessment of tax payable**		total of boxes 70 and 79 minus box 84 86 £ p

Tax reconciliation

91 Tax already paid (and not already repaid)	91 £ p
92 Tax outstanding	box 86 minus box 91 92 £ p
93 Tax overpaid	box 91 minus box 86 93 £ p

Information about capital allowances and balancing charges

Charges and allowances included in calculation of trading profits or losses

	Capital allowances	Balancing charges
105 - 106 Machinery and plant - long-life assets	105 £	106 £
107 - 108 Machinery and plant - other (general pool)	107 £	108 £
109 - 110 Cars outside general pool	109 £	110 £
111 - 112 Industrial buildings and structures	111 £	112 £
113 - 114 Other charges and allowances	113 £	114 £

Charges and allowances not included in calculation of trading profits or losses

	Capital allowances	Balancing charges
115 - 116	115 £	116 £
117 *Put an 'X' in box 117 if box 115 includes flat conversion allowances*	117	

Expenditure

118 Expenditure on machinery and plant on which first year allowance is claimed		118 £
119 *Put an 'X' in box 119 if claim includes enhanced capital allowances for energy-saving investments*	119	
120 Qualifying expenditure on machinery and plant on long-life assets		120 £
121 Qualifying expenditure on machinery and plant on other assets		121 £

Losses, deficits and excess amounts

122 Trading losses Case I	calculated under S393 ICTA 1988 122 £	124 Trading losses Case V	calculated under S393 ICTA 1988 124 £
125 Non-trade deficits on loan relationships and derivative contracts	calculated under S82 FA 1996 125 £	127 Schedule A losses	calculated under S392A ICTA 1988 127 £
129 Overseas property business losses Case V	calculated under S392B ICTA 1988 129 £	130 Losses Case VI	calculated under S396 ICTA 1988 130 £
131 Capital losses	calculated under S16 TCGA 1992 131 £	136 Excess management expenses	calculated under S75(3) ICTA 1988 136 £

CT600 (Short) (2004) **Version 2**

Answers to Full Exam based Assessments

PRACTICE EXAM PAPER 1: ANSWERS

(December 2004 exam)

DO NOT TURN THIS PAGE UNTIL YOU HAVE COMPLETED THE EXAM

SECTION 1

ANSWERS (TASK 1.1)

Capital allowances to the date of cessation

	Pool	Private use car		Allowances
	£	£		£
TWDV b/f	7,330	9,570		
Proceeds	(8,200)	(6,000)		
	(870)	3,570		
Balancing charge	870			(870)
Balancing allowance		(3,570)	× 70%	2,499
Allowances				1,629

ANSWERS (TASK 1.2)

Net taxable trading profits

Final tax year of business is 2005/06, basis period 1 January 2005 – 30 September 2005

	£
Trading profits	53,000
Less capital allowances	(1,629)
	51,371
Overlap profits	(21,050)
Net taxable trading profits	30,321

ANSWERS (TASK 1.3)

Net gain chargeable to capital gains tax, before annual exemption

	£	£
Sale proceeds		225,000
Less: Cost July 1995	82,500	
Improvements February 2003	17,000	
		(99,500)
Unindexed gain		125,500
Less indexation on cost July 1995 – April 1998		
£82,500 × 0.091		(7,508)
Indexed gain		117,992
Business asset owned more than two years tapered gain £117,992 × 25%		29,498

ANSWERS (TASK 1.4)

MEMO

To: Angela Graham **Subject: various queries**

From: Accounting Technician **Date: 30 November 2006**

The net taxable trading profits of a partnership are calculated in the same way as for a sole trader. They are then apportioned between the partners according to the profit sharing ratios in force during the period in which the profit was earned. Each partner is then taxed on her share of the profits as if she were a sole trader.

The tax payable by each partner is determined by adding up that partner's income, ie her share of taxable trading profits from the partnership plus any other income, such as interest and dividends. From this is deducted the personal allowance, and the tax is calculated using the tax rates and bands for the tax year.

You and your sister will need to pay Class 2 and Class 4 National Insurance Contributions.

Class 2 contributions are paid at a flat weekly rate, currently £2.10, but contributions need not be paid if your share of profits are less than £4,345. Class 4 contributions are paid with income tax, and are calculated as 8% of profits between £4,895 and £32,760, and 1% on profits in excess of £32,760.

The records to be maintained will include all the details that you used to prepare accounts, such as copy invoices for income and expenses etc. The records must be kept for almost 6 years from the end of the tax year, and the Revenue may charge a penalty of up to £3,000 for failing to keep adequate records.

ANSWERS (TASK 1.5)

If Angela's final total tax liability for 2005/06 exceeds the £10,000 that she has already paid, the balance will be payable on 31 January 2007.

ANSWERS (TASK 1.6)

Box 3.4	01.01.05
Box 3.5	30.09.05
Box 3.8	30.09.05
Box 3.14	870
Box 3.17	2,499
Box 3.22	870
Box 3.23	2,499
Box3.29	257,200
Box 3.46	79,400
Box 3.49	177,800
Box 3.64	124,800
Box 3.65	53,000
Box 3.68	2,499
Box 3.69	2,499
Box 3.70	870
Box 3.72	870
Box 3.73	51,371

SECTION 2

ANSWERS (TASK 2.1)

Chargeable gain from sale of shares in Yellow Ltd

	£
Proceeds	24,500
Less Cost November 2001	(11,650)
Unindexed gain	12,850
Less indexation November 2001 to March 2006	
£11,650 × 0.110	(1,282)
Chargeable gain	11,568

ANSWERS (TASK 2.2)

Adjusted trading profit, before capital allowances, for the 15 months to 31 March 2006

		£	£
Net profit			49,090
Add:	Gift aid donation	3,500	
	Entertaining customers	8,450	
	Depreciation	14,600	
			26,550
			75,640
Less:	Profit on sale of shares	12,850	
	UK dividends received	4,500	
	Rental income	7,500	
			24,850
Adjusted trading profits			50,790

ANSWERS (TASK 2.3)

(a) PCTCT, 12 months to 31 December 2005

	£
Trading profits 12/15 × £50,790	40,632
Less capital allowances	(8,750)
	31,882
Rental income 12 × £500 = £6,000 – loss b/f £1,000	5,000
Gift aid	(3,500)
PCTCT	33,382

(b) PCTCT, 3 months to 31 March 2006

	£
Trading profits 3/15 × £50,790	10,158
Less capital allowances	(2,600)
	7,558
Rental income 3 × £500	1,500
Chargeable gain	11,568
PCTCT	20,626

ANSWERS (TASK 2.4)

(a) Corporation tax payable 12 months ended 31 December 2006

	£
PCTCT	33,382
FII £4,500 × 100/90	5,000
Profits	38,382
Corporation tax payable: £33,382 × 19%	6,343
Less 19/400 × (50,000 – 38,382) × 33,382/38,382	(480)
	5,863

(b) Corporation tax payable 3 months to 31 March 2006

The starting rate and small companies limits are time apportioned for a three month accounting period:

Starting rate upper limit = £50,000 x 3/12 = £12,500
Small companies lower limit £300,000 x 3/12 = £75,000

Corporation tax payable: £20,626 × 19% = £3,919

ANSWERS (TASK 2.5)

From: AAT@horatio.co.uk
To: MD@horatio.co.UK
Sent 30 November 2006 15.55
Subject: Tax return

The corporation tax return for the year to 31 December 2004 should have been filed by 31 December 2005, and was therefore 9 months late.

The company will be liable to penalties of:

- £200 as the return was more than 6 months late, and
- 10% of the tax unpaid as the returns was between 6 and 12 months late. The tax unpaid is £(19,600 – 15,000) = £4,600, so the penalty is £460.

The additional tax of £4,600 was payable by 30 September 2005. The Revenue will charge interest from the due date until the date before the tax is paid, so the outstanding tax should be paid straight away to prevent further interest from accruing.

BPP
PROFESSIONAL EDUCATION

PRACTICE EXAM PAPER 2: ANSWERS

(June 2004 Exam)

DO NOT TURN THIS PAGE UNTIL YOU HAVE COMPLETED THE EXAM

SECTION 1

ANSWERS (TASK 1.1)

	£	£
Net profit per accounts		87,070
Add: gifts to customers	1,350	
cost of installing machinery	2,200	
increase in general bad debt provision	400	
motor expenses (25% × £4,680 + 15% × £3,200)	1,650	
depreciation	21,080	
		26,680
Adjusted trading profit before capital allowances		113,750

Tutorial note. Gifts of food are never allowable.

ANSWERS (TASK 1.2)

(a)

	FYA	*Pool*	*George's car (75%)*		*Carol's car (85%)*		*Capital allowances*
	£	£	£		£		£
		18,444	15,630		8,780		
WDA @ 25%		(4,611)					4,611
WDA @ £3,000/25%			(3,000)	× 75%	(2,195)	× 85%	4,116
		13,833	12,630		6,585		
Addition	24,200						
Installation	2,200						
	22,000						
FYA @ 40%	(8,800)						8,800
		13,200					
		27,033	12,630		6,585		17,527

(b) IBA = £88,000 × 4% = £3,520

Note. As the period of account is 12 months long, there is no need to time apportion the IBAs.

ANSWERS (TASK 1.3)

	£	£
Trading profit before capital allowances task 1.1)		113,750
Less: capital allowances (task 1.2)	17,527	
IBAs (task 1.2)	3,520	
		(21,047)
Net trading profit		92,703

ANSWERS (TASK 1.4)

Payments on account of income tax for 2005/06 are due on 31 January 2006 and 31 July 2006. Any final balancing payment will be due on 31 January 2007.

ANSWERS (TASK 1.5)

		£
Class 2	NICs (£2.10 × 52)	109.20
Class 4	£(32,760 – 4,895) × 8%	2,229.20
	£(46,352 (note) – 32,760) ×1%	135.92
		2,474.32

Note. As profits are shared equally Carol's profits are £46,352 (£92,703 × 50%)

ANSWERS (TASK 1.6)

Gift relief would be available to defer any gain arising on the gift of the business to George's son, Elliot.

A claim would need to be made for this relief.

The gain deferred by gift relief is calculated assuming that the business is disposed of at market value to George's son.

George's son is then deemed to have acquired the business for the market value less the amount of the deferred gain.

The deferred gain will effectively become chargeable when Elliot disposes of the business.

ANSWERS (TASK 1.7)

Taxable trading profits of the year to 31 January 2006 are taxed in 2005/06.

Profits of the four months to 31 May 2006 will be taxed in 2006/07.

Profits taxed in 2006/07 (the closing year) can be reduced by any overlap profits that arose at the start of the business.

SECTION 2

ANSWERS (TASK 2.1)

FA 1985 pool

	No of shares	Cost	Indexed cost
		£	£
April 1986	2,000	25,000	25,000
Index to June 1991 0.373 × £25,000			9,325
	2,000	25,000	34,425
Addition	2,000	35,000	35,000
	4,000	60,000	69,325
Bonus issue	400	–	–
	4,400	60,000	69,325
Index to September 1999 0.239 × £69,325			16,569
	4,400	60,000	85,894
Rights issue	880	8,800	8,800
	5,280	68,800	94,694
Index to May 2005 0.141 × £94,694			13,352
	5,280	68,800	108,046
Less: sale	(4,000)	(52,121)	(81,853)
	1,280	16,679	26,193

	£
Disposal proceeds	120,000
Less: cost	(52,121)
indexation (£81,853 – £52,121)	(29,732)
Chargeable gain	38,147

Notes

1 For companies, indexation runs to the date of disposal of an asset.
2 There is no need to compute indexation to the date of the bonus issue.

ANSWERS (TASK 2.2)

		£
Sale proceeds		260,000
Less: cost		(150,000)
indexation (£150,000 × 0.136)		(20,400)
Chargeable gain		89,600

	£	£
Purchase cost of new factory		230,000
Capital gain on old factory	89,600	
Restriction on rollover (£260,000 – £230,000)	(30,000)	
Gain rolled over		(59,600)
Base cost of new factory		170,400

ANSWERS (TASK 2.3)

	£
Adjusted trade profit	623,024
Chargeable gain (task 2.1)	38,147
Chargeable gain (task 2,2)	30,000
PCTCT	691,171

There are two associated companies, so the small companies' lower an upper limits must be divided by 2:

Small companies' upper limit = £750,000

Small companies' lower limit = £150,000

Therefore, the small companies' marginal relief applies:

	£
£691,171 × 30%	207,351
Less: 11/400 × (£750,000 – £691,171)	(1,618)
	205,733

£205,733 must be paid by 1 January 2007.

ANSWERS (TASK 2.4)

Box 3	£623,024
Box 5	£623,024
Box 16	£68,147
Box 18	£68,147
Box 21	£691,171
Box 37	£691,171
Box 42	X
Box 39	1
Box 43	2005
Box 44	£691,171
Box 45	30%
Box 46	£207,351.30
Box 63	£207,351.30
Box 64	£1,617.80
Box 65	£205,733.50
Box 70	£205,733.50
Box 86	£205,733.50
Box 93	£205,733.50

ANSWERS (TASK 2.5)

Tell the friend politely that the ethical guideline of confidentiality means that it is not possible to disclose details of the company's profit.

PRACTICE EXAM PAPER 3: ANSWERS

(December 2003 exam)

DO NOT TURN THIS PAGE UNTIL YOU HAVE COMPLETED THE EXAM

SECTION 1

ANSWERS (TASK 1.1)

(a) **Capital allowances**

Period ended 30.9.04	*FYA*	*Pool*	*Private use asset × 75%*		*Allowances*
	£	£	£		£
Addition			13,800		
WDA (£3,000 × 9/12)			(2,250)	× 75%	1,688
Additions	10,200				
FYA @ 50%	(5,100)				5,100
		5,100			6,788
		5,100	11,550		
Year ended 30.9.05					
Addition		10,000			
Disposal		(2,500)			
		12,600	11,550		
WDA @ 25%		(3,150)	(2,888)	× 75%	5,316
Addition	16,902				
FYA @ 50%	(8,451)				8,451
		8,451			
		17,901	8,662		13,767

Tutorial notes

1 FYA are not pro-rated in a short period.

2 The key to getting a capital allowance question right is to set out the proforma as shown here.

3 As the business is a small enterprise, 50% FYA are available on the acquisition in May 2004 and December 2004.

(b) **Industrial buildings**

Period ended 30.9.04

IBAs £95,000 × 4% × 9/12 = £2,850

As the building was in industrial use on 30.9.04, IBAs are available for the period. As the period is only nine months long, time apportionment is needed.

Note that the date of purchase of the building does not effect the IBAs available.

Year ended 30.9.05

IBAs £95,000 × 4% = £3,800

ANSWERS (TASK 1.2)

	Period to 30.9.04	Year to 30.9.05
	£	£
Profits	14,363	38,114
Capital allowances (1.1)	(6,788)	(13,767)
IBAs	(2,850)	(3,800)
Trading profits	4,725	20,547

ANSWERS (TASK 1.3)

		James	Linda
		£	£
Trading profits			
p/e 30.9.04			
£4,725 × 2/3 and 1/3		3,150	1,575
y/e 30.9.05			
£20,597 × 2/3 and 1/3		13,698	6,849
2003/04	(1.1.04 – 5.4.04) £3,150/£1,575 × 3/9	1,050	525
2004/05	(12 m/e 31.12.04)	6,038	3,019
2005/06	(y/e 30.9.05)	13,698	6,849
Overlap profits			
1.1.04 – 5.4.04		1,050	525
1.10.04 – 31.12.04		3,425	1,712
		4,475	2,237

ANSWERS (TASK 1.4)

As James and Linda are self-employed they are required to pay Class 2 and Class 4 NICs.

NICs payable for 2005/06:

	James	Linda
	£	£
Class 2		
£2.10 × 52	109	109
Class 4		
8% (£13,698 – £4,895)	704	
8% (£6,849 – £4,895)		156
	813	265

ANSWERS (TASK 1.5)

The £300 for the new tyres is a revenue expense as it is a cost of repair rather than improvement to the car.

This means that the £300 can be deducted in computing taxable trading profits.

As the £300 is not a capital expense, it is not eligible for capital allowances.

ANSWERS (TASK 1.6)

If the industrial building bought in April 2004 was sold for more than its original cost a chargeable gain will arise on sale.

The gain may be deferred by claiming **rollover relief.** The gains is deferred by deducting it from the cost of the new building. The gain deferred is the gain before rollover relief.

If all of the disposal proceeds are invested in the new building, the full chargeable gain otherwise arising is deferred. If the disposal proceeds are not completely reinvested an amount of the gain equal to the proceeds not reinvested will remain chargeable. The remaining gain is deferred and deducted from the cost of the new building.

SECTION 2

ANSWERS (TASK 2.1)

Capital gain

FA 1985 pool

	No	*Cost*	*Indexed cost*
		£	£
February 1994	5,000	16,900	16,900
Indexation to November 1997			
0.123 × £16,900			2,079
	5,000	16,900	18,979
Rights issue	500	1,000	1,000
	5,500	17,900	19,979
Indexation to May 1999			
0.038 × £19,979			759
May 1999	5,000	21,600	21,600
	10,500	39,500	42,338
Index to August 2005			6,308
0.149 × £42,338	10,500	39,500	48,646

	£
Sale proceeds	72,300
Less indexed cost	(48,646)
Chargeable gain	23,654

ANSWERS (TASK 2.2)

		£
Net profit		162,040
Add:	Entertaining	1,640
	Depreciation	98,320
Less:	Profit on sale of shares	(32,800)
	Decrease in general provision	(1,500)
Capital allowances		(23,700)
Adjusted trading profit		204,000

ANSWERS (TASK 2.3)

	£
Schedule D Case I profit	204,000
Chargeable gains (£23,654 – £3,962)	19,692
PCTCT	223,692

ANSWERS (TASK 2.4)

As 'profits' are below the small companies' lower limit of £300,000 the small companies' rate of tax applies in both FY 2004 and FY 2005. As there is no change in the rate of corporation tax between these two years, there is no need to deal with the financial years separately.

CT Due:
£223,692 × 19% = £42,501

CT of £42,501 is due for payment on 1 October 2006.

ANSWERS (TASK 2.5)

If an associated company is acquired, the rate of tax that had to be paid by Quinten Ltd will change. This is because the companies must share the upper and lower profits limits. The upper limit for Quinten Ltd would be £750,000 and the lower limit £150,000.

If Quinten Ltd had had an associated company in the year to 31 December 2005 tax would have been due at 30% less small companies marginal relief rather than at 19% as shown above.

PRACTICE EXAM 4: ANSWERS

(AAT specimen exam paper)

DO NOT TURN THIS PAGE UNTIL YOU HAVE COMPLETED THE EXAM

NOTE: THESE ANSWERS HAVE BEEN PREPARED BY BPP PROFESSIONAL EDUCATION

SECTION 1

ANSWERS (TASK 1.1)

	FYA @ 40% £	FYA @ 100% £	Pool £	Exp.car £	Private use asset (70%) £	Total £
P/e 30.06.03						
Non-FYA additions						
Cars			11,600		10,000	
WDA @ 25% × 6/12			(1,450)			1,450
			10,150		(1,250) (70%)	875
FYA additions					8,750	
P & M	26,400					
P & M	17,050					
	43,450					
@ 40%	(17,380)					17,380
			26,070			19,705
			36,220			
Y/e 30.06.04						
Disposals			(4,600)			
			31,620			
Non-FYA additions				13,000		
WDA @ 25%			(7,905)	(3,000)		10,905
			23,715	10,000	(2,188) (70%)	1,531
					6,562	
FYA additions						
Computer		3,200				
@ 100%		(3,200)	–			3,200
			23,715			15,636
Y/e 30.06.05						
WDA @ 25%			(5,929)	(2,500)		8,429
			17,786	7,500	(1,640) (70%)	1,148
WDA c/fwd					4,922	9,577

Tutorial notes

1 Writing down allowances are pro-rated in the short period of account but first year allowances are not.

2 The key to getting a capital allowance question right is to learn the above proforma so that in your real examination you can just slot the figures in.

ANSWERS (TASK 1.2)

	Adjusted profit	*CA*	*Taxable trading Profits*
	£	£	£
P/e 30.06.03	27,055	19,705	7,350
Y/e 30.06.04	31,496	15,636	15,860
Y/e 30.06.05	30,047	9,577	20,470

ANSWERS (TASK 1.3)

	£
2002/03	
01.01.03 – 05.04.03	
3/6 × £7,350	3,675
2003/04	
01.01.03 – 31.12.03	
P/e 30.06.03	7,350
6/12 × £15,860	7,930
	15,280
2004/05	
Y/e 30.06.04	15,860
2005/06	
Y/e 30.06.05	20,470
Overlap	
01.01.03 – 0.5.04.03	3,675
01.07.03 – 31.12.03	7,930
	11,605

ANSWERS (TASK 1.4)

(£20,470 – £4,895) × 8% (main rate)	£1,246.00

ANSWERS (TASK 1.5)

1 Joe Dunn's failure to notify the chargeability to tax this will incur a maximum penalty of an amount equal to the tax remaining unpaid on 31 January following the end of the tax year.

2 A £100 fixed penalty is charged if a tax return is submitted late, with a further £100 fixed penalty if the tax return is more than six months late. If the tax return is more than 12 months late, as in this case, an additional penalty may be charged of up to 100% of the tax liability for the year.

3 The due dates for the filing of a tax return are 30 September following the end of the tax year, for taxpayers who want the Revenue to calculate their tax liability, or 31 January following the end of the tax year, for taxpayers who have calculated their own tax liability. If a taxpayer is issued with a short tax return, the Revenue will calculate tax if the return is submitted by 31 January following the tax year.

ANSWERS (TASK 1.6)

The key tax implications of operating a business as a partnership are:

1 The trading profits and losses are calculated in the same way as for an individual
2 The adjusted profit or loss is split between the partners in the agreed profit sharing ratio
3 Each partner is assessed individually on his share of the profits
4 Each partner is responsible for his own tax liability

SECTION 2

ANSWERS (TASK 2.1)

	No. of shares	Cost	Indexed cost
		£	£
June 1995	20,000	12,000	12,000
May 1996 bonus issue	2,000		
	22,000		
November 1999			
IA £12,000 × 0.113			1,356
			13,356
Addition	10,000	16,000	16,000
	32,000	28,000	29,356
January 2006			
IA £29,356 × 0.148			4,345
			33,701
Disposal	(30,000)	(26,250)	(31,595)
Pool to c/fwd	2,000	1,750	2,106

	£
Proceeds	58,500
Cost	(26,250)
	32,250
Indexation allowance (£31,595 – £26,250)	(5,345)
	26,905

Tutorial note. Companies are entitled to indexation until the date of disposal of an asset.

ANSWERS (TASK 2.2)

	£	£
Net profit		318,245
Add: Entertaining customers	2,300	
Gifts	1,000	
Employee loan written off	800	
Increase in general bad debt provision	1,600	
Depreciation	125,630	131,330
		449,575
Less: Profit on sale of shares		(23,800)
Adjusted trading profit before capital allowances		425,775

Tutorial notes

1 Although fines and penalties are not usually deductible, the Revenue will allow an employee's parking fine provided it is incurred whilst parking the employer's car on employer's business. However, such fines are never allowed if incurred by a director.

2 An increase in a general bad debt provision is never allowable.

ANSWERS (TASK 2.3)

	12 months to December 2004	*3 months to 31 March 2005*
	£	£
Profit split 12/3	340,620	85,155
Capital allowances	(35,060)	(9,409)
IBA (£250,000 × 4%)	(10,000)	(2,500)
Trading profits	295,560	73,246
Chargeable gain (task 2.1)	–	26,905
PCTCT	295,560	100,151

ANSWERS (TASK 2.4)

	£
CT payable £295,560 × 19% =	56,156

'Profits' are below the small companies' rate lower limit so the small companies' rate of tax applies.

ANSWERS (TASK 2.5)

	£
£100,151 @ 30%	30,045
SCMR	
(£375,000 – £100,151) × 11/400	(7,558)
CT payable	22,487

Small companies' lower limit £300,000 × 3/12 = £75,000
Small companies' upper limit £1,500,000 × 3/12 = £375,000

'Profits' are between the small companies' upper and lower limits so small companies' marginal relief applies.

ANSWERS (TASK 2.6)

MEMO

To:	Chief Accountant	Date:	1 February 2007
From:	Accounting Technician	Ref:	Corporation tax losses

There are two basic alternatives regarding the loss that you are anticipating.

1. To carry the loss forward under S 393(1) ICTA 1988 and relieve against future trading profits.
2. To relieve the loss under S 393A(1) against total profits. This means that the loss is set against all other profits arising in the year of the trading loss.

If 2 is opted for, the company may also, under S 393A(1), carry the loss back against the total profits arising in the 12 months prior to the loss making period.

I hope this answers your query.

Index

BPP
PROFESSIONAL EDUCATION

Review Form & Free Prize Draw – Unit 18 Preparing Business Taxation Computations Finance Acts 2005 (9/05)

All original review forms from the entire BPP range, completed with genuine comments, will be entered into one of two draws on 31 January 2006 and 31 July 2006. The names on the first four forms picked out on each occasion will be sent a cheque for £50.

Name: ______________________ **Address:** ______________________

____

____

How have you used this Combined Text and Kit?
(Tick one box only)

☐ Home study (book only)

☐ On a course: college ____________

☐ With 'correspondence' package

☐ Other ____________

Why did you decide to purchase this Combined Text and Kit? *(Tick one box only)*

☐ Have used BPP Texts in the past

☐ Recommendation by friend/colleague

☐ Recommendation by a lecturer at college

☐ Saw advertising

☐ Other ____________

During the past six months do you recall seeing/receiving any of the following?
(Tick as many boxes as are relevant)

☐ Our advertisement in *Accounting Technician* magazine

☐ Our advertisement in *Pass*

☐ Our brochure with a letter through the post

Which (if any) aspects of our advertising do you find useful?
(Tick as many boxes as are relevant)

☐ Prices and publication dates of new editions

☐ Information on Interactive Text content

☐ Facility to order books off-the-page

☐ None of the above

Your ratings, comments and suggestions would be appreciated on the following areas

	Very useful	*Useful*	*Not useful*
Introduction	☐	☐	☐
Chapter contents lists	☐	☐	☐
Activities and answers	☐	☐	☐
Key learning points	☐	☐	☐
Quick quizzes and answers	☐	☐	☐
Practice activities	☐	☐	☐
Full skills based assessments	☐	☐	☐
Full exam based assessments	☐	☐	☐
Lecturers' Resource Section	☐	☐	☐

	Excellent	*Good*	*Adequate*	*Poor*
Overall opinion of this Text	☐	☐	☐	☐

Do you intend to continue using BPP Interactive Texts/Assessment Kits? ☐ Yes ☐ No

The BPP author of this edition can be e-mailed at: suedexter@bpp.com

Please return this form to: Janice Ross, BPP Professional Education, FREEPOST, London, W12 8BR

Review Form & Free Prize Draw (continued)

Please note any further comments and suggestions/errors below

Free Prize Draw Rules

1. Closing date for 31 January 2006 draw is 31 December 2005. Closing date for 31 July 2006 draw is 30 June 2006.
2. Restricted to entries with UK and Eire addresses only. BPP employees, their families and business associates are excluded.
3. No purchase necessary. Entry forms are available upon request from BPP Professional Education. No more than one entry per title, per person. Draw restricted to persons aged 16 and over.
4. Winners will be notified by post and receive their cheques not later than 6 weeks after the relevant draw date.
5. The decision of the promoter in all matters is final and binding. No correspondence will be entered into.

See overleaf for information on other
BPP products and how to order

AAT Order

To BPP Professional Education, Aldine Place, London W12 8AW

Tel: 0845 0751 100 (within the UK) Fax: 020 8740 1184

Tel: +44 (0)20 8740 2211 (from overseas) Web: www.bpp.com

Order online: www.bpp.com/mybpp

Mr/Mrs/Ms (Full name)

Daytime delivery address

Postcode

Daytime Tel E-mail

FOUNDATION (£14.95 except as indicated)	5/05 Texts	5/05 Kits	Special offer	8/05 Passcards	Success CDs
Units 1 & 2 Receipts and Payments	☐	☐		Foundation	
Unit 3 Ledger Balances and Initial Trial Balance	☐ (Combined Text & Kit)		Foundation Sage Bookeeping and Excel Spreadsheets CD-ROM free if ordering all Foundation Text and Kits, including Units 21 and 22/23 ☐	£6.95 ☐	£14.95 ☐
Unit 4 Supplying Information for Mgmt Control	☐ (Combined Text & Kit)				
Unit 21 Working with Computers (£9.95)	☐				
Unit 22/23 Healthy Workplace/Personal Effectiveness (£9.95)	☐				
Sage and Excel for Foundation (Workbook with CD-ROM £9.95)	☐				
INTERMEDIATE (£9.95 except as indicated)					
Unit 5 Financial Records and Accounts (for 06/06 exams)	☐	☐		£5.95 ☐	£14.95 ☐
Unit 6/7 Costs and Reports (Combined Text £14.95)	☐			£5.95 ☐	
Unit 6 Costs and Revenues		☐			£14.95 ☐
Unit 7 Reports and Returns		☐			
TECHNICIAN (£9.95 except as indicated)					
Unit 8/9 Core Managing Performance and Controlling Resources	☐	☐		£5.95 ☐	£14.95 ☐
Spreadsheets for Technician (Workbook with CD-ROM)	☐				
Unit 10 Core Managing Systems and People (£14.95)	☐ (Combined Text & Kit)				
Unit 11 Option Financial Statements (A/c Practice) (for 06/06 exams)	☐	☐		£5.95 ☐	£14.95 ☐
Unit 12 Option Financial Statements (Central Govnmt)	☐	☐	Spreadsheets for Technicians CD-ROM free if take Unit 8/9 Text and Kit ☐		
Unit 15 Option Cash Management and Credit Control	☐	☐		£5.95 ☐	
Unit 17 Option Implementing Audit Procedures	☐	☐		£5.95 ☐	
Unit 18 Option Business Tax FA05 (8/05) (£14.95)	☐ (Combined Text & Kit)			£5.95 ☐	
Unit 19 Option Personal Tax FA05 (8/05) (£14.95)	☐ (Combined Text & Kit)			£5.95 ☐	
INTERMEDIATE 2004 (£9.95 except as indicated)					
Unit 5 Financial Records and Accounts (for 12/05 exams)	☐	☐		£5.95 ☐	
TECHNICIAN 2004 (£9.95 except as indicated)					
Unit 11 Option Financial Statements (A/c Practice) (for 12/05 exams)	☐	☐		£5.95 ☐	
Unit 18 Option Business Tax FA04 (8/04)	☐ (Combined Text & Kit)			£5.95 ☐	
Unit 19 Option Personal Tax FA04 (8/04)	☐ (Combined Text & Kit)			£5.95 ☐	
SUBTOTAL	£	£	£	£	£

TOTAL FOR PRODUCTS £

POSTAGE & PACKING

	First	Each extra	
Texts/Kits			
UK	£3.00	£3.00	£
Europe*	£6.00	£4.00	£
Rest of world	£20.00	£10.00	£
Passcards			
UK	£2.00	£1.00	£
Europe*	£3.00	£2.00	£
Rest of world	£8.00	£8.00	£
Success CDs			
UK	£2.00	£1.00	£
Europe*	£3.00	£2.00	£
Rest of world	£8.00	£8.00	£

TOTAL FOR POSTAGE & PACKING £

(Max £12 Texts/Kits/Passcards - deliveries in UK)

Grand Total (Cheques to *BPP Professional Education*)

I enclose a cheque for (incl. Postage) £

Or charge to Access/Visa/Switch

Card Number CV2 No last 3 digits on signature strip

Expiry date Start Date

Issue Number (Switch Only)

Signature

We aim to deliver to all UK addresses inside 5 working days; a signature will be required. Orders to all EU addresses should be delivered within 6 working days. All other orders to overseas addresses should be delivered within 8 working days. * Europe includes the Republic of Ireland and the Channel Islands.

See overleaf for information on other
BPP products and how to order

AAT Order

To BPP Professional Education, Aldine Place, London W12 8AW
Tel: 0845 0751 100 (within the UK) Fax: 020 8740 1184
Tel: +44 (0)20 8740 2211 (from overseas) Web: www.bpp.com
Order online: www.bpp.com/mybpp

Mr/Mrs/Ms (Full name)
Daytime delivery address
Postcode
Daytime Tel E-mail

OTHER MATERIAL FOR AAT STUDENTS	8/04 Texts	6/04 Text	3/03 Text	3/04 Text
FOUNDATION (£5.95)				
Basic Maths and English	☐			
COMPUTER BASED TRAINING				
AAT Bookkeeping Certificate (CD-ROM plus manual) £130 ☐				
INTERMEDIATE (£5.95)				
Basic Bookkeeping (for students exempt from Foundation)	☐			
Business Maths and English (higher level Maths and English, also useful for ACCA/CIMA) £9.95		☐		
FOR ALL STUDENTS (£5.95)				
Building Your Portfolio (old standards)			☐	
Building Your Portfolio (2003 standards)	☐			
Basic Costing				☐

AAT PAYROLL	Finance Act 2005 8/05 December 2005 and June 2006 assessments		Finance Act 2004 8/04 June 2005 exams only	
		Special offer Take Text and Kit together		**Special offer** Take Text and Kit together
LEVEL 2 Text (£30)	☐	£44.95 ☐	☐	£44.95 ☐
LEVEL 2 Kit (£20)	☐		☐	
	For assessments in 2006		For assessments in 2005	
LEVEL 3 Text (£30)	☐	£44.95 ☐	☐	£44.95 ☐
LEVEL 3 Kit (£20)	☐		☐	
SUBTOTAL	£	£	£	£

TOTAL FOR PRODUCTS £

POSTAGE & PACKING

	First	Each extra	
Texts/Kits			
UK	£3.00	£3.00	£
Europe*	£6.00	£4.00	£
Rest of world	£20.00	£10.00	£
Passcards			
UK	£2.00	£1.00	£
Europe*	£3.00	£2.00	£
Rest of world	£8.00	£8.00	£
Tapes			
UK	£2.00	£1.00	£
Europe*	£3.00	£2.00	£
Rest of world	£8.00	£8.00	£

TOTAL FOR POSTAGE & PACKING £
(Max £12 Texts/Kits/Passcards - deliveries in UK)

Grand Total (Cheques to *BPP Professional Education*)

I enclose a cheque for (incl. Postage) £
Or charge to Access/Visa/Switch
Card Number CV2 No (last 3 digits on signature strip)

Expiry date Start Date

Issue Number (Switch Only)

Signature

We aim to deliver to all UK addresses inside 5 working days; a signature will be required. Orders to all EU addresses should be delivered within 6 working days. All other orders to overseas addresses should be delivered within 8 working days. * Europe includes the Republic of Ireland and the Channel Islands.